Modern Approaches to Understanding and Managing Organizations

Lee G. Bolman

Terrence E. Deal

Modern Approaches to Understanding and Managing Organizations

Jossey-Bass Publishers

San Francisco • London • 1986

MODERN APPROACHES TO UNDERSTANDING
AND MANAGING ORGANIZATIONS
by Lee G. Bolman and Terrence E. Deal

Library of Congress Cataloging in Publication Data

Bolman, Lee G.
Modern approaches to understanding and managing
organizations.

Bibliography: p. 301
Includes index.
1. Management. 2. Organizational behavior. I. Deal,
Terrence E. II. Title.
HD31.B613   1984   658   83-49257
ISBN 0-87589-592-1

Manufactured in the United States of America

The paper in this book meets the guidelines for
permanence and durability of the Committee on
Production Guidelines for Book Longevity of the
Council on Library Resources.

JACKET DESIGN BY WILLI BAUM

FIRST EDITION
First printing: April 1984
Second printing: November 1984
Third printing: August 1985
Fourth printing: February 1986

Code 8415

A joint publication in
The Jossey-Bass Management Series
and
The Jossey-Bass Social
and Behavioral Science Series

Contents

Preface

As confidence in American institutions has plummeted, demand for new ideas and insights about management and organization has reached a crescendo. The public has eagerly bought new books on how to find organizational excellence, become a sixty-second manager, build a corporate culture, or apprehend the mysteries of Japanese management.

Readers who keep up with all the new management literature are likely to feel a combination of stimulation, overload, and confusion. The different voices are saying different things and addressing different issues. Are some more reliable than others? Is there some way to put them all in context? Is the popular literature oversimplifying the problems or omitting central issues in management? This book is addressed to such questions. We seek to provide a compact overview of approaches to organizations that are genuinely powerful for management. We present a framework that encompasses much of what is known and that helps to separate the topical from the enduring, the fads from the fundamentals. Along the way, we assess the strengths and limits of many recently popular books and ideas.

Authors are always motivated by something powerful enough to overcome the obstacles and frustrations of writing a book. Our initial motivation was the need for an instructional framework to reconcile our conceptual and stylistic differences. We needed a way to survive each other. We had both studied organizations, but at opposite ends of the United States. We had been educated in very different intellectual traditions at two universities known more for their differences than for their similarities. We both had theories about organizations, but the differences in those theories have historically fueled lively debate and even acrimonious argument.

At Harvard, we found ourselves cast together, jointly responsible for teaching an introductory graduate course with the almost unbounded title "Organizations: Theory and Behavior." Our differences flourished and collided. We became an academic odd couple—intrigued by each other's ideas, dismayed by the problems of professing them in a single classroom to the same students.

The first year, when we were not busy debunking each other's lectures, we were trying to understand why our students seemed so confused. Individually, each of us made some sense, but some students developed dark suspicions that our purpose was to reduce Harvard's population of doctoral students.

We persevered, and learned, and over the years crystallized our different perspectives into a pluralistic way of approaching organizations that transcends its origins. The merging of disparate intellectual traditions has produced a holistic way of understanding the complexities of modern organizations. This approach is reflected in a book with three major objectives: (1) to provide a clear and readable summary and integration of the major conceptual perspectives in the field of organizations, (2) to focus on what organization theory says that is important and useful for managerial practice, and (3) to give equal time to private and public organizations.

The field of organization studies has been divided into a number of distinct traditions that are often isolated from one another. Most of the existing literature focuses on only one or two of those traditions. As a result, these works give the reader an incomplete sense of the state of the field. Even more important, they omit some of the most important aspects of organizations that any manager or student of organizations needs to understand if the goal is better management of human organizations.

The few works that seek to provide a comprehensive overview of organization theory and research are mostly written for other scholars in the field. They are often afflicted with social science jargon and abstraction and have little to say of direct relevance to practitioners.

The bulk of work in organization theory has focused almost exclusively on either the private or the public sector, but not both. We believe it has become essential to give explicit attention to both the similarities and differences between public and private organizations. The two sectors increasingly interpenetrate each other. Public administrators often face problems of "indirect management"—how to influence the behavior of private firms. The controversies in 1983 over the Reagan administration's approach to the Environmental Protection Agency go to the heart of that issue: Much of the EPA's work involves the choice of strategy for influencing the behavior of private corporations, which make most of the decisions that directly influence air and water quality.

On the other side of the same fence, corporate managers face a diverse and often bewildering array of government actions, interventions, and regulations. Private firms need to understand and find ways to manage their relationships with multiple levels of government. Public- and private-sector managers often carry narrow, stereotypic conceptions of each other that impede effectiveness on both sides. At a time when confidence in our nation's institutions has reached a record low, it is imperative that we seek both common ground and a shared understanding that can help to strengthen both public and private organizations.

Our primary audience is managers and future managers. We have tried to write in response to the question: What does organization theory and research have to say that is genuinely important and useful to practitioners? We have used the work successfully in two contexts—in an introductory course for graduate students at Harvard and in our work with practicing

managers in both the public and private sectors. We believe that
the book is also suitable for advanced undergraduate courses.

We have tried to present a large, complex body of theory
and research as clearly and simply as we could, without water-
ing it down or presenting simplistic views of how to solve every
managerial problem. We try to offer not solutions but more
powerful ways of thinking about organizations and understanding the managerial problems that they present.

Part One sets the stage for our approach to organizations.
Chapter One outlines the major perspectives on organization
that will be developed in later chapters. Chapter Two discusses
the basic characteristics of organizations that make them so
challenging and shows why specific approaches or "frames" are
essential to managerial effectiveness.

Part Two is the heart of the book: two chapters devoted
to each of four major frames—structural, human resource, political, and symbolic. The first of each pair of chapters discusses
how the frame or approach developed, specifies core assumptions, and presents the basic elements of the approach. Chapter
Three outlines the structural approach, capturing the rational,
tough-minded side of organizations and clarifying basic issues in
organizational design. Chapter Five explores the human side of
enterprise and examines strengths and weaknesses of current approaches to humanizing the workplace. Chapter Seven presents
the political frame, illuminating the darker side of organizations
—conflict, coalitions, and struggles for power and position.
Chapter Nine discusses organizational symbols and explains the
roles played by myths, rituals, ceremonies, and play at all levels
of the organization. The counterparts of these chapters (Chapters Four, Six, Eight, and Ten) detail how each approach works
in solving organizational problems, with emphasis on ideas that
will be most useful to managers. Case examples from corporations, public agencies, schools, and universities highlight how
the approaches can be effectively applied.

Part Three answers the question, "Where did the frames
come from?" Chapters Eleven and Twelve provide an extensive
review of the theory and research on which the frames were
based, and Chapter Thirteen then integrates that information.

Readers who are already familiar with the organizational literature may want to *start* with those chapters, since they provide
a compact summary of our conceptual approach. Readers who
are more interested in practice than theory will find that they
can skip Part Three and move directly to the final chapters,
which focus on putting the frames into practice.

Part Four provides ways to integrate all four frames into
a comprehensive set of approaches that managers can use. Chapter Fourteen shows how organizational problems can be suc-
cessively reframed to reveal new insights and to avoid managerial ruts. Chapter Fifteen uses a case study to show how managers can generate scripts that provide them with a broader
range of roles in the ongoing drama of everyday life and that
prove there is more than one way to solve almost any managerial muddle. Chapter Sixteen reviews some of the most influential current ideas on excellence in management and in organizations in terms of what they include and what they omit. The
epilogue concludes the book by discussing the paradox of flexibility and commitment that is a fundamental challenge for leaders in modern organizations.

We release the book with intense satisfaction in surviving
our differences productively and with affection. We hope that
our perspective will help others capture and understand the
complexity that makes human organizations immensely frustrating and continually beguiling. Better understanding can produce better use of the power and energy that human institutions create and channel. At the very least, it can help managers
appreciate and accept those aspects of social life that will remain unchanneled and mysterious.

Acknowledgments

Book writing often feels like a lonely process, even when
an odd couple is doing the writing. But we owe much to many
who have contributed ideas, insights, and stimulation. Our students in A-021, the introductory course in organizations at the
Harvard Graduate School of Education, waded through succes-
sive versions of the manuscript. Their criticisms, challenges, de-

mands, and support all helped to produce a much better final product. Bernard Cullen, Millicent P. Daly, Margaret Egan, Joan Gallos, Paul Grigorieff, Cynthia Ingols, Joan La France, Michael Sales, Betsy Schoenherr, and Bari Stauber ably assisted us as members of the A-021 teaching staff, and each made a significant imprint. Millicent Daly deserves special thanks for her insights, warmth, and willingness to stay with us over the long haul. A number of other former students provided significant ideas and critique, including Bud Bilanich, Grady McGonagill, Keith Merron, and Larry Wallace.

We owe much to many present and former colleagues. Chris Argyris provided colleagueship, comments, and his inimitable ability to ask the questions that we did not know how to answer. L. Dave Brown, Philip H. Mirvis, Barry Oshry, and Fritz Steele, all members of the Brookline Guerilla Organization Development Group, provided invaluable support and confrontation.

The Harvard School of Education provided the atmosphere in which our ideas grew, and we want to thank many who helped with ideas, questions, or persistent criticism, including Roland Barth, Steven K. Bailey, Anthony Bryk, David Cohen, Russell Davis, Badi Foster, Robert Herriot, Kenneth Haskins, Gregory Jackson, Fred Jacobs, David Kuechle, Sarah Lightfoot, Walter McCann, Jerome Murphy, John Schlien, Donald Warwick, Charles Willie, and Paul Ylvisaker.

Harvard's Business School has an unusually diverse and talented group of organizational researchers, and we especially thank Louis B. Barnes, John J. Gabarro, and Leonard Schlesinger. Helpful colleagues at the Kennedy School of Government included Walter Broadnax, Michael Dukakis, Charles Kireker, Larry Lynn, Mark Moore, and Peter Zimmerman.

Harvard's president, Derek Bok, provided course development funds at just the right moment to help us put together the first version of the manuscript.

A remarkably creative collection of organizational scholars at Stanford helped in the gestation of our ideas, including J. Victor Baldridge, Ed Bridges, Robert Bush, Elizabeth Cohen,

Sanford Dornbusch, James March, John Meyer, W. Richard Scott, George Spindler, and Larry Thomas. Fritz Mulhauser will recognize ideas in two chapters that were initially developed with the support of the National Institute of Education. His patience in the interim between work on the project at Stanford and the finished book is appreciated. His encouragement has been instrumental in producing the book. We also got important help from Clayton P. Alderfer, David Berg, Richard Hackman, Claire Sokoloff, and Victor Vroom at Yale's School of Organization and Management.

We presented some of these ideas to many of our colleagues attending that best of all professional meetings, the Organizational Behavior Teaching Conference. We wish we could thank everyone, but we especially want to mention David Bradford, Allan Cohen, Esther Hamilton, Todd Jick, Craig Lundberg, John McDonough, Karl Weick, and all the members of the Magic Castle Group.

Barbara Bunker put her expertise in support systems to good use in supporting us, and we have both been enriched by Oron South's wisdom and friendship. Allan Kennedy's insights into the ways of corporate life were a continuing source of stimulation. We owe much to the five horsemen of OD in schools— C. Brooklyn Derr, Dale Lake, Matthew Miles, Philip Runkle, and Richard Schmuck. As the spokesman for OT (Organizational Transformation), Harrison Owen was a stimulating resource for emerging ideas in the field.

A number of students and friends courageously attempted to use some of our ideas in the real world. We hope that we learned as much as they from the results. Thanks are due to Bill Carey, Judy Codding, Gary Dickson, Warren Hayman, Jerry Kohn, Lee Pierce, and Seldon Whittaker. We thank the many participants in executive development programs who helped to keep us connected to the real world. They came from corporations, every level of government, schools and universities—and we learned from them all.

Robert Cordy turned the careful eye of a Navy research manager on the manuscript, with fruitful results. We owe much to our secretary at Harvard, Betty Barnes, for her skill, dedication, and unique personal flair.

Families always bear some of the burden of writing. Steven, Lori, and Scott Bolman have been more tolerant of their always-too-busy father than he has any right to expect. The same can be said for Jane Deal's tolerance of her often-outrageous father.

Our wives, Sandra Deal and Joan Gallos, supported both us and one another through the many trials of collaborative (and sometimes competitive) teaching and writing. We dedicate this book to them as one small way to say thanks, and we love you.

March 1984   Lee G. Bolman
                                                Cambridge, Massachusetts

                                                Terrence E. Deal
                                                Nashville, Tennessee

The Authors

Lee G. Bolman is lecturer on education at the Harvard Graduate School of Education and an independent management consultant. He received his B.A. degree in history (1962) and his Ph.D. degree in administrative sciences (1968) from Yale University.

Bolman's primary research interests have been in organizational behavior, and he has published numerous articles on management development, professional education, organizational conflict, and organization development. He has been a consultant to corporations, public agencies, universities, and public schools. At Harvard, he has taught in numerous executive programs and is faculty chairman for the Institute for Educational Management. He is also a member of the board of directors of the National Training Laboratories Institute for Applied Behavioral Science.

Terrence E. Deal is professor of education at Peabody College of Vanderbilt University. Before joining Peabody, he served on the faculties of Stanford University Graduate School of Education and the Harvard Graduate School of Education. He received his B.A. degree in history from LaVerne College

(1961), his M.A. degree in educational administration from California State University at Los Angeles (1966), and his Ph.D. degree in education and sociology from Stanford University (1972).

Deal has been a public school teacher, high school principal, district office administrator, and university professor. His primary research interests are in organizational symbolism and change. He is the author of five books, including the recent bestseller, *Corporate Cultures* (with Allan A. Kennedy, 1983). He has published numerous articles on change and leadership. He is a consultant to organizations in both public and private sectors, lectures widely, and teaches in a number of executive development programs.

Modern Approaches to Understanding and Managing Organizations

1

Introduction:
Common Views
of Organizations

The difficulties of managing organizations have been well documented and widely recognized. Organizations do not change when we want them to, yet they change rapidly when we wish they would not. They control and stifle with red tape, rigid rules, and bureaucratic lethargy but seem unable to control waste, inefficiency, and misdirected effort. Organizations have huge appetites and can swallow almost unlimited resources but often produce disappointing results. A substantial slice of organizational resources goes to employees in the form of salary, benefits, and perquisites, yet employees are frequently more discontented and apathetic than committed and satisfied.

Solving such organizational problems—and many others—is the appointed task of a special group called managers. To assist them in this awesome task, aspiring managers are armed with decision trees, PERT charts, consultants, management informa-

1

tion systems, "management by objectives" programs, and a panoply of theories and rational techniques. Managers go forth with this arsenal to tame the wild and savage social creations that we mundanely call "organizations." Yet in the end it is often the beast who wins. Defeated and battle-scarred managers retreat to management seminars and universities for tools that may give them a better chance in the next encounter. Often, they are mystified by what went wrong and seek some way to avoid the same mistakes or, at least, to face the same old problems with more confidence and less trauma.

Theories of Organization

The dominance of economic and governmental activity by large organizations is a relatively recent development. It is only in the last twenty-five years that social scientists have devoted significant time and attention to studying organizations and developing ideas about how they work (or why they often fail to work). Within the social sciences, major schools of thought have evolved, each with its own view of organizations, its own well-defended concepts and assumptions, and its own ideas about how managers can best bring social collectives under control.

Rational systems theorists emphasize organizational goals, roles, and technology. They look for ways to develop organizational structures that best fit organizational purpose and the demands of the environment.

Human resource theorists emphasize the interdependence between people and organizations. They focus on ways to develop a better fit between people's needs, skills, and values and the formal roles and relationships required to accomplish collective goals and purposes.

Political theorists see power, conflict, and the distribution of scarce resources as the central issues in organizations. They suggest that organizations are very like jungles and that managers need to understand and manage power, coalitions, bargaining, and conflict.

Symbolic theorists focus on problems of meaning in organizations. They are more likely to find serendipitous virtue in organizational misbehavior and to focus on the limits of managers' abilities to create organizational cohesion through power or rational design. In this view, managers must rely on images, luck, and sometimes the supernatural to bring some semblance of order to organizations.

We summarize these schools at this point only to contrast their basic differences. Each body of theory purports to be based on a scientific foundation—but each is also a theology that offers scripture and preaches its own version of the gospel to modern managers. Each gospel tells them what organizations are like, and each has a vision of how they should be. Each provides a range of ideas and techniques to make organizations better. A modern manager wanting to do better and understand more is consistently confronted with a cacophony of different voices and visions.

Examples of this division and diversity are numerous. A manager of a large corporation recently called several university-based consultants for help in dealing with turnover among middle managers. "It's obvious," said one. "You are probably neglecting your managers' needs for autonomy and opportunities to participate in important decisions. You need an attitude survey to pinpoint the problems."

Another consultant offered different advice. "When did you last reorganize? As your firm has grown, managers' responsibilities have probably become blurred and overlapping. When reporting relationships are confused, you get stress and conflict. You need to restructure."

Still another consultant called attention to the company's recent collective bargaining experience. "What do you expect? You've given up basic management prerogatives. If you want managers to stay, you'll have to get back to the table and fight to restore their power. Why the hell did you give away the store to the unions?"

A final call yielded one more opinion: "Your company has never developed a strong value system, and growth has made the situation worse. Your managers don't find any meaning in their work. You need to revitalize your company culture."

We call this state of organizational consulting—and of organization theory—"conceptual pluralism." In this book we will
not join the battle over which school of thought is better or
more valuable for managers. We do not believe that managers
have to choose the strongest voice or to visit a succession of
organizational gurus in order to obtain a more comprehensive
view. Instead, we advocate the use of diverse outlooks to obtain
a more comprehensive understanding of organizations and a
broader range of options for managerial action.

Theories as Frames

We have consolidated the major schools of organizational
thought into four relatively coherent perspectives. We have
chosen the label "frames" to characterize these different vantage points. Frames are windows on the world. Frames filter
out some things while allowing others to pass through easily.
Frames help us to order the world and decide what action to
take. Every manager uses a personal frame, or image, of organizations to gather information, make judgments, and get things
done.

Understanding organizations is nearly impossible when
the manager is unconsciously wed to a single, narrow perspective. Modern organizations are complicated. Think of the complexities and perils in introducing computers into a small elementary school. Consider the difficulties faced by a large, multi-
divisional company like Johnson & Johnson as it attempts to
integrate more than fifty different, semiautonomous businesses
under one corporate roof. Think of the enormous pressures facing managers in "Ma Bell"—the telephone giant that was forced
to divest all its local operating companies. Ask yourself how
you might try to reduce red tape in government agencies or reform the United States Congress.

Managers in all organizations—large or small, public or
private—can increase their effectiveness and their freedom
through the use of multiple vantage points. To be locked into a
single path is likely to produce error and self-imprisonment. We
believe that managers who understand their own frame—and who

can adeptly rely on more than one limited perspective—are better equipped to understand and manage the complex everyday world of organizations. Sometimes they can make a significant difference in how that world responds.

The four frames described in this book are based on the major schools of organizational research and theory. For each frame, we have provided a label and consolidated the central assumptions and propositions.

The *structural frame* emphasizes the importance of formal roles and relationships. Structures—commonly depicted in organization charts—are created to fit an organization's environment and technology. Organizations allocate responsibilities to participants ("division of labor") and create rules, policies, and management hierarchies to coordinate diverse activities. Problems arise when the structure does not fit the situation. At that point, some form of reorganization is needed to remedy the mismatch.

The *human resource frame* establishes its territory because organizations are inhabited by people. Individuals have needs, feelings, and prejudices. They have both skills and limitations. They have great capacity to learn and a sometimes greater capacity to defend old attitudes and beliefs. From a human resource perspective, the key to effectiveness is to tailor organizations to people—to find an organizational form that will enable people to get the job done while feeling good about what they are doing. Problems arise when human needs are throttled.

The *political frame* views organizations as arenas of scarce resources where power and influence are constantly affecting the allocation of resources among individuals or groups. Conflict is expected because of differences in needs, perspectives, and life-styles among different individuals and groups. Bargaining, coercion, and compromise are all part of everyday organizational life. Coalitions form around specific interests and may change as issues come and go. Problems may arise because power is unevenly distributed or is so broadly dispersed that it is difficult to get anything done. Solutions are developed through political skill and acumen—much as Machiavelli suggested centuries ago.

The *symbolic frame* abandons the assumptions of rationality that appear in each of the other frames and treats the organization as theater or carnival. Organizations are viewed as held together more by shared values and culture than by goals and policies. They are propelled more by rituals, ceremonies, stories, heroes, and myths than by rules, policies, and managerial authority. Organization is drama; the drama engages actors inside, and outside audiences form impressions based on what they see occurring on-stage. Problems arise when actors play their parts badly, when symbols lose their meaning, when ceremonies and rituals lose their potency. Improvements come through symbol, myth, and magic.

Each frame has its own vision of reality. Only when managers can look at organizations through the four are they likely to appreciate the depth and complexity of organizational life. Successful managers rely intuitively on the different frames, blending them into a coherent, pragmatic, personal theory of organizations. We believe that an explicit introduction to and grounding in all four frames can enrich any manager's native intuition. Success becomes possible even for the great majority of us who were not born with the ability to understand and act effectively in such a complicated and ambiguous world.

Learning the Frames

For the past five years, we have taught the four frames to managers in a variety of situations. Our primary setting has been a required introductory course for doctoral students at Harvard's Graduate School of Education. But we have also taught public-sector managers at the Kennedy School of Government and in summer institutes and private-sector managers in university programs and in corporate seminars.

Our experience across these diverse settings has taught us several things about people who manage organizations (at least, those with whom we have had the opportunity to work).

1. Most managers have relatively limited views of organizations. Generally, they are likely to diagnose most organizational problems as caused by the defects of particular individuals

or groups. Although the causes of problems are often seen as personal, the solutions are often rational: restructuring, rational discourse, the use of facts and logic as a basis for influence.

2. A majority of the people we work with have had very powerful negative experiences in organizations. For many, the frustrations of organizational life have outweighed the satisfactions. Attempts to improve organizations have often ended in failure and disillusionment. Feelings of cynicism and impotence are widespread.

3. When we introduce the four frames, people often respond with initial confusion. The frames seem to contradict one another; there is no right answer. Exploration of this issue often produces tension and conflict.

4. As people become more comfortable with the frames and have an opportunity to apply them—particularly in important, real-world situations—they report a liberating feeling of choice and power. They are much better able to understand what is happening around them. Sometimes they are able to develop effective ideas of how things might be changed. They are less often surprised and more often able to predict what will happen.

Our experience encourages us to believe that the frames have a wider audience than the participants in our courses and seminars. The frames can be helpful to any manager—senior executives in large corporations, hospital administrators, agency heads, and junior high assistant principals. They can even help in many of the informal settings of daily life—bridge clubs, sororities and fraternities, marriages, country fairs, or therapy groups. The nature of the setting and an individual's place in the setting will influence the specific application of the ideas, but we hope this book will effectively communicate the frames to managers at whatever level and wherever they confront the challenging but critical tasks that arise from collective activity.

2

⚜ ⚜ ⚜ ⚜ ⚜ ⚜ ⚜ ⚜

New Ways of
Seeing Organizations

Helen Demarco arrived in her office to find a clipping from a local newspaper. The headline read, "Osborne Announces Plan." Paul Osborne had been brought in two months earlier as chief executive of the organization with a mandate to "revitalize, cut costs, and improve efficiency." After twenty years with the organization, Helen had achieved a senior management position. She had not yet talked directly with Paul Osborne, but her boss reported directly to him. Like other long-term employees, Helen waited with curiosity and some apprehension to learn what the new chief would do.

She was startled when she read the plan. Many of its most important aspects rested on technical assumptions that related directly to Helen's area of expertise. Helen knew that Osborne was a professional manager with no particular technical skills, but she immediately saw that the new plan

8

contained fatal technical flaws. "If he tries to implement this, it will be the most expensive management mistake since the Edsel," Helen thought to herself.

Two days later, Helen was one of several senior managers who received a memo from Paul Osborne instructing them to form a committee to begin immediate work on implementation of the Osborne revitalization plan. The group met, and everyone agreed that the plan was "crazy."

"What do we do?" they said to one another.

"Why don't we just tell him that the plan can't work?" said one manager.

Several others rejected that approach: "We can't do that! He already thinks we're too conservative and not really creative. Besides, he's on record saying this plan will be great. If we tell him it's no good, he'll just say that we're defensive."

"Well, we can't just go ahead with it. It's bound to fail!"

"That's true," said Helen, "but we could tell him that we're making a study of how to implement the plan."

Helen's suggestion was overwhelmingly approved by the committee members. They told Paul Osborne that the study was starting, and they received a substantial budget to support the "research." But the real purpose of the study was more subtle (or more sinister): to discover a way to kill the plan without alienating Mr. Osborne.

Over time, the group developed an approach. They developed a very lengthy technical report filled with graphs, tables, numbers, and almost uninterpretable technical jargon. The report presented Paul Osborne with two options. Option A, his original plan, was presented as technically feasible, but the price tag was phenomenal—well beyond anything the organization could possibly afford. Option B, billed as a "modest downscaling" of the original plan, turned out to be much more affordable.

When Paul Osborne pressed the group for an explanation of the extraordinary difference in costs between the two proposals, they responded with extensive quotations from the charts and the technical jargon. They did not mention that if he was able to wade through all the data in the report, he might even notice the well-disguised truth that even Option B would provide very few benefits at a very high cost.

Osborne thought and argued and pressed for more information. He finally agreed to proceed with Option B. Since the plan took more than two years to implement, Paul Osborne had moved on to another organization before the plan was implemented. In fact, the "Osborne plan" was widely described as an extraordinary innovation that proved once again Paul Osborne's ability to revitalize ailing organizations.

Helen came away from this experience with deep feelings of frustration and failure. The Osborne plan, in her view, was a wasteful failure, and she had participated in a charade. But, she said to herself, "I really didn't have much choice. Osborne was determined to go ahead with the plan. It would have been career suicide to try to stop it."

Human organizations can be exciting and challenging. But as the Helen Demarco case demonstrates, they can also be wasteful, inefficient, and frustrating. The case illustrates several major properties of organizations that should be familiar to most managers. They are listed here.

Organizations Are Complex

Organizations are complex for a number of reasons. First and foremost, they are populated by people, and our ability to understand and predict human behavior is still very limited. Second, the interactions among different individuals and groups can be extremely complicated—as the interactions between Paul Osborne and Helen's committee show. Large organizations include a bewildering array of people, departments, technologies, goals, and environments. Almost anything can affect anything else, and it is often difficult to know *what* happened, much less *why*. Paul Osborne thought he knew what was happening on the Osborne Plan. As it turned out, he never did learn the real story.

Organizations Are Surprising

Organizations are full of surprises because they are so hard to predict. Paul Osborne believed his plan was a significant improvement for the organization. Helen Demarco and her group believed the plan was an expensive albatross. If we assume for a moment that Helen, not Paul, was right, the case illustrates something that happens often in organizations: Managers often believe that their efforts are an effective response to existing pathologies. Sometimes they make things worse by trying to improve them and might have made them better by leaving them alone or maybe even by trying to make them worse. Intervening in an organization is often like firing a cue ball into a large and complex array of balls. So many balls bounce off one another in so many directions that it is hard to know whether the final outcome will bear any resemblance to what was intended.

Organizations Are Deceptive

Not only do organizations surprise by defying expectations, they often camouflage the surprise. Paul Osborne expected that Helen Demarco and her colleagues would work hard to implement his plan. He did not expect that they would put most of their energy into sabotage—finding ways to block the plan. They did their best to hide what they were really doing under the form of "research" that was really a holding action and a "technical report" that was really artful camouflage.

Helen did not engage in deception because of a character

flaw or a personality disorder. She felt deception was wrong and felt regret about her actions. Yet she still believed that her behavior was a moral choice under circumstances that seemed to provide no other option. Sophisticated managers know that what happened to Paul Osborne happens often and could happen to them if they are not alert to the risk. Managers' programs for improving the organization might be counterproductive, but subordinates might not say so. They might not want to offend their superior; they might feel that the boss would not listen, or they might fear punishment for being resistant or insubordinate. A friend of ours who occupies a senior position in a large government agency puts it simply: "Communications in organizations are rarely candid, open, or timely."

Organizations Are Ambiguous

Because organizations are complex, surprising, and deceptive, they are often ambiguous—or vice versa. It is surprisingly difficult to know what is happening in businesses, hospitals, schools, or public agencies. Even if we know what is happening, it is hard to know what it means or how we should feel about it. Helen Demarco was not sure how Paul Osborne really felt, how receptive he was to alternative points of view, or what he was willing to accept. She was not sure that the elaborate charade was necessary. But she felt it was too risky to try to find out. Helen and her peers added to the ambiguity by trying to ensure that the director did not really know what was happening either.

As Helen's case illustrates, ambiguity occurs for a number of reasons. Sometimes information is incomplete or ambiguous. Sometimes the same information is interpreted in different ways by different people. At other times ambiguity is deliberately created as a way to hide problems or avoid conflict. Much of the time, organizational events and processes are so complex, scattered, and uncoordinated that no one can fully understand—let alone control—what is happening.

When an event is clear and unambiguous, it is relatively easy for different people to agree on what is happening. It is fairly easy to determine whether a train was on schedule, whether an airplane landed safely, or whether a clock is keeping accurate time. But many of the most important questions that managers ask in organizations are much more difficult to answer. Will a reorganization work? Was a meeting successful? Why did a decision that we all supported turn out not to work? When the issues are complex and the evidence is insufficient to provide definitive answers, individuals must make judgments or interpretations. The judgments they make depend on their perspectives—their beliefs, expectations, and assumptions—about the issues at hand.

To illustrate the influence of individual perspectives, consider a relatively straightforward task—asking people to determine the suit and number of a playing card. In a classic experiment, different playing cards were projected on a screen, and people were asked to call each card. The color of some cards was reversed, so that people saw a red nine of clubs or a black jack of hearts. People usually reinterpreted the reversed cards to make them "right"—the red club became either a black club or a red heart.

When people were given more time to view the anomalous cards, many became uncomfortable. They knew that something was wrong, but they had trouble saying what it was. Some people could not recognize the incorrect cards no matter how much time they were given to study them. People's perspectives influence what they see. What is inside them is as important as what is outside—sometimes more so. If it happens with concrete stimuli like playing cards, it is even truer for the ambiguous realities of everyday life in organizations.

You already have a perspective about organizations: your own beliefs about what organizations are, how they work, and how they should work. Those beliefs represent your personal *theory* about organizations. Next we examine what we mean by a perspective, or personal theory, and how such theories work.

Theories and Frames

Organizations are complex, surprising, deceptive, and ambiguous. But that does not mean they always seem that way to people in them. Keep in mind that people want their world to be understandable, predictable, and manageable. Even in the

face of inconsistent evidence—as in the playing-card experiment
—people will try to make the world fit their current theories
about it. That way, they can see their organizations as clear and
straightforward. They may be right or, like Paul Osborne, they
may be dead wrong. It all depends on whether they have a theory that works for them in the situation they are in. Consider
the following examples:

> A new teacher in an urban junior high school
> is becoming increasingly upset and unnerved by the
> tests, taunts, and tantrums of many of her stu-
> dents. Feeling increasingly confused and ineffec-
> tive, she turns to a more experienced teacher, who
> tells her, "That's normal and it happens to every
> new teacher. It's not your fault. It's the students
> we have at this school. Just stay calm and tell them
> that such behavior is unacceptable. Just remember
> not to let them push you around."

> A middle manager in a large organization has
> spent days trying to figure out how to get authori-
> zation for a nonroutine expenditure. After three
> personal meetings and twelve phone calls, none of
> which helped, she finally locates an obscure official
> in an equally obscure nonroutine expenditures de-
> partment, who tells her, "Oh, sure, that's easy.
> You just have to fill out Form 12-Q-73. Here's a
> couple of copies. Just send it to me, and you should
> get your authorization in a week."

> Over a period of a few weeks, you start to
> notice a novel set of physical symptoms—an un-
> familiar pattern of aches and pains in unusual loca-
> tions. For a while, you worry, wonder, and put off
> seeing a physician. Finally you make an appoint-
> ment. Your doctor makes a brief diagnosis and tells
> you, "Nothing to worry about. Happens all the
> time. Probably a virus. Three of these daily. Should
> clear up in ten days. Call if it doesn't."

The examples suggest that almost any situation can be confusing, worrisome, threatening, or even immobilizing for anyone who lacks a theory or perspective on how to deal with it. It is not always essential that the theory be correct. The experienced teacher's advice may be a poor theory, but it may still help the novice to feel more comfortable and able to cope. She has been assured that she is not responsible for the problem and that it will get better if she stays calm. In fact, if she is able to stay calm, there is a good chance that it *will* get better. Similarly, the doctor's diagnosis may be incorrect and his prescription irrelevant, but there is an excellent chance that you will feel improvement in ten days anyway. The condition might improve on its own, or there might be a placebo effect.

An accurate theory is usually better than an inaccurate one, particularly when accuracy is fairly easy to measure. If the middle manager fills out Form 12-Q-73 and still gets no authorization, her frustration level is likely to skyrocket. Accurate or not, what is most critical about a theory is that it lets us understand situations and take action. The novice teacher could not make sense out of her difficulties and did not know what to do to make things better. The same was true of the middle manager and the puzzled patient. In both cases, it was a relief to find someone who had a theory that made the situation understandable and told them what to do about it.

The theories we learn make all the difference in determining whether a given situation is confusing or clear, meaningful or cryptic, a disaster or a learning experience. Theories are essential because of a simple—but very basic—fact about human perception and thinking. Humans are very good in the long term but extremely limited in the short term. We cannot handle very much information at once, and we cannot learn very much in a short time interval. Typically, we can memorize a list of about seven items after hearing it once. If the list is much longer (say, a nine-digit ZIP code), most of us cannot remember it on one hearing. But if we spend enough time, we can store and remember very large and complicated blocks of information.

Because of the short-term limits on human memory and thinking, too much is happening in any situation for an individual to attend to everything. To understand the situation and to take action, the individual needs theories that do two things:

1. Tell the individual what is important and what can be safely ignored.
2. Group a lot of different pieces of information into patterns or concepts.

Consider the cockpit of a commercial jet airplane. To the nonpilot, it is a very complex and confusing array of controls, switches, gauges, and other mysteries. If the plane is in flight, an experienced pilot can glance at the instruments for a few seconds and know a great deal about the situation of the airplane. A nonpilot could stare at the same instruments for hours and know almost nothing. The pilot and the nonpilot have the same limitation in short-term thinking and memory. But the pilot has learned a set of patterns that group a lot of information into a few manageable chunks. It takes the pilot hundreds of hours to learn the concepts, but once learned, they can be used with enormous ease, speed, and accuracy.

While you are learning a pattern, you have to spend a lot of time concentrating on the information in it. Whether you are learning to program a computer, prove a theorem, play a musical instrument, or return a tennis serve, learning is a slow, frustrating, self-conscious process. But once the pattern is well learned, you can use it quickly and easily without even thinking about it. A person who has good "intuition" can size up a situation very rapidly and know exactly what needs to be done. The intuition is based on prior learning of effective patterns of thought and action.

What this all means is that we have to develop patterns and frames in order to make sense of the complexities of everyday life. It takes time and effort to develop those patterns, so we have an investment in them once they are developed. Helen Demarco had developed a set of theories that enabled her to interpret what Paul Osborne's behavior meant and what she should do about it. Her theory may or may not have been right. She may have misinterpreted the situation, and her actions may have been poorly chosen. But she did not have an alternative theory.

That is why she felt there was nothing else she could do. To give up the theory we have is to sacrifice all the investment that we put into learning it. If we do not have an alternative, we immobilize ourselves if we give up our current theory. Theories shield us from confusion, uncertainty, and anxiety. People get completely stuck when they have tried every theory they know and none of them works.

We are in a dilemma whenever our current theories are not working very well. Revising old patterns is costly in time, effort, and temporary loss of confidence and effectiveness. It is hard to know in advance whether it is more useful to hold on to what we have—at least it is familiar and we already know how to use it—or to develop a new approach.

The dilemma is there even if we do not recognize that our current theory is not working. The card experiment demonstrates that our theory will often block recognition of its own errors. We see the world through the patterns and theories that we already have. Those theories lead us to pay attention to some information, ignore other information, and interpret everything in the light of what we already believe. It is not difficult to see how theories can lead managers into real trouble. Consider the following example of an interaction between a boss and a subordinate.

> A DC-8 jet airplane was approaching the airport in Cold Bay, Alaska, under poor weather conditions. Results from the navigation equipment were erratic because of the mountainous terrain. At 5:36 A.M. the captain asked the first officer, "What's your DME?" (pilot jargon for "How far are we from the airport on the distance-measuring equipment?"). The first officer indicated that he did not have a reading but his previous reading had been 40 miles. The captain, an experienced pilot, was off course for the approved approach into the Cold Bay airport but said nothing to the first officer about what he intended. The following conversation occurred:

First officer: Are you going to make a procedure turn?

Captain: No, I—I wasn't going to.

(Pause)

First officer: What kind of terrain are we flying over?

Captain: Mountains everywhere.

(Pause. At 5:39 A.M.)

First officer: We should be a little higher, shouldn't we?

Captain: No, 40 DME |40 miles from the airport], you're all right.

(At 5:40 A.M.)

Captain: I'll go a little bit higher here. No reason to stay down that low so long.

(The captain climbed briefly to 4,000 feet, then began to descend again)

(At 5:41 A.M.)

First officer: The altimeter is alive. [Translation: "The radio altimeter, which measures the airplane's distance from the ground, shows that we are not very far above the very mountainous local terrain."]

(At 5:42 A.M.)

First officer: Radio altimeter—Hey, John, we're off course! Four hundred feet from something!

(Six seconds later the airplane was destroyed when it crashed into a mountain)

The captain was a senior pilot who had flown into the airport a number of times. He assumed that his knowledge of the terrain and of the approach procedures was accurate. He had a "theory" of how to land the plane safely, but he did not communicate his theory to his copilot.

The first officer, who was in the dark about the captain's intentions, gently probed to suggest that they might not be making a safe approach. Apparently, the probes were too gentle —the captain never responded to the message. The captain did not *expect* difficulty, because he had flown into this airport before. The conversation suggests that he did not *want* to examine the possibility that he might be making a mistake. When the first officer questioned the captain's actions, the captain said, in effect, "I'm in charge here, and I know what I'm doing."

The Cold Bay accident illustrates that experienced and competent people can use theories that are wrong without realizing their error (at least until it is too late to do anything about it). Such errors are most likely to occur in situations that are complex, ambiguous, or stressful—exactly the conditions that organizations often create.

Flying a commercial jet airplane is complicated and requires a lot of training, experience, and skill. But it is actually simpler than much of what happens in most organizations. In an airplane, a serious mistake usually shows up clearly. It may not show up soon enough, but an accident is a clear, unambiguous event. Since organizational processes are often much more ambiguous, administrators need to be able to bring order out of the complexity.

Because of the complexity and ambiguity of organizations, differences in individuals' theories can produce very different interpretations of the same set of circumstances. Most administrators are well aware that the same thing is often seen very differently by different people. What Paul Osborne saw as a great step toward organizational improvement, Helen Demarco saw as a great boondoggle.

People see things differently for a variety of reasons: physical differences (some people are nearsighted, color blind, or hard of hearing), differences in wants and needs (some people seek excitement and challenge; others prefer rest and simplicity), differences in expectations (some people are paranoid and expect the worst, while others are perennial optimists), and differences in position (managers see resistance and lack of cooperation where workers see bureaucratic rigidity and over-control).

Once formed, perceptions can quickly solidify. If you and I attend the same meeting, we might come out with very different views of what happened. Each of us may not see our view as a perception that is influenced by our own theories. Instead, we are likely to think that our view is "the truth."

If we believe that our view is "the truth," we are likely to defend that truth against challenge. The fact that people will defend their views is one reason that decisions in meetings are sometimes left ambiguous. To deal directly with differences in perceptions might produce conflict and dramatically lengthen the meeting. The problem is particularly acute in organizations whose goals and technology are relatively ambiguous. In schools, for example, there is often little agreement among individuals and groups about policies, practices, or procedures. Within the same school there may be little agreement between the principal and the teachers, between the staff and the parents, and among the teachers concerning teaching methods, school policies, and participation in decision making. Even in an airline cockpit (as we have seen) or a stable company that has been making the same product for years, subtle ambiguities and radically different perceptions can make communications difficult at best.

It is commonplace that different people see things differently. It is less widely understood that differences in theory can *create* differences in reality. What people see influences how they define situations and take action. A company president who believes that his board is interfering may act as if anything the board does is an example of interference. In turn, the board may become concerned that the president is so defensive, and they may intervene *more* actively because the president spends so much time trying to keep them from examining management decisions. Rosenthal and Jacobson (1968) studied schoolteachers who were led to expect, and subsequently perceived, dramatic growth by "spurters"—students who were labeled as "about to bloom." Even though the "spurters" had been chosen at random, they made above-average gains on achievement tests. They really *did* spurt. Apparently the teachers' expectations were somehow communicated to and felt by the students. It illustrates the maxim that what you believe can determine what you see and what you get. The same "Pygmalion effect" has been replicated in countless reorganizations, new-product launchings, or new-and-improved approaches to performance appraisal.

A manager is a diagnostician who uses theories, or frames, to focus on certain things while ignoring others. The frame determines the questions asked, the information collected, the problems defined, and, ultimately, the actions taken. When Helen Demarco received instructions to proceed with the "Osborne plan," she had a number of important decisions to make. Is this a problem? Can it be ignored? If not, what does she need to do about it? What actions are likely to be effective?

We have asked a number of students and managers to develop their own diagnoses of Helen's case. We find that most of them use one of the following three common-sense perspectives to develop a diagnosis.

Most common is the *personalistic perspective*. In this view, most of what happens in organizations can be explained by the characteristics of individuals. People do what they do because of their wants, needs, beliefs, attitudes, feelings, and abilities (or lack of abilities). Problems are caused by people: people with the wrong attitudes, with abrasive personalities, or divergent values, or lack of competence. Those with this view blame Paul Osborne for being authoritarian and Helen for not having the "guts" to stand up to her boss.

Another common frame is the *rational perspective*. People should behave rationally in organizations. That means they should examine the relevant information and make the best decision on the basis of the "facts." Sometimes this does not happen because people are not sure what they are supposed to do. That can be solved by clarifying job descriptions, tightening the rules, or providing better supervision. People who view the case in this light believe that both Helen and her boss should approach the situation as two rational managers—that is, sit down, review the facts, and arrive at a decision based on an objective analysis of the situation.

Still a third way to look at the Helen Demarco case is the *power perspective*. People who use this perspective emphasize that it is a dog-eat-dog world and everyone has a vested interest. The way decisions get made depends mostly on who has the most power. For managers, power is the central problem: Who has it, and how can you get it? From this view, both Paul Osborne and Helen Demarco have their own interests: Osborne wants to look good as a manager, while Helen wants to protect her job. Both of them play their own power games, and the winner will be the one who makes the most adroit use of political power.

Each of these three perspectives focuses on important issues in organizations. But administrators who use only one of the perspectives are likely to have an incomplete diagnosis that leads to an incorrect solution.

The personalistic frame assumes that behavior in organizations is caused mostly by personal characteristics—by rigid bosses, charismatic leaders, slothful subordinates, bumbling bureaucrats, greedy labor leaders, insensitive elites, power-hungry politicians, and dedicated public servants. People behave as they do because of internal characteristics, such as emotions, motives, personality conflicts, and unconscious needs.

Several decades of research on personality and individual differences have shown how significant individual characteristics can be. People are different, and their differences have a powerful influence on how they behave. In fact, the personalistic frame is appropriate whenever we are trying to understand why two persons behave differently in the same situation. But what if *different* persons behave the same way when placed in the same situation? For example, what if we replace Helen with a manager who has more "guts," and she then turns out to behave the same way that Helen did? The personalistic frame is no help in explaining such an event.

Another problem with the personalistic frame is that it often provides managers with a diagnosis which they are sure is correct but which they cannot use. If you face a problem that you are sure is caused by someone else's "personality," then the solution is to change the individual's personality or get rid of the individual. Even psychiatrists find personality change a difficult, long-term task, and firing everyone who seems to have a personality problem is rarely a viable solution for managers.

Helen believed that Paul Osborne was too committed to his plan to be influenced. But she did not feel she could say that to him, because he might see her as insubordinate or insulting or attacking. Helen's personalistic diagnosis made the problem seem almost insoluble.

Helen might have tried a rational approach to Paul. She could have made a coherent and systematic presentation of the "facts" that led her to believe Paul's plan would not work. But her diagnosis of Paul led her to believe that that would not work either. She finally settled on a political solution, even though she did not see it as a very effective approach to the situation.

The rational frame has its own limits. It starts from the reasonable assumption that organizations are supposed to achieve certain goals. Organizations will be effective when the goals and policies are clear, jobs are well defined, control systems are in place, and employees behave rationally. In Helen's case, that means she should support Paul's plan if it is based on accurate analysis and information and should persuade him to change it if it is not. Any disagreement between Helen and Paul should be resolved through reasonable discussion. If people always behaved that way, human organizations would presumably work a lot better than most of them do. Paul proposed his plan because he thought the organization was not performing as well as it should. Helen and her fellow managers agreed that the organization needed to become more effective. But they did not agree that Paul's plan would work, and they doubted that reasonable discussion would resolve the difference.

The problem with the rational perspective is that it is very good at explaining how organizations should work but very poor at explaining why they do not work the way they should. In countless organizations, managers who believe in the rational perspective, and sincerely try to make it work become discouraged and frustrated because the organization stubbornly refuses to cooperate. Year after year, there are new job descriptions and control systems, organization studies and reorganizations, management consultants and the introduction of "improved" management methods. Yet the same old problems persist, seemingly immune to every organizational cure that management can devise.

The power perspective points to some important features of organizational life. Helen and Paul do have different self-interests and different forms of power. Helen is a career employee with a stake in protecting her status in the organization. She can afford to take a long-term view of organizational improvement. An unrealistic crash program that fails in the long run is not only harmful to the organization but potentially harmful to her career as well. Paul is in a different situation. He has been brought in with a mandate for change, and he may not stay in this job more than a few years. Long-range programs that take five or ten years to make a difference will not bolster Paul's reputation as a leader who gets action. A dramatic, fast-paced program that promises big improvements in a relatively short time is exactly what he wants to see.

From the power perspective, the relationship between Paul and Helen is a power game. Paul's power derives from his position as the chief executive. Helen's stems from her expertise, her control over information (a power she shares with her colleagues), and her knowledge that she may well outlast the director. The political perspective provides a credible analysis of why the situation turned out the way it did. Helen and her colleagues played their political cards adeptly and, apparently, achieved a significant victory. But Helen and Paul would both prefer to manage organizations so that political games do not dominate decision making. In that sense, both lost, and the power perspective provides little help in knowing how to prevent such an outcome.

The personalistic perspective, the rational perspective, and the power perspective all point to important phenomena in organizations. Each is a useful analytic frame, and each is incomplete. The same is true about almost any theory for understanding anything.

In the past, the prevailing theories about management have had a significant impact on the beliefs and behaviors of practicing managers. Taylor's human engineering approach created an efficiency mind set among many managers, leading to a whole generation of efficiency experts and time-and-motion studies. A generation later, a famous set of experiments at Western Electric highlighted the importance of social factors at work. The result was a new generation of managers who tried to

practice good "human relations." Computers, operations researchers, and systems theorists caused still another generation
of managers to focus on mathematical models and "management information systems."

In Western cultures, there is a tendency to embrace one
theory or ideology and to try to make the world conform. If it
works, we continue in our view. If discrepancies arise, we ra-
tionalize. If others challenge our view, we ignore them or put
them in their place. Only if events go against us dramatically
and over a long period are we likely to question our theories.
Even then, we may quickly convert to a new world view, trig-
gering the cycle again.

In East Asian cultures—Japan in particular—there are four
major religions, each with its own beliefs and assumptions:
Buddhism, Confucianism, Shintoism, and Taoism. Although the
religions conflict dramatically in their basic tenets, the Japanese
do not try to choose one. They use them all, taking advantage
of the strengths of each for suitable purposes or occasions. The
four organizational frames can play a similar role for managers
in modern organizations.

The theories that you take with you in your work as a
manager will influence what you see, what you understand,
what you do, and, ultimately, how effective you are as a manager. We will not attempt to teach you the one true theory of
how to manage, but we will try to present four very important
and powerful perspectives on how organizations work.

In summary: The theories, or frames, that we use determine what we see and what we do. Many organizational problems occur because managers use frames that are too simple or
too narrow. They may employ a "personalistic" frame that
causes them to use "personality" as a catch-all explanation for
everything that happens in organization. They may use a "rational" perspective and believe that everything in organizations
ought to be rational. Or they may use a "power" perspective
and see all of organizational life as a power game in which the
fittest survive.

Any perspective may capture only a limited slice of what
is important in a situation and may lead to faulty diagnoses and

ineffective actions. The world of most managers and administrators is a world of complexity, ambiguity, value dilemmas, political pressures, and multiple constituencies. Such a world is particularly prevalent in public and human service organizations. It is often an easy world in which to feel failure, frustration, cynicism, and powerlessness. If is often a difficult world in which to experience growth, achievement, and progress.

In the next chapters, we will examine four "frames" for analyzing and taking action in organizations. We cannot guarantee your success as a manager, a consultant, or a change agent. We believe, though, that you can improve the odds in your favor with an appreciation of each of the frames and how they can be used in real organizations. You will have a broader understanding of human organizations—how they work, their limitations, and their possibilities. You will have more ways to think and act in any given situation. Some of those situations may still turn out to be impossible, but most of them should reveal surprising possibilities for creativity and effective action.

3

Getting Organized: The Structural Approach

McDonald's, which made the "Big Mac" a household word, dominates the fast food retail business. It is an enormously successful company. Structurally, McDonald's has a relatively small headquarters staff at its world headquarters outside Chicago. The vast majority of its employees are spread across North America and the world in the thousands of McDonald's outlets. Despite its size, McDonald's is a highly centralized organization: Many of the major decisions are made at the headquarters.

The managers and employees of each restaurant have little discretion about how to do their jobs. Much of their work is controlled by technology; machines time the french fries and even measure the soft drinks. Chefs are not encouraged to develop creative new recipes for making a Big Mac or a Quarter-Pounder (although the Egg McMuffin was created by an individual in a local franchise). The parent company makes strenuous efforts to ensure that each McDonald's food item conforms to standard specifications. That assures the customer that a Big

27

Mac will taste virtually identical whether it is purchased in New York or Los Angeles, Toronto or Mexico City, Paris or Hong Kong. But that guarantee of standard quality inevitably limits the latitude of the people who own or work in individual outlets.

McDonald's makes very little effort to offer different products in different markets. The company assumes that its hamburgers will sell in the same form almost anywhere, regardless of local traditions and culture around food. There are occasional concessions to local taste—we once ordered *saimin*, a Japanese noodle soup, from the menu of a McDonald's in Hawaii—but the McDonald's on the Champs Elysées in Paris makes no attempt to conform to Parisian culinary traditions.

Harvard University is also regarded as a very successful organization. Like McDonald's, Harvard has a very small administrative group, but in most other respects the two organizations are structured very differently. Even though Harvard is much more geographically concentrated than McDonald's, its administrative structure is much more decentralized.

Virtually all of Harvard's activities are concentrated in a few square miles of Boston and Cambridge, but most of its employees are spread across the several schools of the university—including Harvard College (the undergraduate school), the graduate Faculty of Arts and Sciences, and the many professional schools. Each of the separate faculties has its own dean and largely controls its own destiny.

Harvard is one of the few universities in the world in which different faculties choose to operate on different academic calendars. The fall semester in the law and business schools usually begins a week or two earlier than in the schools of government and education. Each school also has a large measure of fiscal autonomy and has responsibility for its own budget. Just as the separate schools are highly independent of one another, individual faculty members have enormous autonomy and discretion. In many schools they have almost complete control over what courses they teach, what research they do, and what, if any, university activities they pursue.

The contrasts between McDonald's and Harvard are particularly obvious at the level of service delivery. No one expects that individual personalities will influence the quality of the hamburger you order at McDonald's. But everyone expects that every course at Harvard will be very much the unique creation of the individual professor. Two of Harvard's schools might offer courses with the same title that are entirely different.

Why do McDonald's and Harvard have such radically different structures? Is either structure more effective than the other? Or has each organization evolved an approach to organizing that fits its own task and environment? The structural perspective focuses on questions like these and seeks to understand the complex nature of organizational design and structure.

As Harvard and McDonald's illustrate, different organizations display distinct patterns, tempos, textures, and hues. At the same time, there are a number of characteristics that all organizations share. Organizations have goals, boundaries, levels of authority, communication systems, coordinating mechanisms, and distinctive cultures. This is true whether the organization is a bank, a church, a family, or the United States Army. The profile of those properties varies widely across different types of organizations. Educational organizations, like Harvard, typically have multiple, diffuse goals, unclear boundaries, weak technology, and informal mechanisms for coordination. In contrast, business firms, like McDonald's, are likely to have clearer goals and boundaries, more unified chains of command, and more sophisticated and extensive control systems.

How to structure itself is one of the central issues facing any organization. A formal structure is more than just boxes and lines arranged on an organizational chart. It is a depiction of the formalized pattern of activities, expectations, and exchanges among individuals. The shape of the formal structure enhances or constrains what an organization is able to accomplish. Formal structure also affects the activities, relationships, and mental states of participants who work in the organization.

Structure is important even in small groups, as some research findings illustrate. Small groups trying to accomplish a complicated, nonroutine task (for example, research and education at the frontiers of knowledge) do better with a decentralized structure. Groups working on a simpler, more routine task (for example, producing a Big Mac that is exactly like every other Big Mac) do better with a more centralized structure. Regardless of task, participants generally prefer structures that give them more room to make choices and more options to communicate with other members (Leavitt, 1978).

The purpose of this chapter is to synthesize theory and knowledge of organizational structure. First, we review the intellectual origins of structural thought. Second, we outline the key elements of a structural perspective and explore the conceptual ties among the elements. Third, we highlight some specific theories of organizational structure. In the next chapter we explore some of the common structural pathologies that can make life in organizations difficult and unpleasant.

Structural Beginnings

The ancestry of the structural view of organizations has two main branches. The first arose from the work of industrial psychologists concerned with how organizations could be constructed to obtain maximum efficiency. The work of Frederick W. Taylor (1911) is the best-known example. Taylor's concept of scientific management dealt mostly with his attempts to break tasks into minute detail and to retrain workers to get the most payoff from each motion and second spent at work. Taylor is the intellectual father of the time-and-motion study. Another group of theorists who contributed to the scientific management school included Henri Fayol (1919/1949), Lyndall F. Urwick, and Luther Gulick (Gulick and Urwick, 1937). Their primary focus was on developing a set of principles for managers about specialization, span of control, authority, and delegation of responsibility.

The second branch of the structural tradition began with the work of the German sociologist Max Weber (1947). Weber wrote at the turn of the century, when formal organization was a relatively new pattern that was replacing earlier patriarchal patterns. Patriarchal organizations usually had a father figure—a single individual who had almost unlimited power over others and could reward, punish, promote, or fire solely on personal whim. In popular film and fiction, the image of the Mafia "godfather" suggests that the patriarchal form lives on in some organizations. Weber saw the obvious limitations to rational decision making in patriarchal organizations and sought to conceptualize an ideal form of organization that was constructed to maximize rationality. The model that he developed outlined six major dimensions of "bureaucracy":

1. A fixed division of labor among participants.
2. A hierarchy of offices.
3. A set of general rules that govern performance.
4. Separation of personal from official property and rights.
5. Selection of personnel based on technical qualifications (not such things as family ties or friendship with the leader).
6. Employment viewed as a career by organizational participants.

    After World War II, Weber's work was rediscovered by organization theorists, and it has spawned a substantial body of theory and research. Among others, Blau and Scott (1962), Perrow (1972), and Hall (1963) have contributed significantly to the extension of Weber's model of bureaucracy. Their work has examined the interrelations among the elements of structure, looked closely at why organizations choose one structure or another, and examined the impact of structure on morale, productivity, and effectiveness.

Structural Assumptions

    The structural perspective is based on a set of core assumptions:

1. Organizations exist primarily to accomplish established goals.
2. For any organization, there is a structure appropriate to the goals, the environment, the technology, and the participants.

3. Organizations work most effectively when environmental turbulence and the personal preferences of participants are constrained by norms of rationality.
4. Specialization permits higher levels of individual expertise and performance.
5. Coordination and control are accomplished best through the exercise of authority and impersonal rules.
6. Structures can be systematically designed and implemented.
7. Organizational problems usually reflect an inappropriate structure and can be resolved through redesign and reorganization.

Structuralists tend to see organizations as relatively closed systems pursuing fairly explicit goals. Under those conditions, organizations can operate rationally with high degrees of certainty and predictability. If organizations are highly dependent on the environment, they are continually vulnerable to environmental influence or interference. To reduce their vulnerability, a variety of structural mechanisms are created to protect central activities from fluctuation and uncertainty (Thompson, 1967). Those devices buffer the organization and reduce unpredictability. They include the following:

- *Coding*—creating classification schemes for inputs.
- *Stockpiling*—storing raw materials and products so that inputs and outputs can be regulated.
- *Leveling*—motivating suppliers to provide inputs or creating a demand for outputs.
- *Forecasting*—anticipating changes in supply and demand.
- *Growth*—striving for an economy of scale that will give the organization leverage over the environment.

It is easy to see how business enterprises use these techniques to manage the unpredictable elements in the environment. McDonald's, for example, codes its inputs into categories such as ground beef, potatoes, and condiments. Those inputs are stockpiled as needed to ensure that customer requirements can be met. McDonald's negotiates with suppliers to ensure a steady flow of raw materials and uses extensive marketing and sales efforts to ensure customers in the restaurants. It seeks to anticipate fluctuations in the price or availability of raw materials and to grow through establishing new outlets and adding new products.

The same strategies are used in other types of organizations. Harvard codes its inputs (distinguishing, for example, between undergraduate and graduate students), stockpiles important resources (in Harvard's case, its endowment is a particularly prominent example), and tries to find markets for its outputs (for example, the university established a program several years ago to help graduating Ph.D.s find jobs in the private sector).

Although the word *bureaucracy* often conjures up images of inefficiency and rigidity, the structural perspective is not as machinelike or as inflexible as many believe. Its assumptions reflect a belief in rationality and a faith that the right structure can minimize organizational problems. Where the human resource perspective emphasizes the importance of changing people (through training, rotation, promotion, or dismissal), the structural perspective veers away from training or termination as a key strategy. It focuses instead on how to find some arrangement—a pattern of roles and relationships—that will accommodate organizational needs.

Elements of Structure

Organizations face a major dilemma in structuring work. To get work done, it is necessary to *differentiate*—to divide responsibilities across different individuals and organizational units. But the more an organization differentiates, the more difficult it is to *integrate* all the different parts (Lawrence and Lorsch, 1967). The larger and more diverse the organization, the harder it is to coordinate all the different activities so that the organization can attain the advantages of specialization without becoming chaotic and confused. Achieving a balance between differentiation and integration is one of the most fundamental issues of structural design, and every organization develops its own unique pattern.

McDonald's is highly differentiated geographically, yet each restaurant is very much like the next, and the total organization is very tightly integrated. Harvard is highly differentiated but very loosely integrated both horizontally and vertically. Every organization's pattern of differentiation and integration is reflected in the relations among four major elements of structure: organizational levels, goals, roles, and linkages.

Organizational Levels

Organizations can be viewed as having three major structural levels (Parsons, 1960). The *institutional level* confronts the external environment and maintains the flow of information and resources across the organization's boundaries. In most organizations those are among the major responsibilities of top management. The *managerial level* coordinates and controls the work flow, makes decisions, resolves conflicts, and deals with problems that arise in the work setting. In most organizations those are the primary responsibility of middle managers. The *technical level* performs the specific activities needed to transform raw materials into finished products. That is the responsibility of rank-and-file workers.

Each of the three levels has its own set of functions and constraints. In some ways each level is a distinct organization facing a different environment. But each is also tied to the others as a part of the same organization. In business organizations the ties among the three levels are usually fairly tight. In educational organizations the links are typically loose, so that each level performs its own activities and is substantially disconnected from the other levels (Meyer, Scott, and Deal, 1981).

Goals

Goals are conceptions of desired end states. They are projections of what an organization wants to accomplish, produce, or reach. Goals vary in how specific they are. In business organizations, goals like profitability, growth, and market share are relatively specific and measurable. In educational and human service organizations, goals of "education" or "help" are much more diffuse. Organizations vary in the number and complexity of their goals. Businesses may have fewer and less complex goals, while schools and universities have many. There are also differences among organizations in how much people agree on what the goals are. It is likely that the top management of McDonald's finds it much easier to agree on the basic goals of the institution than the top administrators at Harvard University.

Westerlund and Sjostrand (1979) suggest that organizational goals exist in a variety of different forms and are used for different purposes:

- *Honorific "boy scout" goals*—fictitious goals that credit the organization with desirable qualities.
- *Taboo goals*—goals that are real but are not talked about.
- *Stereotype goals*—goals that any reputable organization *should* have.
- *Existing goals*—a composite of the mixture of goals that are held by organizational participants.
- *Stated goals*—the goals the organization announces for itself.
- *Repressed goals*—goals that are pursued but would not stand up if confronted with the organization's values or self-image.

The list underscores the complexity of organizational goals. Goals can be individual or corporate, overt or covert, conscious or repressed, taboo or honorific. For any organization, disentangling the actual structure of goals is a difficult task. Goals are important in the structural perspective, but their complexity makes them difficult to incorporate into an equation of structural design.

Roles

Differentiation allocates activities and responsibilities across participants. By distributing responsibilities, an organization creates offices, positions, specialties, and subunits. We use the term *role* to refer to differentiation and allocation of work to various individuals or groups. An individual's role involves both activities and expectations. These are generally reflected in job titles or descriptions and in evaluation criteria.

Consider again the familiar McDonald's restaurant. As a customer, you deal directly with counter staff, whose job is to take your order, collect your money, assemble the items ordered, and give them to you. Both McDonald's and you, the customer, have expectations about how counter help will fill their role. If they are slow, surly, or uncooperative, they violate those expectations. If they are efficient, fast, and cheerful, it is likely that you will feel your expectations are being met. If you order a Big Mac and none is available, they will communicate to a cook, whose job is to provide a steady supply of hamburgers and other cooked items. Each restaurant also has managers, who are responsible for hiring and supervising the help, ensuring that the restaurant adheres to standards, and ordering raw materials. The jobs of the counter help are highly structured, narrowly defined, and highly repetitive. Few skills are required, and there is little discretion. The job of the manager is more complex, varied, and demanding.

Harvard University also has role differentiation, but the roles are very different. Whereas the counter help is the primary direct service provider at McDonald's, the professor occupies that role at Harvard. The professor's role definition is complex, ambiguous, and loosely structured. Professors are expected to show up for classes, conduct research, and fulfill vaguely defined goals of "university service." Beyond that, the role is mostly what each individual chooses to make it. In fact, people *expect* professors to be unusual or idiosyncratic.

The structure of roles varies considerably across organizations of different type, size, or location. In some the structure of roles is fairly simple and standardized. Elementary schools typically have a principal, a custodian, perhaps an office secretary, and a group of teachers. Teachers may teach different grade levels, but beyond that the level of specialization is fairly low. Within a classroom, a given teacher is normally responsible for the whole range of subjects.

As organizations become larger and more complex, the level of specialization is higher and the role structure more specialized. Evaluation specialists, computer units, personnel offices, systems analysts, public relations offices, training units, environmental quality departments, and affirmative action officers are only a few examples of the multiplicity of roles likely to be found in any large organization.

The rapid pace of change and development in many technical areas has often made it impossible for a single individual to stay current in a particular field. Such changes create the need for even higher levels of specialization, which make the role structure of the organization even more complicated. Specialization expands the number and range of positions and the level of training and professionalization among participants. A local hamburger stand cannot afford, and probably does not need, to forecast beef prices long-range and worldwide, but such a function is much more critical to McDonald's.

Linkages

Because life in organizations has become increasingly complex, diverse, specialized, and segmented, it has become more difficult to keep the organization together. Linkages keep organizations organized. Otherwise, specialized efforts do not get linked together, and various individuals and units may pursue their own goals while ignoring the larger mission of the organization. Without appropriate coordination and control, organizations become fragmented, fractionated, and ineffective.

Linkages are needed because differentiation leads to interdependence: People and units depend on one another to get work done. Structural theorists (for example, Thompson, 1967) discuss three major forms of interdependence: pooled, sequential, and reciprocal. Pooled interdependence depicts a relationship in which the efforts of one or more individuals or groups make a general contribution to the whole, but the different parts do not have to take one another into account. Two divisions of a bank may have very little to do with each other and may be linked only in the sense that the contribution of each is important to the overall success of the bank. Their efforts are *pooled* to make the bank work more effectively.

The manufacture of an airplane (or an automobile or almost any manufactured product) illustrates *sequential* interdependence. At Boeing Aircraft the design division must outline the overall shape and dimensions of the airplane. The engineering division needs to develop the blueprint and the specifications for individual parts. The parts department needs to purchase or manufacture the essential components. The assembly division needs to put the parts together. The efforts of each role or group are related sequentially. No group can do its work unless the groups "up the line" have done theirs. Assembly cannot put together an airplane until design, engineering, and parts have each done their work.

Reciprocal interdependence exists when interdependence goes in both directions, as illustrated in the relationship between sales and underwriting in an insurance company. The sales department is responsible for finding customers, but the underwriters have to decide whether a given customer is a good risk and how much to charge. Sales is hampered if underwriting rejects too many customers or prices the policies much higher than the competition. Conversely, underwriting is hampered if the sales department keeps finding customers who are very poor risks.

Interdependence increases as it moves from pooled toward reciprocal. The level of interdependence and the complexity of the role structure have important implications for coordination and control. The more complex the specialization and the higher the level of interdependence, the greater the need for coordination and for more sophisticated forms of control.

Organizations attempt to coordinate and control in two primary ways: (1) vertically, through authority and rules, and (2) laterally, through meetings, task forces, and special coordinating roles. Basically, vertical coordination occurs when people at higher levels coordinate and control the work of subordinates. Lateral coordination occurs when the subordinates coordinate with one another. A restaurant manager who instructs cooks and waiters in how to work together is using vertical coordination. When the waiter and the cook talk directly to each other, they are engaging in lateral coordination.

The relative importance of vertical and lateral coordination depends on the task and the environment. Vertical coordination is more likely to be significant when the environment is relatively stable and the task well understood or when uniformity is a critical organization need. McDonald's ensures that each restaurant meets standards almost entirely through vertical coordination mechanisms such as authority, written procedures and quality standards, and regular inspections of every restaurant. Very little coordination occurs laterally between different outlets.

In a university like Harvard, the loose structure and the high levels of faculty autonomy make it very difficult for the president or the deans to use vertical coordination. As a result, Harvard relies extensively on faculty committees for almost every academic decision that requires coordination among faculty members or departments. Professors often lament the loose and inefficient work habits of the proliferating committees, but few would be enthusiastic about tight vertical control as a solution.

A common method for linking the activities of various roles is to create a position with authority over others. Creating a chain of command yields a hierarchy of managers and supervisors. These positions carry out activities designed to keep the organization well integrated and in tune with organizational goals. Executives, managers, and supervisors control activity by making decisions, resolving conflicts, solving problems, evaluating performances and output, and distributing rewards and penalties.

Organizations vary in the number of links in the chain of command and in the centralization of authority. In some, like Harvard, the chain of command is short, and workers or professionals have considerable discretion in dealing with day-to-day operations. Teachers and professors have almost unlimited authority and discretion in the classroom, unless they openly violate accepted norms of practice or the students get out of control. In other organizations, like McDonald's, the chain of command is lengthy, and very detailed decisions are made at the top. In McDonald's, that makes it possible for the customer to buy a hamburger that will meet the same standards and taste basically the same regardless of where it was bought.

The same degree of centralization can be much less effective in a different context. In one mental health organization, decisions to administer any drug were made at the top of the organization. One night a patient became violent, and the staff requested permission to administer a tranquilizer. Unfortunately, by the time permission was granted, the patient was subdued and asleep. Since the staff had no discretion about administering drugs, it was necessary to awaken the patient in order to administer the tranquilizer.

Another way to limit discretion and ensure predictability and uniformity is through rules, policies, and standard operating procedures (SOPs). Rules govern conditions of work, procedures for doing tasks, personnel issues, and relationships with the environment. Rules are intended to minimize differences due to personalities or irrational forces and to ensure that similar situations will be handled the same way regardless of the people, the place, or the time of year. A complaint from a citizen about a tax bill is supposed to be handled by the same procedure whether the citizen is a wealthy politician or a poor shoe clerk. Once a situation is defined as one in which a rule applies, the steps become clear, straightforward, and almost automatic.

The scope and application of rules or SOPs vary widely across different organizations. McDonald's has an extensive set of rules and policies to ensure uniformity across different outlets. Pilots on commercial airlines typically fly with a different crew at the beginning of every month. Since interdependence is high and mistakes are critical, SOPs govern every significant aspect of pilots' work together. Each pilot has been extensively trained in the same procedures. So long as each follows the rules that they all know, they will not surprise one another or fail to coordinate their activities.

Organizations with explicit, well-enforced rules are typically highly formalized places to work. At the other end of the spectrum are highly informal organizations where individuals have nearly unlimited latitude. At Harvard, as in many universities, very few rules or procedures govern the activities of professors. Even where rules exist, they are often not enforced.

The areas in which rules are created differ across organizations. Since rules are a key strategy for coordinating activities, one could expect rules to be established in areas of importance, uncertainty, or conflict—that is, regulating the activities that are most central to an organization's mission or survival. Rules that concern hiring and firing, relationships with the environment, and key aspects of the flow of work are often explicit. But rules sometimes arise in areas that seem less important. In schools, for example, policies and rules pertaining to student discipline are extensive and explicit, but those pertaining to curriculum and instruction are vague or nonexistent. Despite the differences, all organizations have rules. Rules and authority are the two major vertical strategies for coordinating activity and energy in organizations.

As almost anyone who has worked in an organization knows, vertical strategies by themselves are not enough. In many organizations, vertical strategies are relatively ineffective, and many people's actions seem almost untouched by command or rule. Lateral techniques are developed to fill the coordination void. They include (1) formal and informal meetings for developing plans, solving problems, and making decisions, (2) task forces that bring together representatives from different areas and specialties to work together on a particular problem or project, and (3) coordinating roles that work through persuasion and informal negotiation rather than through authority or rules.

Lateral forms of coordination are typically less formalized and more flexible than authority and rules. They are often simpler and quicker as well. If the guards on a basketball team decided that they would pass the ball to the forwards only on direct orders from the coach, the team would provide a vivid demonstration of the limits of vertical coordination. If the guards are not working well with the forwards, the coach may need to intervene, but a successful intervention will be one that establishes effective lateral communications.

Informal communications are the most basic forms of lateral coordination, and they are vital in every organization. Equally necessary are formal meetings. All organizations have formal groups that meet regularly to make decisions. Boards meet to make policy. Executive committees meet to review results and develop strategies. Faculties meet to make academic decisions. In some government agencies, review committees referred to as "murder boards" meet to examine proposals from lower-level officials.

Formal and informal meetings can provide most of the lateral coordination in relatively stable organizations with low differentiation. Examples would include a railroad with a stable market, a company manufacturing a product that changes very little (such as paper clips or cardboard boxes), and a school system in a town with a stable population.

As organizations become more differentiated and their environments more turbulent, the need for horizontal communication increases and is likely to be met by additional devices. Task forces are used when organizations face new problems or opportunities that require the resources of individuals from a number of organizational specialties or functions. High-technology organizations make frequent use of project teams to coordinate the development of new products and services. Those same organizations also make extensive use of coordinating roles and units—individuals and groups whose sole purpose is to help other people work effectively and integrate their work. In the automobile industry, coordinating groups work to build communication among the many departments and specializations involved in the design of a new automobile.

In sum, the organizational structure has two basic axes: (1) differentiation (allocation of tasks and responsibilities across individuals and units), which creates a structure of roles, each with specified responsibilities and expectations, and (2) linkages (relationships between roles that create interdependence). Roles and interdependencies are coordinated vertically by authority and rules and laterally through meetings, task forces, teams, and coordinators.

Technology and Environment

What determines the shape of an organization's structure? Why are Harvard University and McDonald's structured so differently, even though each is viewed as a very effective organization? Current research points to technology and environment as the two most powerful factors in influencing how an organization is structured.

Technology

The technology of an organization is its central activity for transforming inputs into outputs. Although the word *technology* usually evokes images of machinery and hardware, the concept is broader than that. In schools, the basic technology is classroom teaching. In medicine, technology includes the many activities that physicians perform to diagnose and treat illness. In social service agencies, the basic technology is "casework"—a series of encounters between the caseworker and the client.

Technology in organizations has been conceptualized in a number of ways. Dornbusch and Scott (1975), for example, identify three forms of technology. "Materials" technology is the concrete, human, or symbolic materials that form the organization's inputs. "Operations" technology consists of the activities for transforming raw materials into desired ends. "Knowledge" technology comprises the underlying beliefs about cause and effect that link materials, activity, and outcomes. Schools, hospitals, factories, prisons, political organizations, and churches all rely on technologies to transform materials, people, or ideas from one state to another.

Technologies differ in their clarity, predictability, and effectiveness. The technology for assembling an automobile or manufacturing an electric mixer is relatively routine and programmed. The task is clear, most of the potential problems are known in advance, and the probability of successful manufacture is known and assured. Other technologies are much less routine and predictable. In teaching, for example, the day's objectives can be complicated and amorphous; students' needs and skills vary widely; their moods fluctuate in response to weather, time of day, or an immediate distraction; knowing what approach will work with a particular student is often very difficult. In surgery the clarity of the task varies with the difficulty of the procedure. Appendectomies are fairly straightforward, but heart transplants are much less routine. Something can go wrong with any surgical procedure, though, simply because the human body is so complex. The success or failure of an operation can depend on a host of postoperative conditions, including the attitudes of the patient's family, the nursing care, diet, and the presence or absence of numerous complications.

Environment

Environment is typically seen as everything outside the boundaries of an organization, even though the boundaries are often nebulous and poorly drawn. It is the environment that provides raw materials to an organization and receives the organization's outputs. Businesses procure materials and resources from the environment and distribute products or services to customers or clients. Schools receive students from the local community and later return graduates to the community.

The nature of an organization's environment can vary on a number of dimensions. Scott (1981), for example, focuses on the dimensons of uncertainty and dependence. Organizational environments are uncertain when they are diverse, unstable, and unpredictable. Organizations with rapidly changing technologies or markets—for instance, high-technology electronics corporations—must cope with high degrees of environmental uncertainty. A new state-of-the-art product may be outmoded in six months. Any organization that finds itself in rapidly changing economic or political conditions also deals with high levels of uncertainty. In contrast, a stable, mature business such as a railroad or a post office department deals with much lower environmental uncertainty. Organizations that face high uncertainty need high levels of flexibility and adaptability to cope and are likely to be less bureaucratic and more decentralized. A well-known example is Digital Equipment Corporation, a fast-growing manufacturer of minicomputers. Historically, Digital had no organization charts, paid little attention to job titles, and encouraged creative entrepreneurship in its employees. (A representative of the major industry magazines called Digital to check on the title of one of its executives and was surprised to learn that the company was not sure what his title was and did not care because it would probably change soon anyway.) As the company matured and growth began to slow, Digital went through a period of reappraisal, and pressures to tighten up began to appear.

Different parts of the same organization may face very different environments. Lawrence and Lorsch (1967) found that, in the plastics industry, uncertainty was much higher for the research and development departments than for manufacturing, and sales was somewhere between the two. They found corresponding differences in the way each of those functions was organized in the most effective plastics firms. It was only in the ineffective firms that the organization had not found a way to develop different structures for the three functions.

All organizations are dependent on their environment, but the degree of dependence varies. Some organizations have very low power with respect to their environment, and it is difficult for them to get the resources they need. Organizations are likely to be dependent if they are relatively small, if they are surrounded by more powerful competitors or well-organized constituencies, and if they have little flexibility and few slack resources in responding to environmental fluctuations. An organization like Harvard University is insulated from its environment by size, elite status, and a large endowment. A small private college with no endowment is much more dependent on the fluctuations and expectations of the environment. Harvard can afford to give low teaching loads and high freedom to its faculty. A small college with serious financial pressures is likely to have tighter controls, higher work loads, and limited discretion. Harvard can afford to maintain substantial academic programs in classical Greek and Latin even if most of the courses are underenrolled. The poorer college will be forced to eliminate anything that does not attract students and pay its own way.

Relationships Among Structure, Technology, and Environment

The structure of an organization is influenced by, and often influences, its technology and environment. The mutual relationship among the three has led to the development of "contingency theories." Those theories argue that effective organizations develop structures to match the demands or needs of technologies and environments. There is no one best way to organize, because a workable structure for one combination of technology and environment may be inappropriate for another. The key to organizational effectiveness is to tailor the structure to fit the situation.

Two major examples of contingency theory (Lawrence and Lorsch, 1967; Galbraith, 1977) both focus on one basic idea: The structure of an organization depends particularly on the amount of *uncertainty* the organization has to deal with. Organizations that live in relatively simple, stable environments can develop relatively simple, stable structures. Organizations that live in turbulent, changing, uncertain environments need structures that are more complex, differentiated, and flexible.

Lawrence and Lorsch studied organizations in three industries: box containers, foods, and plastics. The container industry is a slow-growth sector in which the main objectives are consistent quality and prompt service. Innovation is not emphasized, because proven containers produced rapidly and at low cost give organizations a competitive edge. The packaged foods industry is in a more rapidly changing environment; innovative marketing approaches are a major factor in success. Plastics, in the 1960s, was a rapidly changing, high-growth environment. The dominant competitive issue was the development and introduction of new and revised products.

Each industry had a different environment and relied on different technologies. Lawrence and Lorsch discussed three major dimensions of the task environment: clarity of information, uncertainty of cause-and-effect relations, and the time span for feedback. When information is unclear, knowledge is limited, and feedback is slow, an organization has to deal with very high levels of uncertainty.

Lawrence and Lorsch believed that environmental uncertainty would have a major impact on four major organizational characteristics: the degree of formality and bureaucracy in the structure, how people related to each other, how people dealt with time, and what goals the organization sought.

They reasoned that it is much easier for an organization to have accurate information about its environment if the environment is stable. Jobs can be specified through predetermined rules. Communications can be handled through the formal channels. A straightforward, task-oriented managerial style is likely to be effective.

If the environment is complex and rapidly changing, the task is more difficult. Rules may be outmoded as soon as they are made. The organization needs more points of contact with the environment, so a flatter hierarchy is needed. Much more information needs to be communicated, and the traditional channels cannot handle all of it, so that a much more complex, multiple-channel communications system is needed. Such a system is likely to work better with an interpersonal style that emphasizes building effective relationships.

Lawrence and Lorsch added an additional element: In most large organizations, different subunits face different environments. In the plastics industry, the research units face much more uncertainty than the manufacturing units. If the two units are structured the same way, at least one of them will have a poor fit with its own task environment. In order for the research and the manufacturing departments each to do its own job well, the two departments need different structures and different management styles. The more diverse the environments that different units face, the more differentiation in structure is needed.

But as differentiation increases, integration becomes more difficult. The more different two units are, the harder it will be for them to work together. A researcher with a long time orientation may become very frustrated with a manufacturing manager who rarely thinks more than a day or so into the future. If an organization has little internal differentiation, then rules, procedures, and hierarchy may provide sufficient integration. But if an organization has high uncertainty and diversity, then task forces, integrating units, coordinators, and more face-to-face interaction become necessary.

Lawrence and Lorsch's research generally confirmed their theory. Within industries, organizations with structures that fit the environment were found to be more effective. Effective container organizations were more centralized and formalized than effective plastics organizations. The effective plastics firms had higher levels of differentiation and more complex approaches to integration.

Galbraith (1977) also viewed uncertainty as central in determining organizational structure. He defined uncertainty as the difference between the information that an organization already has and the information that it needs. How much it needs depends on three things: the diversity of its output, the diversity of its input (which Galbraith measured in terms of the number of specialties included within the organization), and the level of goal difficulty. As uncertainty increases, more information is needed to make decisions—information that the organization may not have. For simple, predictable tasks, an organization can plan in advance how things are to be handled. But planning is harder when uncertainty is high, and decisions have to be made as the task moves along.

As uncertainty increases, Galbraith argues, organizations are confronted with two choices: either reduce the need for information processing or increase the capacity to process information. Organizations can reduce information processing by creating slack resources or by creating self-contained units that can work on their own without depending on other units in the organization. If each project in a research firm is given its own editor instead of relying on one editorial department, the organization has created a slack resource (more editors than it needs) and made each department more self-contained. By spending more money on editors, the organization reduces the need for researchers to spend time coordinating with the editorial department.

An organization can increase its capacity to process information by investing in vertical information systems (computers and staff personnel to collect information and direct it to decision makers) or by developing lateral relations (direct contacts, liaison roles, project teams, and matrix structures).

As organizations face more complicated tasks, they must choose one or a combination of the strategies. If no choice is made, slack resources are automatically created and organizational costs increase. But each of the strategies has costs as well as benefits.

Lawrence and Lorsch and Galbraith share the view that effective organizations are those that build structures to meet technological and environmental demands. Both focus on the role of uncertainty and the way it affects the information needs of organizations. Both argue that simpler, more "bureaucratic" organizations are most likely to be effective in relatively stable, predictable environments, while environments that are turbulent and uncertain breed more complex organizational structures.

4

Applying the
Structural Approach

"We need some help," he said almost pleadingly, "to resolve personality conflicts in our staff." The caller was the principal of an alternative high school who telephoned us several years ago. Over the course of the phone call, we learned that the school felt its problems were so serious that only a neutral outsider could help. Several internal initiatives, including one by the superintendent of schools, had failed to define or resolve the issues.

"Maybe your personality difficulties stem from problems in the way the school is structured," we responded, knowing that such problems commonly plagued alternative schools.

"Maybe we should talk to someone else," was the principal's reply. The conversation ended.

A week later, we received a second call. This time the entire staff was huddled around a telephone speaker for a conference call. The staff wanted to give us a second chance as consultants. In a meeting the previous day, staff member A had moved that staff member B be fired. The measure failed by a narrow margin of three to four. In retaliation, B moved to terminate A. That motion failed by the same margin.

If personalities could not be changed and there was no agreement as to whom should be fired, what could be done to solve the school's problems? After protracted discussion, the staff had reached one consensus: it needed help. The conversation to pinpoint the form of the help lasted an hour and a half. The staff finally agreed to a study of its organization.

To make a long story short, the study revealed significant flaws in the school's formal structure. Authority was distributed equally among all staff members. Everyone claimed responsibility for some tasks, while no one felt responsible for others. There were no explicit procedures for making decisions. Most decisions were made by the staff as a group in daily meetings that usually lasted two to three hours. Although there were a few rough edges, the personalities of the participants were far more serviceable than the structural arrangements that almost guaranteed conflicts, frustration, exhaustion, and burnout.

The alternative high school was an unusual organization because of its small size and unique ideology, but its problems were only an exaggerated form of common structural maladies. Similar patterns arise time and time again in our work in organizations, whether they are corporations, churches, hospitals, public agencies, or schools.

Problems of communication, apparently petty bickering, conflict, sabotage, alienation, overconformity, unresponsiveness, and excessive rigidity are common in organizations. They are the typical pathologies that make collective action more frustrating and less productive than anyone would wish. Frequently the problems are attributed to people—with the implication that the solution is to change the people. We need to retrain them, or rotate them, or get rid of them. The hope is that somehow the right people will make things work.

The structural perspective emphasizes that even the right people will have difficulties if they are enmeshed in the wrong structure. Structural consultants assume that a variety of organizational problems arise from hidden structural flaws. They try to map the roles, relationships, and linkages within a setting.

How are responsibilities divided? Whom do people depend on in carrying out their work? How are activities coordinated? What does the organization do? In what environment does it operate? By asking such questions, structural consultants often uncover problems like the following:

- *Overlap.* Two or more individuals are doing the same thing, often without realizing it. Duplicate activities waste effort, and territorial disputes are common.
- *Gaps.* Important tasks or responsibilities are not assigned to any particular person or unit, and things fall through the cracks.
- *Underuse.* Some individuals or units have too little work. They often become bored and get in other people's way.
- *Overload.* Some individuals or units are so overloaded that it is impossible for them to get it all done.
- *Excessive interdependence.* Some units are more tightly connected than they should be. Each group has difficulty concentrating on its own work, and much time is wasted in coordinating activities.
- *Excessive autonomy.* Individuals or groups are too loosely coupled, so that they feel isolated and unsupported, and their efforts are uncoordinated with other people's.
- *Too many meetings.* It is common to hold a meeting or form a committee for every new problem. In some organizations, people spend so much time in meetings that they get little else done.
- *Too many rules.* When rules become excessive, people tend to lose track of them and to resist them.
- *Diffuse authority.* No one knows, or everyone disagrees about, who is in charge of an important activity. The confusion often limits initiative and creates conflict.
- *Too loose versus too tight.* In some organizations the structure is so loose that no one knows what it is, and people go off in all kinds of different, uncoordinated directions. In other organizations the structure is too tight, so that flexibility is stifled, and people spend much of their time trying to evade, beat, or escape the structure.

- *Structure/technology mismatch.* The structure is inappropriate for the technology, or vice versa. This is often the result of drift in one or the other.
- *Structure/environment mismatch.* Environments often change quickly, and organizational structure may lag behind. It is fairly common to find organizations well structured to meet challenges that vanished years earlier—wondering why things do not work as well as they once did.

The list could be expanded, but the point is that many organizational problems are caused by structure more than by people.

Clarifying and Shaping Structure

What can be done to resolve structural problems? One frequently used alternative is to clarify and shape the structure to fit the participants and their work. In the case of the alternative high school, the staff met for two days to discuss structural problems that were identified by a survey instrument. After considering the data and crystallizing several issues, staff members agreed to grant more authority to the principal, clarified the role of individuals in making decisions, developed some policies for recurring issues, reduced the frequency of staff meetings, structured the remaining meetings more carefully, and encouraged informal communication to coordinate day-to-day activities.

Responsibility charting (Galbraith, 1973) has been used by a variety of organizations—from Baskin-Robbins to the Office of the Vice-President of the United States—to clarify and shape their formal structure. Responsibility charting takes the various tasks of an organization or subunit and provides a language for pinpointing authority, roles, and relationships. Figure 1 illustrates how the process worked for a small school district.

The language is referred to as RACI. The letter "R" denotes operating *responsibility*. The person with the "R" is directly accountable for a particular task. The figure shows that operating responsibility is assigned differently for various tasks.

Figure 1. Responsibility Charting in a School District.

Tasks		Roles				
	Superin-tendent	Assistant Superin-tendent	Principals	Teachers as Group	Individual Teachers	Parents
Prepare budget	A	R	C	I	I	I
Report to school board	R	C	C	I	I	I
Respond to parent complaints	I	C	C	I	C	I
Define curriculum	A	C	R	A	C	I
Prepare instructional materials	I	I	A	C	R	I

The assistant superintendent, for example, is responsible for preparing the budget. Individual teachers are accountable for preparing instructional materials.

The other three letters—A, C, and I—stand for *approve, consult,* and *inform*. The superintendent's "A" for the budget means that the superintendent must approve the budget after the assistant superintendent has put it together. Principals are responsible for developing curriculum, but teachers must approve it. The principals' "C" on the budget indicates that they are to be consulted by the assistant superintendent while the budget is being prepared. "I" indicates that persons in a particular role are to be informed as decisions are made or actions are taken. The superintendent informs teachers and parents about important developments at school board meetings. Principals keep parents informed about curriculum developments.

Responsibility charting enables an organization to talk about structure by relating it to specific tasks or areas. When most organizations first attempt it, they are surprised to find that people hold radically different images of roles and relationships. As a result, major tasks do not get done, duplicated effort is common, and conflicts develop over who is responsible for what. The gaps, overlaps, and conflicts are commonly attributed to such individual personal characteristics as irresponsibility, power grabbing, or abrasiveness rather than seen as problems in the formal structure. Responsibility charting, like management by objectives (MBO) and similar approaches, is an effort to clarify and shape the formal structure of organizations.

Reorganizing

Few organizations have never been reorganized. Most have been reorganized a number of times. Some are restructured so often that participants feel they are in a perpetual state of reorganization. That thought was in the mind of a federal government employee who told us that the primary activity in his agency was "orging off." We think he was trying to depict a process that leads to a degree of self-satisfaction without producing any other significant outcome.

Organizations restructure for a number of important reasons:

- *The environment changes.* In the case of American Telephone and Telegraph ("Ma Bell"), a shift in the environment from regulation to competition has required a major reorganization of the Bell System.
- *The technology changes.* The introduction of the silicon chip into the electronic industry spawned the need for more flexible, decentralized structural patterns.
- *Organizations grow.* Digital Equipment Corporation (DEC) thrived with a very informal and flexible structure during the company's early years, but the same structure produced major problems when DEC grew into a multibillion dollar corporation. Reluctantly at first, Digital was forced to develop more formal procedures and relationships.
- *The political climate changes.* Public agencies often reorganize to attune their structure to the priorities and expectations of the legislature. In recent years, for example, the National Institute of Education was reorganized to tailor its research units to the areas that were most prominent for Congress.
- *Leadership changes.* Reorganization is often one of the first initiatives of new leaders. Sometimes there are clear task-related reasons for a new structure. In a recent case following a change in the White House, other forces were more prominent.

Reorganization takes a variety of forms. One of the most common is divisionalization. Divisions are frequently created around product lines or geographic areas in an effort to consolidate different functions into more manageable units. In environments of turbulence and uncertainty, reorganization often takes one or another form of decentralization: moving decisions from the top toward the operating level. The reorganization of the New York City public schools, for example, created divisions (district areas) and decentralized authority by giving local schools more autonomy in day-to-day decision making.

In the rational mind-set of the structural frame, reorganization is a fundamental approach to improving organizational effectiveness. Often, it works. And often, it fails. In some organizations, reorganization occurs every year or so in an effort to solve problems that never do get solved.

Reorganization also serves other purposes, particularly for organizations in fuzzy environments where goals are hard to pin down and effectiveness is hard to measure. In the case of the reorganization of the National Institute of Education, the main goal of the effort was "cleaning up the mess." The reorganization may not have accomplished all its objectives, but it was followed by increased levels of congressional support. Similarly, responsibility charting in a small school district led to little structural change but still appeared to reduce conflict and provide individuals a better understanding of how they could work together.

Rational Blinders: Critiques of the Structural Frame

The structural frame helps to capture the more stable and formal aspects of human behavior in organizations. Activities and relationships are influenced by goals, roles, rules, and procedures. But much of organizational life falls outside the jurisdiction of organization charts, policy, and formal authority. Slippage between structure and reality occurs for three primary reasons:

1. The structural frame has put little emphasis on the complex, nonrational sides of human behavior that keep intruding into the most sophisticated of structures.
2. Power and conflict have usually been seen as things to be avoided rather than exercised and encouraged.
3. Rationality has been stressed as a complete virtue rather than a partial logic that governs only under conditions of reasonable certainty and predictability.

Argyris (1957, 1964) is an outspoken critic of the structural frame's inattention to human needs and personality. He argues that structural assumptions lead in the long run to inefficiency and organizational dry rot because they fail to provide room for human needs for self-expression, creativity, and independence. Taken to the extreme, structural logic creates the machinelike monotony of the assembly line and the mindless inflexibility of bureaucratic red tape. In response to programming and control, people find remarkably ingenious ways to deviate from, undermine, and even sabotage dictates from above. Structuralists often forget that structure can govern behavior only if it is endorsed from below as well as delegated from above.

In the structural ideal, the regulated use of power makes it possible for authorities to keep self-interests from overriding collective goals, but the ideal rarely matches reality. Organizations are always coalitions of special interests, each struggling for power and its share of the organizational pie. Political scientists like Baldridge (1971) underscore the tendency of the structural frame to ignore power and minimize conflict, reducing its usefulness to managers who grapple every day with political realities.

An even more glaring weakness is the structural frame's reluctance to acknowledge that much human activity is expressive. Empirically, we know that structure does not always control activity (Meyer, Scott, and Deal, 1981), that planning rarely shapes the future (Cohen and March, 1974), and that meetings frequently fail to make decisions or solve problems (March and Olsen, 1976). Structuralists often define such realities as error and dysfunction and seek to reinforce the virtues of a narrow definition of rationality, thus limiting the frame's application in a world that is often imperfect, uncertain, and nonrational.

Despite those limits, the structural frame is a powerful source of both explanations and solutions for a wide range of organizational problems. Structure shapes behavior, as long as the frame is applied with a realistic appreciation of both its strengths and its limits.

Structural Analysis Applied: Case Examples

Helen Demarco

Examine the list of structural pathologies and ask yourself which ones might apply to Helen's case. When we performed

that exercise, three items from the list seemed particularly perti-
nent: gaps, diffuse authority, and "too loose."

Paul Osborne's position is at the institutional level of the
organization, while Helen Demarco and her colleagues are managers with responsibilities for internal, technical issues. The different levels have different tasks and different knowledge, beliefs, and perceptions. Paul's initiative may have been his effort
to get the organization to respond quickly to a serious environmental challenge, whereas Helen saw it as a direct encroachment
on her area of responsibility. Perhaps because of the differences
in level, perhaps because Paul was new to the organization and
brought a different set of assumptions about management, Paul
and Helen disagreed about who should have authority and responsibility and how the different levels should relate to one another in the decision-making process. Should Paul have informed Helen, consulted her, or asked for her approval before
moving ahead with the Osborne plan? Ambiguity or disagreement about such issues leads inevitably to "diffuse authority."

When Helen learned of Paul's plan, there was no obvious
mechanism or forum for confronting and resolving the conflict.
The issue might have been aired in a regular staff meeting. Helen
might have gone to someone (for instance, her boss) who had
the responsibility for coordinating such a disagreement. The absence of an official channel created a structural gap. Helen and
her colleagues filled the gap with subterfuge and politics.

Gaps and diffuse authority are symptoms of a structure
that is too loose and ill defined. Paul is trying to head in one direction while Helen is headed in the opposite direction, but there
is nothing in the structure to detect and resolve the divergence.

Fairness in Marriage

Helen's case involves senior managers and a large organization. It may seem natural to use a structural lens in such a
case but less so in the case of the small, two-person relationship
known as marriage. Consider the following example:

A husband (it could have been a wife or a
lover) arrives home one night, relishing the day's

victories at work and carrying a bottle of champagne to celebrate the triumphs. Over candlelight, he pops the cork and lifts his glass for a toast, when the other partner says emphatically, "This marriage is unfair!" A potentially joyous occasion quickly degenerates into acrimonious debate. Then the couple lapses into strained silence.

Organizational structure is probably the last thing to which most couples would turn in such a situation. The husband might interpret the wife's statement as a statement about him, "*You* are unfair," and a bitter discussion of each other's personal flaws might easily follow. But the structural frame suggests that the problem might be better solved through an explicit examination of roles and responsibilities.

In this case, the husband tried to salvage the evening by taking a piece of paper and dividing it into three columns: husband, wife, and both. The various tasks of daily living—cleaning, shopping, lawnmowing, bill paying—were then entered into the appropriate columns. A role problem quickly emerged: The wife was doing almost everything, the husband almost nothing. Shared tasks were nonexistent. The wife was overloaded, the husband underloaded, and coordination was absent. The marriage really was unfair.

That evening, the couple restructured their marriage. The husband took on some tasks from the wife, and joint tasks were created so that they would spend more time together. In one hour the problem was solved—for a while, at least. The marriage is still a happy one, and the couple periodically check to see how their pattern of roles and relationships has evolved over time.

New Technology in a Newspaper

The "information revolution" has had an enormous impact on organizations in the last two decades, and the revolution is continuing. The dizzying pace of development of such technologies as microcomputers, office automation, data net-

works, and optical scanning will affect virtually every organization during the next decade. All of us have experienced—or
soon will experience—a case like the following:

> A large newspaper replaced typewriters with
> computer consoles that make it possible for report-
> ers to type stories directly into a word processor.
> Once a story is in the computer, it can be edited,
> typeset, and printed without the material ever leav-
> ing the computer. The major goals of the innova-
> tion were to cut costs and to save reporters' time
> so that they could spend more time in the field.
> Six months later, a study showed that the new
> technology had produced a significant *increase* in
> the amount of time reporters needed to write their
> stories.

As we said earlier, organizations are often surprising. In
this situation, several structural options seem clear: create a role
to help reporters enter their stories, designate a task force to
study the problem, or appoint someone to lean on reporters so
that they use the computers more efficiently (an "implementation czar"). All were tried. None worked. Perhaps this was not a
structural problem.

In each of the three cases we have examined, the structural perspective suggested options for solving the problems that
people faced. In the marital case, they were effective. In the Demarco case, they might have been. In the introduction of word
processors, they failed. We will return to each of these cases in
subsequent chapters and examine them through the other three
frames.

Conclusion

The structural perspective probes behind the individuals
to examine the context in which they relate and work together.
This perspective is sometimes undervalued because it is equated

with excessive bureaucracy and rigidity. It is frequently under-used as organizations develop massive people-change programs when the basic problems are somewhere else. Conversely, re-structuring has often been overused as a solution for all sorts of organizational ills, without taking adequate account of non-structural factors that need to be addressed. Using the perspective in conjunction with others to understand and remedy problems can help to create structures that work for, rather than against, both people and purpose in organizations.

5

⚜⚜⚜⚜⚜⚜⚜⚜

Fitting Organizations to People: The Human Resource Approach

The more monotonous and mechanical, the more tiring and soul-deadening daily work becomes, the more difficult it is to engage in more creative occupations with cohesive relationships and meaningful goals, and the easier it is to seek substitutes for the daily burdens in titillating amusements, in idle dreams and fantasies, lacking connection with reality.

—Ernst Wigforss, 1923

Wigforss, a Norwegian politician, made one of the earlier statements of the human resource frame. His statement built on

63

the Marxian analysis of alienation in the workplace brought on by factory technology, division of labor, and the capitalists' ownership of the means of production. Marx and Wigforss were both ahead of their time. Ideas about class struggle made little headway in nineteenth-century England or Germany, and concepts of freedom and democracy in the workplace found little acceptance in Norway or anywhere else in the 1920s. But Marx and Wigforss anticipated a set of ideas about management that have become more and more influential during the last thirty years.

In the previous two chapters we described the structural frame, which focuses particularly on the way structure develops in response to an organization's task and environment. Rationality is a central motif in the structural perspective. The human resource frame adds an additional dimension—the interplay between organizations and people. The frame starts from the premise that people are the most critical resource in an organization. Their skills, insights, ideas, energy, and commitment can make or break an organization. Organizations can and do create environments that are so alienating, dehumanizing, and frustrating that human talents are wasted and human lives distorted. Humans can respond by devoting much of their effort to beating the system—or one another. But it does not have to be that way. At their best, organizations can be energizing, exciting, productive, and rewarding for the individual—and for the system as well.

Literature and film offer many depictions of the relationship between individual and organization. Most of them focus on the alienating and brutalizing aspects of systems. In Kafka's *The Trial*, the protagonist faces a mysterious, impersonal, unpredictable, and hostile organization that destroys individuals at its own time and for its own mysterious reasons. Frederick Wiseman's documentary film *High School* shows a world in which insensitive adults tyrannize students. The same filmmaker's *Welfare* shows scenes from an urban welfare agency in which virtually every encounter between welfare workers and clients produces frustration for both. Is reality as bleak as it is often depicted? Are human beings inevitably the pawns of organizations, used for whatever the organization needs, only to be thrown out when they are no longer needed? Can individuals do no better than to protect themselves and to hope to exploit the system before it exploits them?

Those questions are particularly important and poignant in the light of the enormous size and power of modern institutions, both public and private. Public spending represents a steadily increasing percentage of the total wealth of virtually every developed nation, and much of that spending goes to feed large public bureaucracies. The twentieth century has witnessed an extraordinary growth of large private corporations, including giant multinational companies. One of the largest of these, General Motors, generates revenues each year that exceed the gross national product of most of the world's nations. Is there much possibility for the individual to find freedom and dignity in a world whose political and economic decisions are increasingly dominated by such gigantic institutions?

Answering such questions is not easy, and it requires an understanding of humans, of human organizations, and of the complex relation between the two. The human resource frame draws from a body of research and theory built around several major assumptions:

1. Organizations exist to serve *human needs* (and humans do not exist to serve organizational needs).
2. Organizations and people need each other. Organizations need the ideas, energy, and talent that people provide, while people need the careers, salaries, and work opportunities that organizations provide.
3. When the fit between the individual and the organization is poor, one or both will suffer: The individual will be exploited or will seek to exploit the organization or both.
4. When the fit is good between the individual and the organization, both benefit: Humans are able to do meaningful and satisfying work while providing the resources the organization needs to accomplish its mission.

A good place to begin exploring the fit between people

and organizations is to examine the concept of need. What in fact do people need from their experiences with organizations?

Human Needs

The concept of need is a controversial one in the study of organizational behavior. Some writers reject the whole idea. They argue that the concept of need is too vague, that it refers to something that is difficult to observe, and that human behavior is so strongly influenced by environmental factors that the idea of need is no help in explaining how people behave (Salancik and Pfeffer, 1977).

From a human resource perspective, the concept of need is important, even though it is hard to define what needs people have or how those needs can be measured. The idea that people have needs is consistent with common-sense psychology. Parents talk about the needs of their children, politicians try to respond to the needs of their constituents, and managers try to meet the needs of their workers.

Common sense makes sense in this case, but in everyday language the term *need* is used in a variety of ways, many of them imprecise and ambiguous. An analogy may help to define what we mean by the term *need*. Gardeners know that each plant has "needs" for certain combinations of temperature, moisture, soil conditions, and sunlight. When a plant's needs are well met, the plant flourishes and grows. When its needs are poorly met, the plant grows poorly or dies. A plant's needs are defined by the environmental conditions it needs in order to grow and to reach its full potential. Within the limits of its capabilities, the plant will do the best it can to get its needs met. It will orient its leaves toward the sun to get more light. It will send roots deeper into the soil to get more water. The plant's capabilities generally increase as it matures. Plants that are highly vulnerable in infancy usually become better able to take care of themselves (for example, to fend off insect damage and crowding from other plants) as they reach maturity. Those capabilities decline later as the plant nears the end of its life cycle.

It is reasonable to argue that human needs can be defined

in the same way—there are conditions in the environment that people need in order to survive and develop. The case is simpler with physiological needs. Without adequate oxygen, water, and food, humans survive badly or not at all. A more complicated question is whether psychic needs also exist that are inherent in human beings. There are two sides, which often battle over the issue.

One position is that certain psychological needs are basic to the fact of being human. Those needs are presumably present in some form in everyone. The opposite argument is that humans are so influenceable by environment, socialization, and culture that it is fruitless to talk about generic human needs. The question is one form of the "nature/nurture controversy" that has been a hotly contested issue in the social sciences. In this particular contest, one side (the Nature team) has argued that human behavior is mostly determined by biological and genetic factors. The Nurture team has taken the other side—that human behavior is almost completely determined by learning from the experiences that people have.

The issue has often been an emotional one, for good reason. The stakes are high. If members of one group (such as black Americans) get lower scores than members of another group (such as white Americans) on tests of "intelligence," does that mean that members of the one group are genetically less intelligent? Or do the tests simply capture the effects of social and economic pressures? The answer has implications for social policy. Is mental illness determined by genes or by growing up in environments that would drive anyone crazy? The answer makes an important difference in determining whether drugs or conversation is a more appropriate form of therapy. Are behavioral differences between men and women determined by biology or culture? (Do women have greater maternal needs? Do men have greater needs for combat and competition?) The answers are important in understanding the possibilities for redefining male and female roles.

The available evidence is pretty clear: Neither the nature nor the nurture argument is correct in its extreme version. Perhaps the most surprising thing about the nature/nurture contro-

versy is that it has produced so much polarization and dichoto-
mous thinking. It does not take a degree in psychology to know
that people are capable of enormous amounts of learning and
adaptation. What people learn is certainly very much influenced
by the situations in which they find themselves. Similarly, however, it does not require advanced training in biology to recognize that there are a lot of differences among people that are
present at birth. It is clear that significant physical differences
are genetically determined. It is surprising that many environ-
mentalists become so wedded to the argument that differences
in behavior are *always* caused by environmental factors.

A consensus is emerging in the social sciences around the
belief that human behavior is always the result of an interaction
between heredity and environment. An individual's genes determine an initial trajectory, but subsequent learning has a profound
effect in modifying or even reversing the original instructions.

The idea of a nature/nurture interaction suggests a way of
thinking about human needs. A need can be defined as a genetic
predisposition to prefer some experiences over others. Needs
energize and guide behavior, and they vary in strength at different times. We prefer temperatures that are neither too hot nor
too cold. We do not like being alone all the time, but we are not
happy if we are constantly surrounded by people. Since the
genetic instructions cannot anticipate all the specific situations
that the individual will encounter in life, the form and expression of each person's needs will be significantly modified by
what happens after birth.

Needs also influence how we feel and guide learning. We
are likely to have positive emotions—happiness, contentment,
joy, and love—in situations that are need-fulfilling for us. We
are likely to have negative emotions—anger, fear, depression,
and boredom—in situations in which we are unable to meet important needs. We are also likely to learn things that are relevant
to our needs. If you have a strong desire to be a successful manager, and if you believe that understanding organizational behavior will help you succeed, then you are likely to learn a lot
about the subject. If you have no desire to be a manager, or if
you believe that social science is mostly common sense dis-

guised with a lot of polysyllabic words, you are not likely to learn very much about it.

The concept of need provides a way to talk about conditions that are more favorable or unfavorable for humans in organization. A simple "theory" of needs assumes that everyone has needs and that there is some commonality across people in their basic biological needs. People behave in an effort to satisfy their needs, become unhappy when their needs are frustrated, and are more likely to learn things that are relevant to their needs than things that are irrelevant. Individuals are likely to flourish and develop in environments where they have a good probability of satisfying their important needs. They are likely to become psychologically undernourished in situations in which major needs are difficult or impossible to satisfy.

What Needs Do People Have?

If all humans have needs, what needs do they have? What needs are common to everyone? A number of investigators have grappled with these questions, and no single answer is universally accepted.

One of the most influential theories about human needs was developed by Maslow (1970). Maslow started from the notion that humans have a variety of needs and that some of them are more fundamental than others. He noted that when people are chronically hungry, the desire for food dominates their lives. But for people who are used to being well fed, eating is usually less prominent, and other forms of satisfaction become more significant.

Maslow grouped human needs into five basic categories, arranged in a hierarchy from "lower" to "higher." Lower needs dominate behavior when they are not satisfied. Higher needs become important only after the lower needs have been satisfied. Maslow proposed the following categories: (1) physiological needs (such as needs for oxygen, water, food, physical health and comfort), (2) safety needs (needs to be safe from danger, attack, threat), (3) belongingness and love needs (needs for positive and loving relationships with other people), (4) esteem needs

(needs to feel valued and to value oneself), and (5) needs for self-actualization (needs to develop to one's fullest, to actualize one's potential).

Maslow argued that normally the lower needs are "prepotent"—they have to be satisfied first. He did not assume that they have to be completely satisfied: It is a matter of degree. The better a lower need is satisfied, the more an individual is likely to focus on higher needs. He also acknowledged that there are exceptions. Parents who sacrifice themselves for their children and martyrs who give their lives for a cause are examples in which higher needs dominate lower ones. Maslow believed that such exceptions occur only for people whose lower needs were very well satisfied early in life, so that they fall into the background. For such people, needs for belongingness, esteem, and self-actualization come to dominate.

Maslow's ideas on motivation have had an enormous impact on the thinking of both managers and behavioral scientists. They seem intuitively reasonable, but that does not necessarily mean the theory is correct. In fact, a number of researchers have tried to assess the validity of Maslow's theory, never with complete success. The problem is that it is very hard to measure people's needs. To test the theory, you have to be able to assess both the strength and the level of satisfaction of each need. The question is how to do that. Do you ask people questions like "How strong is your need for self-actualization, and how well is that need met?"? Do people really know that much about their own needs? What if some of their needs are unconscious? Even if they know, will they give truthful answers? What if people think the researcher will have a better opinion of them if they say they are concerned about self-actualization rather than mundane things like salary and benefits?

There have been several systematic attempts to assess the validity of Maslow's theory (Alderfer, 1972; Schneider and Alderfer, 1973), but none of the research has succeeded in demonstrating that Maslow's theory is right or wrong. Even though no one is very sure the theory is right, it has still become the most influential single view of motivation in organizations. It has become, in effect, a widely accepted myth. Its validity is often assumed, despite the lack of convincing empirical evidence.

Theory X and Theory Y

Douglas McGregor (1960) developed a set of ideas about motivation in organizations that is one of the most widely read set of ideas in the history of organizational behavior. To Maslow's theory of motivation, McGregor added another central idea: that the perspective or theory that a manager holds about other people determines how the others will respond. McGregor suggested that most managers hold a theory that he called "Theory X." The central proposition of Theory X is that managers need to actively direct and control the work of subordinates. According to Theory X, subordinates are passive, resist work because they are lazy, have little ambition, prefer to be led, and are self-centered and resistant to change.

McGregor believed that virtually all conventional management practices were built on Theory X assumptions. He said that if managers held Theory X assumptions, the range of possible management approaches varied from "hard" Theory X to "soft" Theory X. The hard version of Theory X involves coercion, tight controls, threats, and punishments. Hard management, in McGregor's view, leads to low productivity, antagonism, militant unions, and subtle sabotage of management goals. The other possibility is a "soft" style that uses permissiveness, tries to satisfy people's every need, and avoids conflict. Soft management might lead to superficial harmony, but in McGregor's view it also leads to apathy, indifference, and people's expecting more and more from the organization while giving less and less in return. Either way—hard or soft—Theory X creates its own self-fulfilling prophecies. Both approaches produce signs that the theory is correct and that even more Theory X management is needed to cope with workers who "just don't seem to give a damn any more" and "are never satisfied."

McGregor argued that new knowledge from the behavioral sciences challenged the conventional view. The evidence was inconclusive, he acknowledged, but it suggested a different view that he called "Theory Y." Maslow's need hierarchy served as the foundation for Theory Y: "We recognize readily enough that a man suffering from a severe dietary deficiency is sick. The deprivation of physiological needs has behavioral consequences. The same is true—although less well recognized—of deprivation of higher-level needs. The man whose needs for safety, association, independence, or status are thwarted is sick just as surely as the man who has rickets. And his sickness will have behavioral consequences. We will be mistaken if we attribute his resultant passivity, his hostility, his refusal to accept responsibility to his inherent 'human nature.' These forms of behavior are symptoms of illness—of deprivation of his social and egoistic needs" (McGregor, 1960, pp. 35–36).

McGregor suggested that managers needed a new theory about people. Theory Y, like Theory X, accepted the proposition that "management is responsible for organizing the elements of enterprise . . . in the interest of economic ends." McGregor did not challenge capitalism or the purposes of private industry. He was challenging managers to behave differently. Theory Y argues that people are not passive or indifferent by nature; they sometimes become so as a result of experience in organizations. Motivation is always present in people. Management cannot put it there.

The key proposition of Theory Y is that "the essential task of management is to arrange organizational conditions so that people can achieve their own goals best by directing their efforts toward organizational rewards" (p. 61). In other words, the job of management is to arrange things so that the organization's interests and the employee's self-interest coincide as closely as possible. In McGregor's view, Theory X relies too much on external control of people, while Theory Y relies on self-control and self-direction. Theory X treats people like children; Theory Y treats them like adults.

McGregor expected that moving toward Theory Y would be a monumental and very slow process after decades of Theory X. But he saw a number of emerging trends that were headed in the right direction. Those included management by objectives, decentralization, job enlargement, and participative management. (Several of these applications of the human resource frame will be discussed later.)

Personality and Organization

McGregor's Theory X, Theory Y was one classic, early statement of the human resource frame. Another such statement was provided by Chris Argyris (1957, 1964). Argyris saw a basic conflict between the human personality and the ways that organizations were traditionally structured and managed. Argyris did not base his view of human personality directly on Maslow's need hierarchy, but his ideas were similar to Maslow's. Argyris believed that basic "self-actualization trends" are common to most people. In his view, people tend to develop in particular directions as they mature from infancy into adulthood. They move from passivity as infants to activity as adults; from high levels of dependence on others toward relatively high levels of independence; from having a narrow range of skills and interests to having an increasingly diverse range; from a short time perspective (in which interests are quickly developed and quickly forgotten and there is little ability to anticipate the future) to a much longer time perspective. People tend to develop from low levels of self-awareness and self-control to higher levels. Argyris proposed that all individuals are predisposed to move from the infant toward the adult end of each continuum, "barring unhealthy personality development" (1957, p. 51). This position is similar to Maslow's idea that people tend to move up the need hierarchy unless their lower-level needs are frustrated.

Argyris viewed the developmental trends as predispositions that could be modified as a result of experience. Since different individuals would have different experiences in the course of their development, Argyris did not expect that his theory would be useful for making predictions about individuals; rather, it could be used to describe individuals' levels of development.

Like McGregor, Argyris said that there is a conflict between individuals and organizations because organizations often treat people like children. Employees are expected to be passive and dependent. The view was anticipated in Charlie Chaplin's film *Modern Times*. Early in the film, Charlie has a job on an assembly line. He works furiously trying to tighten each bolt on each piece that goes past him. The time perspective of the job can be measured in a few seconds. The range of skills is so minimal that Charlie has difficulty doing anything other than tightening bolts. He has virtually no control over the pace of his work. A researcher uses Charlie as the guinea pig for a new machine to increase efficiency. The new machine will feed Charlie his lunch while he continues to tighten bolts, thereby reducing idle time. The machine goes haywire and begins to assault Charlie with the food rather than feed it to him. The message is clear— the logic of industrial organization is to treat adults as much like infants as is technologically possible.

Argyris argued that these problems were built into traditional principles of organizational design and management. The principle of task specialization, carried to its logical extreme, leads to defining jobs as narrowly as possible. "You put the right front tire on the car; Joe will tighten the bolts; and Bill will check to see that it was done right." Task specialization produces the need for a chain of command to coordinate the work of all the people doing narrowly specialized jobs. The chain of command requires that people at higher levels be able to direct and control people at lower levels, creating a situation of passivity and dependence. Argyris believed that under such conditions people experience "psychological failure." They are unable to define their own goals or the way they will achieve their goals.

The result, said Argyris, is that organizations create a situation that is fundamentally in conflict with the needs of healthy human beings. The conflict gets worse as one moves down the hierarchy, as jobs become more mechanized, as leadership becomes more directive, as formal structure becomes tighter, and as people attain increasing maturity.

Argyris carried his argument a step further. If there is a basic conflict between the individual and the organization, and if the conflict frustrates employees, then employees can be expected to find some way to resist or adapt to the frustration. Argyris suggested several likely ways for employees to respond: (1) They might withdraw from the organization, through quitting or frequent absenteeism. (2) They might stay on the job but withdraw psychologically, becoming indifferent, passive, and apathetic. (3) They might resist the organization through restricting output, deception, featherbedding, or sabotage. (4) They might try to climb the hierarchy to better jobs. (But, Argyris cautioned, the pyramidal structure of most organizations means that there are far more jobs at the bottom than at the top.) (5) They might create groups and organizations (for example, labor unions) that can help to redress the power imbalance between the individual and the organization. (But, Argyris cautioned, those new organizations are likely to be designed and managed the same way as the old ones. In the long run, the employees may feel powerless with both the company and the union.) (6) They may socialize their children to believe that work is unrewarding and that hopes for advancement are slim.

The theories of Argyris and McGregor dovetail closely at several points. Both hold that management practices are inconsistent with employee needs and that the conflict produces resistance and withdrawal. Both believe that managers often misinterpret such employee behavior to mean that something is wrong with the employees rather than the organization. Withdrawal and resistance confirm Theory X assumptions that employees are lazy, uninterested, incompetent, or greedy. If managers assume that the problem is "in" the employees, then the solution usually means some effort to change the employees. Argyris said that managers typically use three major strategies and that all three tend to make the problem worse instead of better.

One approach is "strong, dynamic leadership." The assumption is that the employees are a relatively passive flock of sheep who will respond to strong leadership. Argyris argued that the strategy is self-defeating—it puts more and more responsibility on managers and less and less on workers.

A second solution is to install tighter controls—quality

control inspectors, time-and-motion studies, and so on. But tighter controls deepen and reinforce the conflict between individual and organization and lead to an escalation of competitive games between managers and employees.

Both of the first two solutions correspond to the "tough" version of Theory X. The third one is a softer version, involving the use of a variety of "human relations" programs. In Argyris' view, "human relations" often takes the form of selling management's philosophy (through company newspapers, films, and so forth), pseudo participation ("Make the employees *feel* that their ideas are valued"), and communications programs that rarely communicate what employees really wanted to know. The human relations approaches try to make employees feel better without changing the basic conflict. In the long run, that makes the situation worse.

How can the conflict be reduced? Argyris suggested that both "job enlargement" and participative management have the potential to reduce the conflict. But he said that there are limits to those strategies. Many employees are already socialized to be passive and dependent at work. They might resent and resist efforts to make the work more challenging and responsible. Ultimately, said Argyris, "reality-centered leadership" is needed —leadership that takes into account the actual needs of the employees and the needs of the organization. Argyris and McGregor both believed that much more must be learned about the design and management of organizations in order to reduce the conflict between the system and the individual.

Interpersonal and Group Dynamics

Individuals rarely see themselves relating to "the organization." Much of the time, they relate to one another, often in the context of groups (such as work groups, committees, task forces, and project teams). Managers, in particular, spend virtually all of their time in interpersonal exchanges (Kotter, 1982; Mintzberg, 1973).

Social psychologists and folk wisdom agree that individuals' social needs and interpersonal styles are substantially influenced by experiences in infancy and childhood and do not change quickly or easily in response to organizational requirements. Thompson (1967) and others have argued that the socializing institutions of a bureaucratic society will shape individuals to make them better suited to organizational life. But organizations' human inputs are created by a decentralized cottage industry known as the family, which seldom produces raw materials exactly to organizational specifications.

People bring to the workplace at least two characteristics that complicate organizational life. First, individuals conduct their interpersonal relationships in ways that fit their own styles and preferences, often disregarding what the organization or anyone around them wants. Second, when individuals are in interpersonal or group settings, they may work on organizational tasks, but they never work *only* on organizational tasks. They also work on whatever interpersonal and social needs are important for them.

Both individual differences and the intrusion of interpersonal dynamics are continual sources of organizational muddles. A project is on the rocks because no one on the team likes the manager's style; only a mid-stream change in leadership can save it. Two departments are constantly battling because of interpersonal friction between their respective heads. The company's executive committee rarely gets anything done because of interpersonal tensions that everyone recognizes but no one discusses. A school principal spends an inordinate amount of time trying to deal with a handful of abrasive or ineffectual teachers who are responsible for most of the discipline problems and almost all the parental complaints.

The reality of persistent individual differences has led to a long line of research on the kinds of personal characteristics and interpersonal behavior that will be more effective in task settings. A classic study was Lewin, Lippitt, and White's (1939) research on autocratic, democratic, and laissez-faire styles of leadership. In a study of adult leaders in experimentally created boys' clubs, the researchers found that autocratic leadership produced substantial discontent and either dependent apathy or rebellious hostility. Laissez-faire leadership led to aimlessness

and confusion, while democratic leadership was strongly preferred by the boys and produced a much more positive group
climate.

A number of subsequent researchers examined leadership
in work settings (much of this work is reviewed in Stogdill,
1974). Fleishman and Harris (1962) conducted a series of studies focusing on two dimensions of leadership: consideration
(how well a leader showed concern for and sensitivity to people) and initiating structure (how much a leader actively structured subordinates' activities). A series of studies produced a
complex pattern of findings, but high consideration generally
produced lower turnover, fewer grievances, and less absenteeism. Overall, supervisors who were high on both consideration
and structure were the most effective. Similar results were produced by Likert (1961), who presented evidence that "employee-
centered" managers were more effective in the long run than
"task-centered" managers.

An almost endless series of theories, books, workshops,
and tests have been developed to help managers identify their
own or others' personal or interpersonal styles. Are they intro-
verts or extroverts? Are they friendly helpers, tough battlers, or
objective thinkers? Do they care more about control, inclusion,
or affection? Do they behave more like a parent, an adult, or a
child? Are they 9,9 (superstars who are concerned for both people and production), 1,9 ("country club" managers concerned
only about people), or 9,1 (hard-driving taskmasters who are insensitive to human needs and feelings)? There is the risk of turning managers into undertrained amateur psychologists, but such
ideas do provide a language that enables managers to talk about
an elusive, complex, and sensitive phenomenon. A number of
studies have shown that managers are often blind to their own
management styles (Argyris, 1962; Argyris and Schön, 1974)
and unable to learn about it without some help from their
friends. Their friends may be more helpful if they have some
way to talk about the issues.

Argyris (1962) emphasized the importance of "interpersonal competence" as a basic managerial skill. His research
showed that managers' effectiveness was often impaired because

they were overcontrolling, excessively competitive, uncomfort-able with feelings, and closed to ideas other than their own (Argyris, 1962; Argyris and Schön, 1974). In effect, his research suggested that most of the managers he studied were too much like Lewin, Lippitt, and White's "autocratic" managers, and in-sufficiently skilled in democratic leadership.

Argyris and Schön (1974) carried the issue of interper-sonal effectiveness one step further. They argued that individ-uals' behavior is controlled by personal "theories for action": assumptions and ideas that people have about the nature of ef-fective behavior. Their research found that there was a signifi-cant discrepancy between the theory that most managers es-poused and the theory that they used. Managers' explanations and predictions of their own behavior were often unconnected to their actions. Managers typically saw themselves as rational, open, concerned for others, and democratic. Yet their behav-ior was generally governed by values of competition, control, and self-protection. Most managers were unaware of the discrep-ancy and followed a behavioral program that was designed to make it unlikely that they would learn of discrepancies or of in-effectiveness in their behavior.

In a subsequent work, Argyris and Schön (1978) argued that individuals' theories for action were a major impediment to organizational learning. When faced with conditions of ambigu-ity and uncertainty, managers often felt inadequate and devel-oped organizational games to camouflage the inadequacy. To avoid being caught in the game playing, they piled camouflage on top of the camouflage, which made conditions in the organi-zation even more uncertain and ambiguous and also made detec-tion of error difficult or impossible. Argyris and Schön provided a number of cases in which organizations persisted in a course of action for months or years even though many in the organi-zation knew they were on a path to disaster.

Such issues are critical in implementing many organiza-tional reforms toward greater employee participation and in-volvement—efforts that have little chance of success if managers lack needed skills. Argyris and Schön suggest that such skills are, in fact, very rare. The result is that many change efforts will fail not because the intentions are incorrect or insincere but because managers lack the skills and understandings necessary for implementation. A good example is management by objectives (MBO). MBO suggests that an effective approach to management and evaluation focuses not on how a manager performs but on what the manager accomplishes. MBO programs ask that managers and subordinates meet at the beginning of a year to discuss what are the subordinates' major objectives for the year and reach an agreement that is acceptable to both. At the end of the year, they meet again to evaluate how well the objectives are being accomplished. The theory of MBO calls for putting more responsibility on the subordinate to develop realistic goals and to evaluate effectiveness. Evaluation will be fairer because subordinates will not be evaluated on highly subjective personality traits but on objective, observable results.

That is the theory. We once were talking to a group of managers in a company with an extensive MBO program, and we asked them how MBO was working. The first answer was, "We don't have MBO. We have MBT."

"What is MBT?", we asked.

"Management by terror," was the reply. The managers said that, in practice, they were manipulated into agreeing to goals that they felt were unrealistic and then punished for not achieving the goals that they had "set for themselves." In effect, the intentions of the program may have been fine, but managers' ability to carry out the intentions was missing.

The inevitability of groups being the vehicle for accomplishing all sorts of tasks has also spawned a long tradition of research on how groups work. A number of theorists have emphasized that groups always operate at two different levels: a more overt, conscious level of focus on the *task* and a more subtle, implicit level of group maintenance and interpersonal dynamics (Bion, 1961; Leavitt, 1978; Maier, 1967; Schein, 1969).

One of the oldest of management jokes defines a camel as "a horse put together by a committee," reflecting a common view that groups are inefficient, confused, and frustrating vehicles for accomplishing anything. Research on task groups (Collins and Guetzkow, 1964) has demonstrated convincingly that such images are unduly harsh and that groups can be wonderful or terrible, productive or hopeless, imprisoning or freeing, conformist or creative. Group effectiveness depends mostly on who the members are, what resources they bring, and how well they are able to work together. Many group problems are related to the interpersonal and group dynamics, but those problems can be solved if they are identified and explicitly managed.

As an example, group members need to find a role within the group that is personally comfortable and satisfying. Individuals who feel that their ideas are not heard or their feelings are not considered are likely to be unproductive or disruptive. In some groups, everyone has such feelings, and little is accomplished. In others, everyone feels appropriately recognized and valued, and productivity is very high. Maier (1967) has shown that group leadership makes a critical difference. Leaders who overcontrol or understructure tend to produce frustration and ineffectiveness. Effective leaders are sensitive to both the task and the process dynamics and enlist the group in actively managing both.

6

⛥⛥⛥⛥⛥⛥⛥⛥⛥⛥

Applying the
Human Resource
Approach

The theories of Maslow, McGregor, and Argyris suggest that conflict between individual and organization will get worse as organizations become larger (with greater impersonality, longer chains of command, increasing number and complexity of rules and control systems) and as society becomes better educated and more affluent (producing more people whose higher-level needs are salient). One source of indirect confirmation for that prediction has appeared. More and more organizations, including many of the largest, are committing resources to address human resource issues. An example is General Motors, which had little investment in applications of the human resource frame until the late 1960s and early 1970s. Then GM encountered a period when profits were declining even though sales were increasing, because internal costs were increasing disproportionately. Just as Argyris and McGregor had predicted, the

internal system was becoming increasingly expensive and difficult to manage. In 1972 GM's new plant at Lordstown, Ohio,
became one of the notorious examples of conflict between individual and system.

The Lordstown plant went into operation in 1970. It was
GM's newest and most heavily automated plant. After a year in
operation, the plant had failed to achieve its production targets.
New management came in to solve the problem. They reduced
the number of workers and increased the work load for those
who remained. Although wages and benefits were excellent, the
grievance rate soared (from 500 grievances a year to more than
500 each month). There were several instances of employee
sabotage to slow or stop the assembly line, and the local union
voted to strike over working conditions. One of the major issues
was an employee practice known as "doubling up." One employee would cover two jobs on the line for a period of time so
that another could take a break. Then the second person would
cover both jobs so that the first could take a break. Since cars
moved down the line at a rate of 100 per hour, each worker
normally had 36 seconds to perform one job. Doubling up
meant only 18 seconds to perform a job. That was a fast pace,
but many employees preferred to work faster with intermittent
breaks rather than face another car every half minute all day
long. When employees were interviewed about the strike vote,
everyone said wages were not the issue: "The job pays good,
but it's driving me crazy." "It's just like the army. No, it's
worse than the army, 'cause you're welded to the line. You just
about need a pass to piss."

After a costly wildcat strike at Lordstown, General Motors began to get the message. Since that time, GM has made a
very substantial investment in its "Quality of Work Life" program. The program has had its failures as well as its successes,
but GM is convinced that the program is essential to corporate
well-being. The extent of the change in philosophy is symbolized by appointment in 1982 of a plant manager who is a woman (in itself a remarkable break from automotive tradition)
trained in clinical psychology and a specialist in human resource
management.

General Motors is only one example of a trend that can be seen in almost every major organization—public or private—in the United States and in many other nations. Attempts to implement better "human resource management" have taken a variety of forms. The most prominent have been job enrichment, participative management, organizational democracy, organization development, and "Theory Z." Each of those approaches is discussed below.

Job Enrichment

If jobs are too narrow, fragmented, and restrictive, one approach to reducing person/system conflict is redesign of work. "Job enlargement" and "job enrichment" are two labels often used to describe efforts in this direction.

An influential exponent of such efforts was Frederick Herzberg (1966). Herzberg developed a "two-factor" theory of motivation based on his research with managers and workers. Herzberg's research approach was simple and direct: He asked employees to talk about the times when they felt best about their jobs and the times when they felt worst. He found that people talked about different themes when they talked about positive and negative experiences.

The most dominant themes in "good feelings" stories were things like achievement, recognition for performance, satisfactions intrinsic to the work, responsibility, advancement, and learning. The "bad feelings" stories were most likely to feature such themes as company policy and administration, supervision, and working conditions. Herzberg concluded that there was a difference between the things that produced job satisfaction (he called them "motivators") and the things that produce job dissatisfaction (which he called "hygiene factors"). In effect, Herzberg proposed another need hierarchy, but one with only two levels. The "hygiene" level included Maslow's physiological, safety, and belongingness needs. The "motivator" level included primarily self-esteem and self-actualization.

Herzberg argued that the hygiene factors relate to people's "animal nature," while the motivators relate to the "unique human characteristic, the ability to achieve and, through achievement, to experience psychological growth" (p. 56). Herzberg's hygiene factors all have to do with the work environment, while the motivators mostly deal with the work itself. From this Herzberg argued that attempts to motivate workers with more pay and fringe benefits, with improvements in working conditions, with communications programs or human relations training are all based on what he called the "KITA" approach to motivation—the belief that the quickest and surest way to get someone to do something is to kick the person in the tail. In Herzberg's view, KITA approaches do not motivate. They may get the person to move, but to get the person to move again requires another kick.

Herzberg saw job enrichment as the way to motivate. Enrichment is not the same as "horizontal job enlargement." Adding more dull tasks to an already dull job does not enrich it. Herzberg argued for "vertical job loading"—giving the individual more freedom and authority, more accountability, more feedback, more challenge, and the use of more skills.

Herzberg's theory has been heavily criticized, particularly because the research was based entirely on what people said about good and bad work experiences. Several commentators have noted that people often attribute unpleasant events to forces outside themselves while taking personal credit for successes. Psychologists call this systematic distortion the "attributional bias." Even if Herzberg's theory oversimplifies questions of human motivation, it is broadly consistent with the work of Maslow, McGregor, Argyris, and other human resource theorists. All the theories point in the direction of job enrichment as a way to produce a better fit between individual and organization.

Does job redesign work? A number of experiments have been tried (some going back to the middle 1940s), and the answer has been mostly yes. In most of the experiments, the majority of workers have preferred the redesigned jobs, although there has usually been a minority who preferred the old jobs. (The latter finding is consistent with the prediction of both Argyris and McGregor that many workers have been trained to accept Theory X assumptions and would therefore resist a change toward more responsibility.) In some cases, job redesign has led to greater productivity and lower costs. In others, costs have been roughly comparable under both systems.

Overall, the track record for job redesign efforts has been good in many of the organizations that have tried it. It is likely that the next decade will see a significant expansion of such efforts and a gradual reduction in the percentage of jobs that are overwhelmingly dull, routine, and unchallenging. Increasingly, such jobs will be either redesigned or turned over to computers and other machines (whose needs are generally simpler). But there are significant barriers to the progress of job enlargement, and dull jobs will not entirely disappear in the future. One source of resistance is the philosophy of "technological determinism"—the belief that jobs should be organized on the basis of technical imperatives, and people then trained to perform the jobs correctly. Another barrier is the durability of Theory X. Right or wrong, many managers continue to believe that their workers will be most productive in a Theory X environment. A third barrier is economic. Many jobs cannot be significantly altered without major investments in the redesign of physical plant and machinery. The barriers will slow the movement toward job enrichment, but they are not likely to stop it.

Participative Management

McGregor and Argyris both believed that organizations create a world that forces employees to be highly dependent on their bosses and gives them very little control over their work situations. Adults are asked to take on the status of children. One possible solution to that problem is *participation*—giving employees more opportunity to influence decisions that affect their work.

The basic idea behind participation is illustrated in a classic case from the organizational literature (Whyte, 1955). The case involved a group of manual workers, all women, who were responsible for painting dolls in a toy factory. The job had just been reengineered. In the new system, each woman took a toy from a tray, painted it, and put it on a hook passing by on an endless belt. The women received an hourly rate, a group bonus, and a learning bonus because the job was new.

Although management had expected no difficulty with the new system, production was well below prediction and many hooks went by empty. Morale among the women was very poor. The women especially complained about the heat and the speed of the belt. A consultant suggested that the foreman meet with the women to discuss the problems. Reluctantly, the foreman followed this advice. After several meetings, the foreman agreed to bring in fans, even though he and the industrial engineer both doubted that fans would help. The fans produced a significant improvement in morale. Discussions continued and the employees developed a genuinely radical suggestion—they asked that they be allowed to control the speed of the belt. The engineer strongly opposed the idea, since he had carefully calculated the optimal speed. The foreman was doubtful but agreed to install a control. The employees met and developed a complicated schedule so that the belt ran fast at some times of the day and slow at other times.

Morale shot up, and so did production. So, in fact, did the women's pay. Production went up so much that it far exceeded the engineer's calculations and began to overload the rest of the plant. Pay went up so much that the women were now earning more than many workers with more skill and experience. The high production and high pay upset the rest of the plant. The experiment did not have a happy ending. In order to solve the overpay/overproduction problems, management decided to revert to a fixed speed on the belt. Production dropped again; morale plummeted; most of the employees quit in a few months.

The doll-painting case was not in itself a definitive experiment, but the case illustrates two major findings of subsequent research about the effects of participation:

1. Many studies of participation at work have found significant improvements in both morale and productivity. Par-

ticipation is one of the very few ways to increase both at the same time. (For a review of this literature, see Blumberg, 1969, and Katzell and Yankelovich, 1975.)

2. Participation can fail, even when it is working, because it creates the need for changes that are resisted by other parts of the organization.

"Participative management" has become a fad in the last decade. Managers throughout the world go off to seminars to learn how to be more participative. A recent example was the sudden "discovery" of quality circles. Even though the Japanese had originally gotten the idea from the United States a decade earlier, hundreds of companies jumped at the chance to employ the latest example of Japanese success in managing human resources. The participation fad has made it more difficult to find managers who forthrightly proclaim their belief in autocratic supervision. There is evidence (Argyris and Schön, 1974; Bolman, 1975) that participative management often exists more at the level of myth than at that of reality. At virtually any level in any organization, managers believe in participation for themselves more than they believe in it for their subordinates. Many efforts at fostering participation have failed not because participation did not work but because it was not implemented. The failure of implementation often reflects both the difficulties of designing a workable participative system and managers' ambivalence about power—they may believe in sharing power but fear that subordinates will misuse it.

Organizational Democracy

Particularly in the United States, "participative management" has usually been viewed as a matter of style and climate rather than a matter of formal authority. A manager may choose to be participative or choose not to, but there is no formal change in managerial prerogatives. In both public and private organizations in the United States, most managerial thinking has been resistant to the idea of "organizational democracy," in which the rights of workers to participate in decisions are built into the formal decision-making process and are not subject to managerial discretion.

Organizational democracy has been carried further in a number of European nations and in Israel. In Norway and Sweden, "industrial democracy" is increasingly accepted as a fact of life by both managers and workers. Organizational democracy has been successful in Israeli *kibbutzim,* although the system has not yet had much impact on management practice in other Israeli organizations.

One of the earliest and most far-reaching formal systems of organizational democracy is "self-management" in Yugoslavia. Yugoslavia went through significant ideological changes after its rejection from the Soviet camp by Stalin. The Yugoslav government came to the view that worker alienation was not eliminated simply by transferring ownership of factories from capitalists to central state bureaucrats. Such a system changed the identity of the master but did not reduce powerlessness and dependency at work. Yugoslavia made a subtle change in the official definition of who owns the workplace: It was owned not by the state but by the entire society. That shift was mostly symbolic, but it signaled a shift away from centralized control of managerial decision making.

Beginning in the early 1950s, a legally mandated system of worker self-management was gradually introduced into all Yugoslav work organizations. Every work organization was required to have a workers' council, elected by the employees, with essentially the formal power that is usually held by the board of directors in a corporation. The workers' council can set basic policy, hire and fire management, and set wages and salaries.

Formal authority and real power are not always the same thing (a lesson some managers have difficulty appreciating). Extensive research on the Yugoslav experience (summarized in Blumberg, 1969, and Jenkins, 1973) suggests that the workers' councils often have less power in practice than in law. Members of the Communist party and better-educated workers often exercise influence out of proportion to their numbers. Management expertise dominates workers' legal power in many decisions. If a group of workers is asked to review management policies on complex financial matters, they may agree to anything the financial manager suggests simply because the topic is mysterious to them. An additional source of erosion of workers' power is the size of the council and the fact that it is a part-time body. In large organizations the council may have fifty or a hundred members and may meet only a few hours a month. It is difficult for a large group with limited time to go into much depth on most issues.

Despite all the limitations, the evidence also suggests that the workers' councils have had a significant impact on how Yugoslav organizations make decisions. Chief executives have resigned or been dismissed because they were unable to satisfy the wishes of the council. Even though the council members might not fully understand highly technical issues, they are able to understand basic issues like wages and salaries.

Since the Yugoslavian system is an unorthodox way to manage anything when viewed from the perspective of most Western thinking, an obvious question arises: Can such a system work? Yugoslavia was one of the more economically backward nations in Europe and was severely devastated by World War II. During the period since worker self-management was instituted, economic growth and productivity gains have been excellent by almost any standard. During the first twenty years of worker self-management, Yugoslavia's increase in industrial production was second only to Japan's. There is no way to prove what the rate would have been in the absence of self-management, but the evidence strongly suggests that the Yugoslavian approach is no barrier to economic efficiency.

Perhaps the greatest limitation of the Yugoslavian system has been its highly formalized and remote nature. The Yugo-slavian workers have formal control of the workplace, but the workers' council generally focuses its attention on broad, organizationwide decisions. Particularly in large organizations, most of those decisions are remote from the individual workers and their jobs. Many Yugoslav organizations are a reverse image of United States experiments in participation. In many United States organizations, management's formal authority remains absolute, but workers have considerable informal opportunity to participate in decisions affecting their jobs. In Yugoslavia the workers have formal control of the organization but may have little chance to participate in job-level decisions.

In Sweden and Norway, serious efforts to introduce organizational democracy began later than in Yugoslavia but have moved very rapidly. Ironically, one reason for rapid success was that the Scandinavian nations were able to make use of the expertise of a number of British social scientists who had gained considerable understanding of participative systems but whose ideas were not particularly welcome in Britain. One of the ideas they brought to Norway was that legal participation in the management of the enterprise is not enough. Changes are also needed in what they called the "sociotechnical system": the interplay between the social and the technical aspects of how work is performed.

In both Sweden and Norway, worker participation in decision making is now legally mandated, and there is extensive experimentation with new forms of work and employee participation. As one example, both of the major Swedish auto makers —Saab and Volvo—have experimented with radical alterations of the traditional assembly-line approach to producing automobiles. Rather than tying each worker to a limited, repetitive job on the assembly line, both auto makers have experimented with the use of work teams that are responsible for a complete subassembly (for example, an engine or a transmission). A system in which three or four workers produce an entire engine, rotating jobs among themselves as they choose, is a dramatic change from traditional work arrangements in automobile plants.

Industrial democracy is viewed by some as an enormously powerful idea whose time has finally come, by others as an overrated fad. The debate has often been clouded by an oversupply of rhetoric, ideology, and emotion and a shortage of empirical data. The idea implies fundamental changes in power relations. Changes of that magnitude are likely to produce fear and resistance in those who benefit from existing social arrangements. But several things seem reasonably clear:

- There has been an enormous increase in experiments in industrial democracy. (Before the late 1950s, there were many experiments in benevolent paternalism, as well as state ownership of work organizations, but neither did much to increase employees' controls over decisions.)

- Most of the empirical investigations show more positive than negative consequences. Workers almost always prefer more power to less.

- Experiments with industrial democracy sometimes show an initial decline in productivity, but in the long run most experiments produce either a gain in productivity or a level that is roughly comparable to productivity under the previous system.

- The process is usually irreversible. When workers gain more power, they are rarely willing to give it up, and they often press for its expansion.

- Despite the mostly favorable evidence, many managers, scholars, and trade union leaders continue to oppose the idea.

Participation and organizational democracy have both shown enough successes that they will continue to spread, but the changes will come slowly. Managers resist democracy for fear of losing many of the powers and prerogatives that they currently enjoy (and sincerely believe to be essential to organizational success). Union leaders sometimes see organizational democracy as a management trick—a way of getting workers to accept gimmicks instead of real gains in wages and benefits. Resistance by unions may also stem from a fear that organizational democracy will produce closer collaboration between workers and management that might undermine the role of the union. Union leaders who hold a basically adversarial conception of the management/labor relationship often view participation and democracy with profound suspicion. Moreover, some unions are formally democratic but are internally as authoritarian as their corporate counterparts. Democracy in the corporation almost inevitably leads to questions about democracy in the union as well.

Training and Organizational Development

One result of early research on human relations in industry was the belief that managers needed more skills in human

relations. Training programs and departments began to proliferate rapidly in the 1950s and 1960s. Many of the programs focused on training managers how to be more sensitive, how to be
better listeners, and how to communicate more effectively.

The early programs usually consisted mostly of lectures
about the importance of good human relations. Participants
often left those programs with more enthusiasm, but no more
skills, for improving their human relations. The programs assumed that human relations skills could be improved with a
good lecture. After enough failures, the question was asked:
Isn't there a problem with the way we are trying to teach human relations? If people cannot learn to play tennis or a violin
by listening to a lecture, why should they be able to develop human relations skills that way?

The question gave birth to the idea of experiential learning: training programs that tried to give learners the chance to
"learn by doing." One of the most provocative examples of experiential learning was "laboratory human relations training,"
often known as "sensitivity training" or "T-groups."

The T-group was a serendipitous discovery. A group of
social psychologists sponsored a conference on race relations,
held in Connecticut in the late 1940s. During the conference,
participants met in groups to discuss the issues, and researchers
were stationed in each group to take notes on the discussion. In
the evening, the researchers reported their observations to the
program staff. When the participants learned about the evening
sessions, they asked to be invited. At the sessions they were fascinated to hear reports about themselves and their behavior in
groups that they had never heard before.

The researchers recognized that they had discovered
something and began a program of "human relations laboratories" that attempted to provide both human relations training
for participants and research opportunities for social scientists.
The first such laboratory, held in 1946, had six trainers and
thirty researchers on the staff. The participants were divided
into "Basic Skills Training Groups," which met for several hours
a day. Each group had a trainer and a training observer. The observer discussed his observations of the group during the last
half hour of each meeting. One year later, when another labora-

tory was held, the observer had become a trainer, and the observations were reported as events occurred. Trainers and participants were joined in the common task of working in a group and learning from the work at the same time. That became the basic model for the T-group. It was a powerful, even startling, educational model.

Particularly during the early years, few who came to T-groups were expecting what unfolded when they arrived. As soon as the group began, they found themselves in a group with approximately twelve other participants and one or two trainers. The opening often went something like the following:

Trainer: We'll be together for many hours during the laboratory. This gives each of us a chance to learn more about ourselves and how we can participate effectively in groups. I think the best way for us to do that is to focus on the here and now: on what we do and how we do it. I'm here to help as much as I can, but I don't plan to serve as the group leader.

(Silence ensues, becomes increasingly uncomfortable for group members, and lasts for anything from a few seconds to a few minutes)

Member A: I don't think I understood everything you said, Trainer. Could you repeat it?

Trainer: (Repeats, in essentially the same words)

Member B: What are we supposed to work on?

Trainer: I see that as something for the group to decide.

(Another silence)

Member C: Well, I think this whole thing is a waste of time! If we're going to get anything done, we have to get organized. We need a leader. Every group has to have a leader to get anything done. Why don't we choose someone to chair the meeting?

(More silence)

Member D: (Carefully) Maybe it would be a good idea if we all introduced ourselves.

Member A: Yeah, I don't know anyone's name.

Member D: (More confidently) Good, A. Why don't you start? Then we'll go around the table.

(A introduces himself, and others follow around the circle)

Later the trainer would ask the group to examine how they had felt when C suggested a leader. C would be surprised to learn that there were many who agreed with him but that others had mistrusted his motives for making the suggestion. The group might examine how D, with a little help from A, had made a decision that everyone followed. They might discover that many members disagreed with D's procedure but no one felt willing to question it.

The T-group had several features that made it a powerful experience for many participants. The trainer's failure to fill the customary role for group leaders created a vacuum: The group began with little in the way of rules, organization, leadership, or content. The only definition of the task was to learn from examining events in the group, and this definition had little meaning for most participants. In order to function, the group had to create its own agenda, goals, and procedures.

This situation was enormously frustrating and unsettling at first but led to a great sense of achievement and satisfaction when groups began to create for themselves a structure that worked. It also came as a surprise to many that a group with so little structure and such unorthodox leadership could actually work.

A second source of the power of the T-groups was interpersonal feedback. In a culture where it is rare for people to communicate direct reactions to one another's behavior, the high levels of feedback in a T-group constitute a powerful intervention. Countless members of T-groups found themselves saying, "I never knew that was how people saw me."

As word spread, T-groups began to replace lectures as an approach to producing human relations skills in organizations. T-groups also attracted a large body of research on their impact (mostly because so many T-group leaders were trained as social and behavioral scientists). Through a haze of controversy, charges, and countercharges (T-groups had more than their share of zealous proponents and equally zealous critics), the evidence began to suggest two basic things: T-groups could and did have an effect on people's feelings about themselves, their self-perceptions, and even their behavior. But those effects rarely led to very much organizational change (Gibb, 1975; Campbell and Dunnette, 1968).

As research and experience showed that the training effect often faded out, many laboratory trainers began to experiment with new approaches. If participants were not applying learnings in their organizations, perhaps it was because the individual needed support from others in the workplace. If so, might the effects be better if an entire work team were included in the same T-group? A number of such experiments were tried, and they represented a very important early experiment in what has come to be called "organization development," or OD for short.

Many of those "family" T-groups worked very well in promoting communication and trust within the group, sometimes at the cost of an in-group climate that alienated others in the organization. The research evidence was never very clear (and still is not) about the presence or absence of benefits from the use of T-groups in work organizations, but many practitioners increasingly came to believe that the T-group was too specialized and rarefied to respond to the variety of situations and problems present in work organizations. Increasingly, OD separated itself from T-groups as practitioners took some of the basic elements of laboratory training (for example, use of face-to-face groups, emphasis on open communication, use of interpersonal feedback) and adapted them to a variety of organizational contexts. "Conflict laboratories" were designed for situations involving conflict between departments. "Team-building" programs were designed for groups that wished to increase their ability to work as a team. A host of other OD intervention techniques were gradually created.

At about the same time that laboratory training was getting its start (the late 1940s), a group of researchers at the University of Michigan began the first of a long series of efforts to develop questionnaires that would measure important human elements in organizations: motivation, communications, leadership styles, and organizational climate. Rensis Likert was a founding member of the Survey Research Center at Michigan, and his 1961 book, *New Patterns of Management,* became a classic work in the human resource tradition.

In that book Likert argued that many common-sense beliefs about effective management were wrong. He distinguished between "job-centered" and "employee-centered" management styles. The job-centered manager decides how the job should be done, instructs the employee, and monitors to make sure the employee does it right. The employee-centered manager focuses on the human aspects of employee performance and on building effective work groups with high performance goals. Likert pointed to a large body of evidence—most of it derived from survey research—showing that employee-centered supervisors usually managed higher-producing units than job-centered supervisors. The issue was *not* satisfaction, said Likert. In some studies of jobs that were routine and required a low skill level, job satisfaction was a little higher in units that were low in production.

Likert's distinction between job-centered and production-centered supervision bears a strong resemblance to McGregor's conception of Theory X and Theory Y. Likert developed a prescription for organizational effectiveness that included employee-centered supervision and "overlapping group" organizational structure. The overlapping group structure viewed every manager as a member of two work groups and as a "linking pin" between those groups. One group consisted of the manager's boss and peers; the other group included the manager's subordinates. Each was to be a "high-performing group," with openness, cohesiveness, democratic supervision, and high production goals. Likert's view of a new management system retained the basic hierarchal structure of organizations but put great emphasis on groups and on the quality of interpersonal relationships. If every supervisor were an effective, employee-centered leader, the quality of life in organizations would be dramatically improved.

Likert's theory, based in part on survey data, was instrumental in the evolution of survey feedback as an approach to organizational improvement. The survey feedback process begins with administration of questionnaires to members of an organization. The questions ask about a variety of human and organizational issues. The questionnaires are tabulated and results computed for each work unit and subunit. A consultant meets with each unit to report the results for that group and for similar work units in the company. The consultant asks the group to discuss the results, test the data against their own experience, and talk about what they can do to solve any problems that have appeared. In a given unit, the results might show that information flows well and that members of the group are highly motivated but that decisions are often made in the wrong place with the wrong information.

Where Is OD, and Where Is It Going?

Likert's emphasis on openness, interpersonal relations, and effective groups was consistent with the basic assumptions of laboratory training. T-groups and survey research became the parents of organization development. Understanding the parentage helps to understand why OD has developed into its current form. Both parents were very much in the human resource tradition. The only other major frame in organization theory at the time was the structural approach, and most structural theorists were more interested in studying organizations than in trying to improve them. Human resource theorists had the field of organization development almost to themselves, and that parentage is still reflected in current OD practice.

OD consultation has grown enormously since the middle 1960s. In 1965 few managers or organizations had heard of OD. By 1975 there were few managers who had not heard of it and few major organizations (particularly in the United States) that had not tried it in some form or other. General Motors and the United States Post Office, IBM and the Internal Revenue Service, Texas Instruments and the United States Navy had all made significant investments in one or another form of OD.

OD's popularity does not result entirely from its enormous success. Both the research evidence and the feelings of clients point to a mixed record—there have been notable successes and dramatic failures. There is still scanty evidence to provide firm conclusions about what form of OD works under what conditions.

Yet OD continues to grow in significance, for a fairly simple reason. OD may not be the best solution to human resource problems, but it is just about the only solution. A professor of medicine once offered the opinion that doctors probably killed more patients than they cured until about 1940. For centuries, physicians used cures that did not work to cure illnesses that they did not understand, because no one else could do better. The public recognized many of the limitations of the medical profession, which was held in much lower repute in the past than now. But people still went to doctors.

Something similar is happening to OD. The enormous dominance of social life by large institutions is primarily a twentieth-century phenomenon. Systematic research on organizations is at most a few decades old, and most OD practice has evolved during the past ten or fifteen years. It is not surprising that OD, like air, is all around us but hard to define or pin down. The research base is growing, but it is still primitive and controversial. OD is also a highly personalized activity—the style of the consultant is a significant determinant of the nature of the consultation.

Fullan, Miles, and Taylor (1981) provided an excellent recent review of OD practice, although they focused mainly on OD in public schools. They concluded that OD is sufficiently ill defined and amorphous that it is important to distinguish OD from organizational training and from other organizational improvement approaches. Fullan and associates argue that the label "OD" should be reserved for programs that have all the following characteristics: "*simultaneously* is planned, long-range, involves a change agent or agents, focuses on organizational processes, tasks, and structures; addresses the development of individuals as well as the organization; and uses behavioral science techniques to generate valid data for both individual and organizational decisions" (1981, p. 6).

On the basis of their review of the literature, Fullan and associates concluded that the probability of any given OD project's being successful is 0.5 or less. But many of the failures appear to have been "ineptly conducted," and the success rate is high for those programs that adequately meet their definition of a systematic approach to OD.

It is fairly safe to predict the general future of OD. It will continue to grow, and it will evolve as its knowledge base improves. It will become more precise and differentiated and will develop more specific cures for specific organizational illnesses. It is also likely to become more professionalized. Currently, OD is primarily a two-tier profession.

One tier consists of a relatively small number of researchers and theorists, mostly based in universities, who write most of the books and garner most of the prestige. The second tier consists of a much larger number of OD consultants who work full-time as practitioners. Some are internal consultants who work full-time for one organization. Others are external consultants who enter a number of organizations as outside consultants. Members of the university tier typically have doctoral degrees and extensive training in the social sciences. Members of the consultant tier have learned much of their craft from hands-on experience and from attendance at occasional workshops. OD training programs are becoming more common in universities, and more than one organization has attempted to certify the competence of OD practitioners. Even though there are counterpressures from within the field, the future is likely to bring more formalization of training, credentials, and emphasis on professionalism.

Theory Z

William Ouchi's *Theory Z,* published in 1981, was the first book by an organizational behavior researcher to attain a long stay on the nonfiction bestseller lists in the United States. The book was published at a time when the American economy was sagging, and many were comparing American organizations and American management unfavorably with the Japanese.

Ouchi, a Japanese-American, studied both Japanese and American approaches to management. He described several major differences between American and Japanese organizations:

1. Whereas American organizations have high mobility and turnover, Japanese organizations provide lifetime employment for their basic work force.

2. In American organizations, evaluation is relatively explicit, and promotion is often rapid. In Japanese organizations, performance evaluation is relatively subtle and implicit, and promotion is infrequent.

3. American organizations are much more likely to provide highly specialized career paths for different managers—so that a financial manager always works in finance, and a manufacturing manager never leaves manufacturing. In Japanese organizations, specialized career paths are unusual, and most employees move through a variety of functions in the course of their careers.

4. Whereas decision making in American organizations is frequently seen as the individual responsibility of the appropriate manager, decision making in Japanese organizations is a collective process that involves everyone who is affected by the decision. This leads to an important contrast: American organizations often make decisions more quickly but encounter great problems in getting the decisions implemented. Japanese organizations are often much slower to make decisions but are able to implement those decisions smoothly and rapidly once made.

5. Whereas American culture highly prizes individuality, Japanese culture prizes collective effort.

Ouchi believes that there are important differences between American and Japanese culture that make it impossible to import all of the Japanese approach to American organizations. But his research also led to two additional conclusions: (1) a number of Japanese organizations had successfully adapted their system when they created subsidiaries in the United States; (2) a number of very successful American businesses followed an approach to management that closely resembled that of Japanese organizations.

Ouchi, mindful of McGregor's Theory Y, coined the term

Theory Z to describe a management philosophy that success-fully blended Japanese and American approaches to manage-ment. His description of Theory Z incorporates many of the cen-tral assumptions of the human resource frame: "Of all its values, commitment of a Z culture to its people—its workers—is the most important. . . . Theory Z assumes that any worker's life is a whole, not a Jekyll-Hyde personality, half machine from nine to five and half human in the hours preceding and follow-ing. Theory Z suggests that humanized working conditions not only increase productivity and profits to the company but also the self-esteem for employees. . . . Up to now American man-agers have assumed that technology makes for increased produc-tivity. What Theory Z calls for instead is a redirection of atten-tion to *human* relations in the corporate world" (Ouchi, 1981, p. 165).

Ouchi's view of the basic characteristics of a Theory Z or-ganization can be seen in his prescription for how to move an organization toward Theory Z. The first step in the process in-volves the development and implementation of a company phi-losophy. One of the basic elements of a Z corporation is a strong emphasis on corporate philosophy and culture (a topic that will be explored later in the symbolic frame). The philos-ophy needs to include both a statement of the organization's basic goal and mission and a statement of its commitment to its people. Once the philosophy is in place, the organization can begin to work on developing interpersonal skills, including skills in understanding group processes. A next step is to "test your-self and the system"—collect evidence to see how well the new system is working. Use of questionnaires is one method that Ouchi recommends. Other steps include involving the union in the process, stabilizing employment, and developing a system for slow evaluation and promotion.

Ouchi acknowledges that Theory Z organizations have potential weaknesses. Because they put strong emphasis on close, harmonious working relations, they often tend to ex-clude people who are different. That can lead to the exclusion of ideas from outside the organization. It can also lead to racism and sexism—a paradoxical result because Z organizations emphasize egalitarian relations within the organization. A predominantly white male management might exclude women and nonwhites because they might disrupt the existing interpersonal relationships.

The process of implementing Theory Z is time-consuming and not well understood: "Going from A to Z reaches down to touch every worker in every plant within perhaps ten to fifteen years. The large-scale successful developments are to date so small in number that it is not possible to gauge these estimates reliably. The process of participative management, once begun, is largely self-sustaining because it appeals to the basic values of all employees. And in fact the process promotes greater productivity and efficiency through better coordination and will flourish unless intentionally stopped by a disenchanted or threatened union or by top management" (Ouchi, 1981, p. 110).

Ouchi's theory incorporates and restates many classical elements of the human resource frame, but it also makes important additions, particularly in its emphasis on organizational philosophy and culture and in its explicit questioning of many implicit values in American management theory. American organizations will never become mirror images of their Japanese counterparts because of the significant differences between the cultures, but in the same way that the Japanese have shown an ability to learn from other cultures, Americans may learn a great deal in return from the Japanese that can help in enhancing the effectiveness of American management and organization.

Critiques of the Human Resource Frame

Almost as soon as human resource theorists began to have a significant impact on management thinking, critics began to question the validity of their ideas. Human resource theories have been criticized mainly on two grounds: naiveté and alliance with power elites (Morrow and Thayer, 1977; Nord, 1974).

The naiveté criticism has appeared in several forms: (1) Human resource theorists hold a mistaken conception of human nature and seek to impose an academic, middle-class value system on everyone else. (2) The theorists ignore individual differences and the imperatives of organizational structure. (3) Human resource theorists are too optimistic about the possibility of integrating individual and organizational needs. They underplay issues of power and scarcity in organizations.

The first criticism is difficult to assess. Assessment requires agreement about "human nature," and such agreement is difficult because the human resource theorists and many of their critics have different theories about human nature. Is Theory X more valid than Theory Y? It is possible to cite evidence in support of either view. McGregor believed that either theory could become a self-fulfilling prophecy. Managers could make either theory valid through their expectations and their behaviors. There is ample evidence to validate the "Pygmalion effect"—namely, our ability to get other people to behave the way we expect them to.

Human resource theorists have been criticized for ignoring individual differences, but that criticism often rests on a misunderstanding of their work. Argyris and McGregor were both careful to acknowledge the existence and importance of individual differences, even though neither of them made such differences a central issue in his theory. Similarly, human resource theorists have not entirely ignored structure, but it has usually not been at the center of their concerns. Structural theorists often emphasize the ways in which structure constrains choice. Human resource theorists tend to take the opposite tack and argue that choice can constrain structure. Thoroughgoing structuralists (for example, Perrow, 1970) often argue that structural imperatives impose very serious limits on the possibility of creating organizations that are significantly different from existing ones. Human resource theorists have usually preferred to think of structure as something that can and should be changed to meet human needs.

In their more glowing moods, human resource theorists may indeed become too optimistic about the possibilities for congruence between individual and system. In part, this tendency may derive from the need for a positive myth. Even if integration of individual and organization is as much dream as reality, believing that such a thing is possible and worthwhile can energize efforts to go beyond the status quo.

It is fair to say that human resource theorists have generally had little to say about power and the allocation of scarce resources. The works of Argyris, McGregor, and Likert devote much attention to concepts like communication, feedback, and leadership but rarely mention power. Organizational politics, if mentioned at all, is usually viewed as a problem to be solved rather than a natural and basic phenomenon in organizations.

The limited attention to power and politics may reflect predominant belief systems in the United States and Western Europe. By and large, human resource theorists have worked with management on the premise that it is possible to make improvements that benefit both employer and employee at the same time. They have focused on improvements in organizational climate, management style, and management skills but not on radical changes in the distribution of power. Their theories have often received a hospitable welcome in American management circles. Why not, if the theories promise to improve productivity and morale without any loss of management authority? Power and the politics of scarcity are a fundamental barrier to increasing the congruence between individual and organization, and human resource theorists will have to tackle that issue more directly than they have in the past.

Three Cases Revisited

We applied the structural perspective to three cases: Helen Demarco, the "unfair marriage," and the newspaper with new word processors. What can we learn by viewing those same cases as problems of human needs and interaction rather than formal roles and relationships?

It seems likely that Helen and Paul had significantly different needs. Helen seemed to value technical excellence and job security, whereas Paul was concerned about quick, major improvements in the organization. The differences in needs presumably colored each one's reactions to the situation and to each other. Neither was necessarily wrong, but they wanted different things.

At the same time, neither Paul nor Helen ever made an effort to make sure that they really understood each other.

Paul appeared to be operating in the "hard" version of Theory X—he assumed that the managers needed to be directed and controlled in order to make improvements. The likely subordinate response to directive management is resistance, deception, and sabotage, exactly the path that Helen and her colleagues chose. The human resource frame counsels Paul to involve his subordinates before making unilateral announcements of major changes and suggests to Helen that she communicate openly when she has serious reservations about a top management initiative. Both chose other approaches, with less than happy outcomes.

In the case of the sparring couple, one common-sense possibility is to seek outside assistance to help the couple learn what each of them is doing to create the problems. If that does not work, there is always divorce. Those approaches are consistent with the human resource emphasis on learning and improving communications.

It is clear, however, that this couple had not been talking for a long time about key issues in their relationship. They might want to establish regular times to share needs, communicate feelings, and give each person a voice. Restructuring may be less important than understanding each other and providing each a chance to influence the quality of the relationship. When the wife says the marriage is unfair, the husband might respond by asking, "What do you feel is unfair?" He might learn that the division of labor has been inequitable, and she might feel better if only because he is listening.

The newspaper missed the opportunity to involve reporters before the technology was introduced—a key mistake from a human resource perspective. Early participation might have ensured that reporters understood the new technology and felt that their views had been considered. Lack of involvement generated suspicion and mistrust that tended to undermine subsequent efforts to build reporters' commitment to the new system. The newspaper did employ another human resource strategy —training. Reporters were given orientation and practice sessions. The publisher presented the rationale for the new equipment. Proponents of the new system explained its advantages and conducted group discussions of concerns, fears, and problems with the new system. But the potentially more efficient system continued to be inefficient.

The human resource approach to the three cases emphasizes an understanding of individual needs, open communications, and participative management. Compared with the structural frame, the human resource view is less formal, more focused on people and relationships, and more focused on influencing or educating people than on changing the setting in which they function.

Summary

The human resource frame focuses on the fit between individual and organization. Humans are viewed as having needs that energize their behavior. These include physiological needs, social needs, and needs for self-esteem and self-actualization. An organization may meet the needs of its participants well or badly. When the fit is poor, the human resource frame predicts underutilization of human energy and talent, frustration, and psychological conflict for the individual. Individuals may respond with apathy, resistance, sabotage, or attempts to exploit the organization in return.

Large organizations increasingly face many of the problems predicted by the human resource frame, and more and more effort is being devoted to attempts to solve those problems. Job enrichment, participative management, organizational democracy, organization development, and "Theory Z" all represent efforts in that direction.

The knowledge base in organizational behavior is still too limited to make a conclusive determination of the validity of the human resource frame and particularly of the solutions developed for human problems in organizations. But existing evidence suggests that the problems are real, even if some of the reasoning of human resource theorists is faulty. Many of the currently popular cures for organizational ills may eventually prove to be inadequate or misdirected, but the need for such cures will continue, and it is likely that further research and experiment will develop a more valid and comprehensive science of human resource management in organizations.

7

Managing Power,
Conflict, and Coalitions:
The Political Approach

*People often call university administrators
bureaucrats, implying that they are red-tape specialists, but that is a childishly naive understanding
of our role. Sure, there are indeed lower-level administrators who are paper pushers and bureaucrats
in the old sense of the word, but the men in the
critical roles are not bureaucrats, they are* politicians, *struggling to make dreams come true and
fighting to balance interest groups off against each
other. This place is more like a political jungle,
alive and screaming, than a rigid, quiet bureaucracy.*

—A senior administrator at
New York University, cited in
Baldridge, 1971, pp. 20–21

108

*Political realists see the world as it is: an
arena of power politics moved primarily by perceived immediate self-interests, where morality is
rhetorical rationale for expedient action and self-
interest. It is a world not of angels but of angles,
where men speak of moral principles but act on
power principles; a world where we are always
moral and our enemies always immoral.*
                    —Saul Alinsky, 1971, pp. 12–13

From a structural perspective, organizations are designed
to be rational systems. The central question is how to design a
structure that is appropriate to achieving the organizational purposes. The human resource frame also views organizations as in-
tending to be rational but emphasizes the malfunctions that
occur because of mismatch between the needs of organizations
and the needs of individuals.

The political frame views organizations as "alive and
screaming" political arenas that house a complex variety of individuals and interest groups. Five propositions summarize the political perspective:

1. Most of the important decisions in organizations involve
    the allocation of scarce resources.
2. Organizations are coalitions composed of a number of indi-
    viduals and interest groups (for example, hierarchal levels,
    departments, professional groups, ethnic groups).
3. Individuals and interest groups differ in their values, pref-
    erences, beliefs, information, and perceptions of reality.
    Such differences are usually enduring and change slowly if
    at all.
4. Organizational goals and decisions emerge from ongoing
    processes of bargaining, negotiation, and jockeying for po-
    sition among individuals and groups.
5. Because of scarce resources and enduring differences, pow-
    er and conflict are central features of organizational life.

An example of a political view of organizations is Baldridge's political analysis of the university. Baldridge (1971, p. 23) defines universities as configurations of "social groups with basically different life-styles and political interests." Each of those groups wants to have an impact on organizational decisions and attempts to do so by participating in a multistage process that includes articulation of interests, efforts to get those interests translated into institutional policy, resolution of conflicting forces into an accepted policy, and implementation of decisions that have been attained.

Organizations as Coalitions

Baldridge and other political theorists see organizations as coalitions that include a diverse set of individuals and interest groups. Because they are coalitions, organizations inevitably have multiple, conflicting goals, which change as the balance of power in the organization shifts.

Traditional views of organizations—both academic and common-sense—have mostly assumed that organizations either have or ought to have clear, consistent goals. Generally, the goals are presumed to be established by those in authority. In business firms, the authorities are the owners, and they are typically assumed to set a goal of maximizing profits. Public agencies are viewed as having purposes that are set by the legislature or the executive to whom the agency is accountable. In a parliamentary system, for example, the goals of a ministry are presumably set by the chief administrator in ways that are consistent with the policies of the government in power. In systems with an independent executive—as in the United States at both the federal and state levels—agencies are presumed accountable to an executive (for example, the director of an agency) who sets goals that are consistent with the policies of the executive and with the agency's legislative mandate.

The view that organizational goals are set by authorities is usually explicit in structural conceptions of organization. The purpose of bureaucracy is to enhance rationality. Rationality is definable only with respect to a reasonably clear sense of organizational mission and task. A similar view has generally been im-

plicit in most human resource approaches. Human resource theorists have rarely treated organizational goals as a major topic.
They have tended to assume that the goals are reasonably well
established and understood. The focus has been on how to
achieve the goals in a way that is congruent with the needs of
organizational participants.

The political frame offers a very different view of organizations. Rather than seeing them primarily as authority systems
in which the authority at the top has the right to set goals, the
political frame views organizations as coalitions of individuals
and interest groups. Different individuals and groups have different objectives and resources, and each attempts to bargain
with other members or coalitions in order to influence the goals
and decision making of the system. Cyert and March (1963, p.
30) spell out the difference between the structural and political
view of organizational goals: "To what extent is it arbitrary, in
conventional accounting, that we call wage payments 'costs' and
dividend payments 'profit,' rather than the other way around?
Why is it that in our quasi-genetic moments we are inclined to
say that in the beginning there was a manager, and he recruited
workers and capital? . . . The emphasis on the asymmetry has
seriously confused the understanding of organizational goals.
The confusion arises because ultimately it makes only slightly
more sense to say that the goal of a business enterprise is to
maximize profit than to say that its goal is to maximize the salary of Sam Smith, Assistant to the Janitor."

What Cyert and March are saying is something like this:
Smith, the assistant janitor, Schwartz, the foreman, and March,
the company president, are all members of a grand coalition,
March Enterprises. All of them have certain demands that they
make on the coalition, and each bargains to get those demands
met. March is in a more powerful position than Smith or
Schwartz and can get her demands met more easily. But March
does not have a divine or inalienable right to determine the
goals of the organization. Her ability to determine goals depends on how much power she can mobilize compared with
that of Smith and Schwartz.

There will be times when Smith, in combination with his

colleagues in the union, will be able to mobilize more power than March can. At those times, Smith and friends will be able to leverage their own demands into the organization's goals. March, Schwartz, and Smith may all continue to believe that the goals are what March says they are (for example, "to make a fair profit while providing high-quality goods and services to customers and meeting our social responsibilities"). But March's goals statements are, at best, a partial statement of the organizational objectives, and they may be mostly ceremonial. An analyst who relied on public goal statements to predict organizational decision making would probably conclude that the organization is "irrational"—it gives things to the workers that reduce profits and gives things to top executives that hamper organizational efficiency. From a political view, that is to be expected in a world of divergent interest groups, each doing its best to impose its own demands on the organizational agenda.

If political pressures on organizational goals are visible in private organizations, they are often blatant in the public sector. Public agencies typically operate amid a complex welter of constituencies, each making policy demands and using whatever resources it can muster to enforce those demands. The result, typically, is a confusing multiplicity of goals, many of which are in conflict.

Universities, for example, are commonly assumed to have a primary goal of educating students. This view was implicit in the puzzlement of a university administrator when the faculty resisted his suggestion for a more systematic approach to scheduling courses. He said, while scratching his head, "I often get the feeling that the faculty seem to be scheduling their classes for their own convenience." The administrator felt that this was a surprising and deviant practice, but he was relatively new to the university. After more political lessons, he may appreciate that educating students is only one of many goals, each representing the interests of one or more of the university's major constituencies. Universities do have to make a reasonable gesture of providing learning, because students and their allies often have significant power to enforce some of their demands on institutional policy processes. But faculty members are also powerful and, particularly in many of the high-prestige institutions, are not hesitant to use their power to ensure, for example, that class schedules do not unduly interfere with their research or, in some cases, their consulting activities. Is the university's goal education or research or the enhancement of faculty lifestyles? From a political perspective, it is all of these, so long as all three agendas have an important impact on the decisions that are made.

Power and Decision Making

In analyzing power, structural theorists have typically been fascinated with authority: the legitimate, formal prerogative of making decisions that are binding on others. Managers make decisions that subordinates must accept. School principals make decisions for teachers, and teachers, in turn, exercise authority over students. Welfare workers make decisions for clients, and union leaders make decisions for their membership. From a structural perspective, authority is often viewed as the principal influence mechanism for getting organizational goals implemented. Managers make rational decisions (decisions that are consistent with the organization's purposes), monitor to be sure the decisions are implemented, and evaluate how well subordinates carry out the directives of those in authority.

Human resource theorists have traditionally placed little emphasis on power, even though they focus extensively on decision making. Unlike structuralists, they tend to emphasize the limits and difficulties inherent in the exercise of authority. Since authority is primarily a one-way influence mechanism, it often impedes the integration of organizational and individual needs. When A can influence B but not vice versa, there is a good chance that the relationship will be more satisfying for A than for B. Human resource theorists have tended to focus on forms of influence that enhance mutuality and collaboration in decision making. The hope is that managers and workers can make decisions jointly to meet the needs of both. Decisions, of course, need to be technically sound and consistent with the organizational mission. But they also need to respond to individual needs and make effective use of the organization's human resources.

The political frame acknowledges the existence and importance of authority but views it as only one among a number of important forms of power. The political frame acknowledges the existence and importance of human (and group) needs but focuses on situations of scarce resources and incompatible preferences where different needs collide. To illustrate the difference between the human resource and political preferences, consider a case of policy conflict in an organization. Say that one group (for example, graduate students in a university department) wants the organization to become more democratic and responsive, while another (for example, the faculty in the same department) insists that it needs to tighten its controls and standards. The human resource theorist is likely to ask: What are the needs and perspectives of each group? How can these two groups engage in a productive dialogue so that they can learn from each other, explore the differences between their positions, and seek a solution that integrates their views? The human resource view rests on two important but implicit assumptions: (1) that the incompatibility of preferences is reducible (that there is a possibility for "win/win" outcomes); (2) that some solutions are "better" than others (for example, because they are based on better analysis or because they produce better outcomes for both parties) and that the parties can learn to recognize better solutions through exploration and open dialogue.

The political theorist is more likely to view divergent interests and conflict over scarce resources as an enduring fact of life and is less likely to be optimistic about distinguishing among better and worse solutions. The question becomes: How does each group articulate its own policy preferences and mobilize power to enforce its demands on organizational decision-making processes?

Gamson's (1968) analysis of political processes focuses on two major players in a social system: authorities and partisans. Authorities are defined essentially as the people who are entitled to make binding decisions. Gamson describes the relationship between authorities and partisans as follows: "Authorities are the recipients or targets of influence, and the agents or initiators of social control. Potential partisans have the opposite roles—as agents or initiators of influence, and targets or recipients of social control" (pp. 36-37). As an example, parents often function as authorities, while children function as potential partisans in a family. Parents make binding decisions about such things as who goes to bed when, whether the television set may be turned on, and which child gets to use a particular toy. Parents initiate social control, and children are the targets, or recipients, of parental decisions. Precisely because the children are affected significantly by those decisions, they often attempt to exert influence on the decision makers. They will argue for a later bedtime or for the unfairness of giving one sibling something that another does not have. They may try to split the authorities by getting something from one parent after the other has refused. They may form coalitions (with siblings, grandparents, and so on) in an attempt to strengthen their bargaining position.

Social control is essential to authorities, because their capacity to make decisions depends on it. Officeholders retain authority only if the organization remains viable. If partisan conflict becomes too powerful for the authorities to control, their positions are undermined. Partisans, in contrast, may or may not have a stake in maintaining existing authority systems. Gamson (1968) and Baldridge (1971) both suggest that it depends on how much a given group of partisans trusts the authority.

During the early years of the Roosevelt "New Deal," the United States Supreme Court consistently invalidated major pieces of economic and social legislation that the Roosevelt administration was able to pass through Congress. Political conservatives were aghast when Roosevelt proposed to increase the size of the Court (which would have permitted him to appoint justices who were more likely to vote his way). During the 1930s, conservatives trusted the Court and wanted to protect its authority. Twenty years later, the tables were turned, and a much more liberal Supreme Court was attracting the wrath of political conservatives. They began to argue for curbing the power of a "runaway" Court, while liberals became staunch defenders of the Court's legitimacy.

The shifts in views of the Court illustrate Gamson's suggestion that partisans will trust authorities when they expect them to make "correct" decisions. When trust is high, potential partisans are unlikely to become mobilized; they will leave the authorities alone and support the authorities if they are attacked. When trust is low, and partisan groups expect any decisions of the authority to be bad, they are likely to try to wrest power away.

Partisans do not have authority, but they do have a number of potential sources of power. Some social scientists (French and Raven, 1959; Baldridge, 1971; Kanter, 1977) have tried to address the question "what do individuals and groups have to have in order to be powerful?" Among the most significant forms of power are these:

1. *Authority.* The higher an individual's position in an authority hierarchy, the more power the individual typically has.
2. *Expertise.* Expertise is the power of information and knowledge. People who have important information, people who know how to do things or get things done, can use their expertise as a source of power. Sometimes the expertise may be more symbolic than real—we might not be able to assess our lawyer's competence, but we will probably not initiate a lawsuit without legal counsel.
3. *Control of rewards.* People who can deliver jobs, money, political support, and other valued rewards can be extremely powerful.
4. *Coercive power.* The union's ability to walk out, the student's ability to sit in, and the air controller's ability to slow down (so that planes stack up for miles) are all examples of coercive power in action.
5. *Personal power.* Individuals with charisma, political skills, verbal facility, or the capacity to articulate visions are powerful by virtue of personal characteristics, in addition to whatever other power they may have.

The existence of multiple forms of power means that the capacity of authorities to make decisions is constrained. In practice, people who rely solely on their authority often undermine their own power—they generate resistance and are outflanked, outmaneuvered, or overrun by individuals and groups who are more versatile in the exercise of multiple forms of power. The multiple pressures operating on authorities help to explain why so many administrators seem more powerful to their subordinates than to themselves.

University presidents, for example, are often seen as exalted, remote, and very powerful figures by students and faculty. Yet one president remarked ruefully that his primary job seemed to be to provide "sex for the students, parking for the faculty, and football for the alumni." The remark was half facetious, but it reflects an important reality: It is costly for the president to make any decision, however correct and necessary, that produces rebellion among any of the major constituencies. Students can sit in, faculty members can boycott classes and make damaging statements in the press, and alumni can stop giving. The president's power lies particularly in a "zone of indifference"—those areas in which few people care deeply about what the president decides. On other issues, the president is so heavily constrained by partisan pressures that it may be all he can do to keep conflict down to a manageable level so that the university can continue to function.

Chief executives do not always feel hemmed in by a welter of political forces. The political constraints on a decision maker will vary with the power of the decision maker and with the satisfaction or dissatisfaction of potential partisans. The chief executive who owns the company will feel fewer constraints than a chief executive who is watched closely by someone else who owns most of the stock. Individuals with expertise, strong track records, or high charisma are likely to have a wide range of room to make decisions. This is particularly true when things are going well and constituencies are basically satisfied. If an organization sets new profit records every year, it is unlikely that stockholders will besiege the management with complaints and demands for change. As many company presidents have learned, however, the first bad quarter will suddenly elicit a steady stream of letters and telephone calls from board members, stockholders, and financial analysts. In effect, the "zone of indifference" can expand or contract markedly, depending on how the organization is doing in the eyes of its major constituents.

Summary

The traditional view of organizations is that they are created and controlled by legitimate authorities, who set the goals, design the structure, hire and manage the employees, and seek to ensure that the organization functions in ways that are consistent with their objectives. The political frame offers a different perspective. Authorities have exclusive access to the power of position, but they are only one among many contenders for power in the organization. Each contender has different preferences and beliefs. All contenders have access to various forms of power, and all compete for their share of scarce resources in a limited organizational pie.

The political perspective suggests that goals, structure, and policy emerge from an ongoing process of bargaining and negotiation among the major interest groups. Sometimes the legitimate authorities are in fact the dominant members of the organizational coalition; this is likely to be the case in a small, entrepreneurial organization where the chief executive is also the owner. But large corporations are often controlled by senior management, rather than by the stockholders or the board of directors. Government agencies may be controlled more by the permanent civil servants than by the political leaders at the top. The dominant group in a school district may be the teachers' union rather than the school board or the superintendent. In all such cases, naive, rational observers will feel that something is wrong. Like the puzzled university administrator who was surprised by faculty resistance to coordinated class schedules, they will feel that the wrong people are moving the organizational agenda in the wrong direction. But the political view suggests that the exercise of power is a natural part of an ongoing contest. Those who exercise it best are likely to be winners.

Conflict in Organizations

The structural perspective emphasizes social control and norms of rationality. Conflict is a problem that interferes with the accomplishment of organizational purposes. Hierarchal conflict raises the possibility that the lower levels will ignore or subvert management directives. Conflict among major partisan groups can undermine an organization's effectiveness and the ability of its leadership to function. Such dangers are precisely why the structural perspective emphasizes the need for a hierarchy of authority. A basic function of authorities is to resolve conflict. If two individuals or departments cannot resolve conflict between them, they take it to higher authorities, who adjudicate and make a final decision that is consistent with the organization's goals.

From a political perspective, conflict is not necessarily a problem or a sign that something is amiss in an organization. Organizational resources are in short supply—there is not enough money to give all members what they want; there are too many jobs at the bottom and too few at the top; if one group controls the policy process, others may be frozen out. Individuals compete for jobs, titles, and prestige. Departments compete for resources and power. Interest groups vie for policy concessions. Under such conditions, conflict is natural and inevitable.

The focus in the political frame is not on the resolution of conflict (as it often is in both the structural and human resource frames) but on the strategy and tactics of conflict. Since conflict is not going to go away, the question is how individuals and groups can make the best of it. Several bodies of literature have evolved that deal with the question of conflict strategies and tactics, including the literature on "game theory," theories of bargaining, and theories of coalition formation.

Game Theory

Game theory is not about games in the usual sense of the word. It is not a theory about how to play chess, bridge, or baseball. It is a more general set of ideas about any situation in which one party's decisions affect someone else's gains or losses. Game theory focuses particularly on situations in which two parties—A and B—are in a relationship with the following characteristics:

1. A knows the choices that are available to both A and B.
2. A's fate depends on both A's and B's actions.
3. A is not sure what B is going to do.

The case of Helen Demarco fits all three characteristics. Her boss, Paul Osborne, announced a bold new program to improve the organization's effectiveness, but he had consulted none of the career administrators before announcing the plan publicly. Helen believed the plan to be a serious error that would produce a substantial waste of money. One intriguing question in a case like this is: What led Paul Osborne to make a public announcement before consulting with the career administrators? Was this a sensible way to proceed? A game-theoretic analysis might shed some light on the situation.

Suppose that Osborne had two choices: announce the plan first or consult with the senior managers before announcing it. Suppose that the managers also had two choices: support the new plan or oppose it. What are the payoffs to the new chief executive? They can be represented in a payoff matrix as in Table 1.

Table 1. Expected Payoffs of Two Courses of Action
by Osborne and by Managers.

| | | Osborne | |
		Consult First	Announce First
	Support	8 (8)	10 (2)
Managers			
	Resist	0 (4)	5 (5)

The matrix represents the choices for both Paul and the managers (including Helen). The first number in each box represents Paul's payoff. If this were a negotiation over the sale of an automobile, the numbers might represent the dollar value of the transaction. In this case, the numbers are arbitrary but might reflect something like "reputation points" that Paul can cash in for a future job.

The payoffs are structured under the assumption that the best situation for Paul is to announce without consulting, *if* the managers support his decision. In that case, he can take all the credit for the new program, and he still gets cooperation from the staff. The worst situation for him is if he consults first and the organization resists. Consultation takes time, and it will be difficult for him to go public with a plan after the experts have said it will fail. If he announces first and the managers resist, he still gets political points for his attempt to exercise bold leadership.

Under those assumptions, if the staff is going to resist, Paul is better off announcing first. If the staff is not going to resist, he is still better off announcing first. If he is better off announcing first regardless of what the staff does, did he make the only rational choice?

Maybe not, if he has not considered the payoffs for the managers, represented by the numbers in parentheses in the chart. The managers do best when Paul consults and they support, worst when Paul announces and they support (on the assumption that, in that situation, Paul gets political points, but they have to take the rap when the plan fails). In this game, Paul moves first. If he is aware of the staff payoffs, he can reasonably expect that the staff will resist if he announces first but will support if he consults first. If the predictions are correct, then Paul and Helen are *both* better off if he consults. He would be happier if he could maneuver the managers into the upper right-hand box (he announces, they support), but that is their worst option.

The case represented here is an example of what game theorists call a "mixed motive" game—a situation in which the players have incentives both to compete and to collaborate. The matrix in Helen's game has a good possibility of producing a collaborative outcome, *if* the players take account of each other's payoffs. Often, players in real-world games do not know each other's payoffs. Paul's strategy was sensible when viewed only in terms of his own payoffs, but he might have made a different and better choice if he had thought through the situation for the other players.

As the illustration suggests, game theory provides a way of modeling the structure of a conflict situation. Application of game theory to real situations requires simplifying assumptions about the players and their payoffs, but the model can be useful in analyzing such questions as these: Who are the players? What options do they have? What does the payoff matrix look like?

Game theory has focused more on the structure of conflict than on the process that players go through in dealing with conflict. Theories of bargaining and coalition formation have focused more on those process issues.

Bargaining

Because of its prominence in both labor relations and international negotiations (for example, between the United States and the Soviet Union), bargaining has received substantial research attention during the last several decades. (Representative examples of the literature include Boulding, 1962; Schelling, 1960; Walton and McKersie, 1965; Deutsch, 1973; Rubin and Brown, 1975.) To varying degrees all the research has focused on two basic questions: (1) How *do* players normally behave in bargaining situations? (2) How *should* they behave?

Theorists who focus on the "should" question generally split into two somewhat separate groups: those who focus on how conflict participants can bargain to their own best advantage and those who focus on how *both* parties should behave in order to achieve a more collaborative, integrative solution. The "conflict resolution" stance (Deutsch, 1973; Fisher and Ury, 1981) is analogous to the human resource frame because of its concern for collaboration and "win/win" outcomes. The "bargaining tactics" stance better represents the political perspective. A classic example is Schelling's (1960) essay on bargaining. Schelling focuses particularly on the problem of how to make credible threats.

Suppose that I am buying a house from you, and I am willing to pay $75,000 for it (although you do not necessarily know what my highest offer would be). If I want to convince you that I am willing to pay only $65,000, how could I make such a threat credible? Schelling notes that, contrary to a common assumption, I am not always better off in such a situation if I am stronger and have more resources. If you know that I am very wealthy, you might take my threat less seriously than if you know (or I can get you to believe) that it is barely possible for me to scrape up $65,000. Common sense also suggests that I should be better off if I have considerable freedom of action, rather than having limited options. Yet I may be able to get a better price if I can convince you that my hands are tied—for example, that I am negotiating for a very stubborn buyer who cannot go above $65,000, even though the house is worth much more. Such examples suggest that the ideal situation for bargainers is to have considerable resources and freedom yet be able to convince the other side that they do not.

Such depictions of the bargaining process lead to a picture that has the following major characteristics:

1. Bargaining is a mixed-motive game: Both parties have a stake in reaching an agreement, but they have very different preferences about which agreement.
2. Bargaining is a process of interdependent decisions: What each party does affects the other. Each player wants, as much as possible, to be able to predict the other while limiting the other's ability to predict.
3. Generally, the more player A can control player B's level of uncertainty, the more powerful A is.
4. Bargaining is primarily a process of judicious use of *threats* rather than sanctions. Players may threaten the use of force, a strike, a breakoff in negotiations, and all kinds of terrible outcomes. Mostly, though, players much prefer not to have to carry out the threats.

5. A critical bargaining skill is the ability to make threats credible. A threat will be influential only if your opponent thinks you might actually carry it out. Noncredible threats may actually weaken your bargaining position.
6. Calculation of the appropriate threat level is also critical. If I underthreaten, I may weaken my own position; if I overthreaten, you may not believe me, or break off the negotiations, or escalate your own threats.

Bellow and Moulton (1978) present an example of such a bargaining process—the discussions between lawyers for the justice department and lawyers for Vice-President Spiro Agnew. The legal case against Agnew developed partly by accident. A group of federal attorneys was investigating corruption in Baltimore County (Maryland), without fully knowing where the trail would lead.

Agnew made an early tactical error. Only a few weeks after the prosecutors had begun to subpoena witnesses, Agnew expressed concern about the investigation to the attorney general. The prosecutors had not been looking for Agnew, but they immediately became suspicious when they heard that he was trying to influence the investigation. Until then, the prosecutors had not realized they were making the vice-president nervous. Once they knew, their curiosity was aroused.

One of the first breaks came when an attorney for William Fornoff, a potential defendant, came to the prosecutors and said, "I know you have A, B, and C, but what else do you have?" At the time, the prosecutors had nothing else, but they chose not to say so. They played a hunch—that an unknown case (a "black box") was more threatening than a known one. They attempted to control Fornoff's uncertainty, and it worked. They insisted that they would make a deal only after Fornoff told what he knew. He did, providing information that led to several persons who, in turn, provided evidence against Agnew.

As Agnew realized that some of his former friends were cooperating with the prosecutors, he sent his attorneys to negotiate. Both sides had reasons to want a deal. The attorney general (Eliot Richardson, a Nixon appointee) was anxious to get Agnew out of office before something occurred that might permit him to become president. Agnew wanted to avoid a trial and possible conviction. Both sides had reasons not to go to trial, since trial creates uncertainties that neither side can control. The bargaining came down to three issues: Agnew's resignation, how much Agnew would admit in court, and whether Agnew would go to jail. Initially, the prosecutors asked for all three, and Agnew refused all three.

During the negotiations, a newspaper published the news that plea bargaining was underway. Someone in the prosecutor's office apparently leaked the information, perhaps as a way to increase the pressure on Agnew. Agnew responded by promising that he would not resign, even if indicted. Agnew's statement was a threat that made indictment less attractive to the attorney general. Richardson, a Republican, was anxious to avoid the symbolic damage of a convicted felon—and a Republican felon selected by Richardson's boss, President Nixon—in the office of the vice-president. The prosecution, meanwhile, continued to keep much of its evidence secret—once again using the "black box" technique to put pressure on Agnew.

Agnew continued to make public statements that he was being harassed and tried in the press, but he also sent his attorneys to make another try for a plea bargain. Most members of the prosecution wanted to hold out for a full public confession, if not a jail term. They reasoned that Agnew had to strike a bargain. Agnew's attorneys continued to hold out, and Richardson finally agreed to settle for a resignation and minimal admissions in court. Richardson's position was softer than his subordinates wanted, but he was determined to avoid bringing an incumbent vice-president to trial. The deal was struck. Agnew resigned, appeared briefly in court, and made a nationwide television appearance in which he minimized any wrongdoing on his part.

Bargaining is often thought to apply primarily to commercial, legal, and labor relations settings. From a political perspective, though, bargaining is central to decision making in organizations. Consider Helen Demarco's case again. Paul Osborne's public announcement can be viewed as an initial step in a bargaining process. His failure to consult any of the senior managers adds to their uncertainty about how to respond. It is possible that he never expected his plan to be implemented.

Helen and her colleagues faced considerable uncertainty. They were not sure what Osborne really wanted or would accept. They were not sure how he would respond if they resisted his plan. They were not sure what they could do that would be effective for the organization and for their own careers. They chose to use the camouflage of a study team conducting research in order to buy time and prevent the director from knowing what they had in mind.

Helen and her colleagues deserve credit for a sophisticated approach to bargaining. The "study team" strategy allowed them to manage Paul's uncertainty, rather than vice versa, while lulling him into the belief that the project was moving well. They produced a report that began with a threat disguised as an endorsement, the threat being that Osborne could have his plan only if he wanted to be laughed at because of its exorbitant costs. The report followed with rejection disguised as acceptance (an example of the bargaining tactic of making a superficially attractive offer while camouflaging the fact that the offer has more holes than Swiss cheese). Finally, the staff gave Paul Osborne a "choice." Instead of telling him his plan was impossible, they asked him to choose between his plan and an alternative.

So Paul reluctantly accepted the modified plan, and the managers won a major victory. Or maybe they did not. The effectiveness of their approach ultimately rested on their chief power base—the control of technical information about the organization and its task. But it is possible that Osborne recognized the study team and the report for exactly what they were —the bureaucrats' efforts to beat him in the bargaining process. Perhaps he accepted their new plan because it gave him 20 percent of his original plan and he never expected to get more than that. He also got a staff who were committed to the new plan, because *they* had said it would work.

Coalition Formation

> Allen, Barbara, and Carol are the three can-
> didates for the top job in a local human service
> agency. It is a close race, but Allen is the strongest
> candidate, with Barbara and Carol second and third,
> in that order. All three have friends on the agency's
> board of directors. If any two of the candidates
> agreed on a choice, they could swing the vote.

What is likely to happen in such a case? Coalition theory focuses on questions like the following: In a case like this one,
will a coalition form? If so, who will be in it?

There are four possible winning coalitions: Allen and Barbara, Allen and Carol, Barbara and Carol, or Allen, Barbara, and
Carol. Since there are so many possible winning alliances, coalition theory suggests that one or another is likely to form. One
theory suggests that coalitions do not form with more resources
than they need. Only two persons are needed to win, so the
Allen/Barbara/Carol coalition includes a redundant third member. The theory says that ABC will not form but does not say
which of the two-person coalitions is most likely.

Gamson's (1961) "minimal resources" hypothesis says
that the coalition that will form is the one that can win with
the least resources. Allen, as the strongest candidate, would
probably demand more from a coalition partner than Barbara or
Carol would. Allen would probably prefer to ally with Carol,
because Carol is in the weakest position and should demand
less. But Carol might prefer to ally with Barbara, because Barbara might be more accommodating than Allen. Barbara might
offer a significant increase in job responsibilities to Carol,
whereas Allen might offer nothing more than his heartfelt appreciation.

According to the minimal-resources hypothesis, Barbara
and Carol should unite. In experimental research, that is usually
what happens, *at first*. But then the players begin to notice a
paradox: Allen's supposed strength is turning out to be a weakness. Because he demands more, he gets less. Allen realizes that

he needs to moderate his demands, and others then become more willing to unite with him.

In organizations there are far more variables that affect who allies with whom than coalition theory has yet been able to deal with. Will Barbara and Carol coalesce because they are both women, uniting against male dominance? Will Barbara or Carol unite with Allen because she thinks he will be the most effective leader for the agency? Will one or more of the players refuse to form any alliance on the ground that it is unprofessional and unethical? If Allen declines to participate in the coalition process, but Barbara and Carol unite, then Allen loses (and the agency may also lose, if the Barbara/Carol coalition really does represent an unprofessional way to influence the choice of a leader). If Barbara and Carol both decline to form a coalition, but Allen tries to form an alliance with each of them in turn, they may conclude that it is *now* essential for the two of them to unite to prevent the unethical Allen from becoming director.

Why and how alliances form, stay together, have an impact, or fall apart is important whenever there are scarce resources that need to be distributed and individuals or groups can strengthen their bargaining position by forming alliances. Examples include these:

> The senior managers of an organization believe that the chief executive is destructive and needs to be removed for the well-being of the organization. They and the chief executive both seek to obtain the support of the organization's board of directors. With whom will the board ally?

> In response to a mandate from the board of education, a superintendent of schools has proposed that principals make more classroom visits and provide detailed, public evaluations of classroom teachers. The teachers are uniformly and vehemently opposed to the proposal and seek the support of their principals. With whom will the principals ally?

A regulatory agency is responsible for regulating an industry on behalf of consumers. The industry is well organized, finances an extensive and sophisticated lobbying effort (including a continuing willingness to provide meals and entertainment for staff members of the agency), and can provide excellent jobs to agency staff when they retire from public service. The consumers are diffuse, unorganized, and mostly unaware of the agency's activities. With whom will the agency ally itself?

Coalition formation and bargaining both represent central aspects of the tactics of conflict. They are consistent with a basic assumption of the political frame: In a world of scarcity, there will be winners and losers. People who understand the strategic implications of conflict have a better shot at being winners.

Population Ecology: A Macro Perspective

To this point, we have mostly discussed the internal politics of organizations, but the political frame can also be applied to relations among organizations. If we change our level of analysis, organizations can be viewed as political actors who compete in an environment of scarce resources. The "population ecology model" (Aldrich and Pfeffer, 1976; Pfeffer and Salancik, 1978) applies the concept of natural selection to organizations. It takes the view that organizations, like biological species, evolve and change relatively slowly. There may be periodic "mutations" when a new kind of organization—for example, an organization like Apple Computer that creates an entirely new market—enters the field. If organizations change slowly, those that are best fitted to their environment will survive, while those that are less fitted will be selected out. In this view, the survival of the fittest occurs in society as in nature.

The population ecology perspective does not necessarily imply a Social Darwinist view that the fittest are also the best or the most worthy. They are simply those organizations that are better adapted to the world around them. The perspective does suggest that organizational adaptation is often *not* caused by internal changes and improvements. Poor organizations do not necessarily get better, they simply die. The organizations that were better in the first place are the ones that survive and grow.

The evidence suggests that the population ecology model applies best to small private-sector organizations, which die at a substantial rate. Large organizations and public organizations are rarely selected out. In effect, natural selection works for infant firms, but older organizations manage to survive by developing the power and resources necessary to survive in a political environment.

8

Applying the
Political Approach

*Whenever we think about social change, the
question of means and ends arises. The man of action views the issue of means and ends in pragmatic
and strategic terms. He has no other problem. He
thinks only of his actual resources and the possibilities of various choices of action. He asks of ends
only whether they are achievable and worth the
cost; of means, only whether they will work. To
say that corrupt means will corrupt the ends is to
believe in the immaculate conception of ends and
principles. The real arena is corrupt and bloody.
Life is a corrupting process from the time a child
learns to play his mother off against his father in
the politics of when to go to bed. The real and
only question is, and always has been, "Does this
particular end justify this particular means?"*
—Saul Alinsky, 1971, p. 24

131

*Many have dreamed up republics and princi-
palities which have never in truth been known to
exist; the gulf between how one should live and
how does live is so wide that a man who neglects
what is actually done for what should be done
learns the way to self-destruction rather than self-
preservation. The fact is that a man who wants to
act virtuously in every way necessarily comes to
grief among many who are not virtuous. Therefore
if a prince wants to maintain his rule he must learn
how not to be virtuous, and to make use of this or
that according to need.*
                    —Machiavelli, 1961 (1514), p. 163

Suppose that you want to improve organizations: to
make them better places than they sometimes are. If you turn
to the structural frame for guidance, it leads you to consider
the goals of the system, its tasks, and how the system is structured to achieve those tasks. Organizational improvement is defined as an improvement in the fit between the goals and the
structure. The human resource frame suggests that there are
fundamental conflicts between individual and organization but
that those conflicts can be reduced, if not reconciled, through
greater levels of collaboration and learning, more meaningful
work, and genuine exercise of participation in important decisions.

The political frame says that the pursuit of self-interest
and power is the basic process in organizations. Organizational
change is always political—it occurs when a particular individual or group is able to impose its agenda on the organization.
Those who create change may clothe their efforts in a variety
of ethical or technical disguises, but that is window dressing.
What they are really trying to do is to redesign the world to make
it better express their self-interests. Consider some examples:

A public agency recruits a group of analysts
and computer experts, who enter and discover that
decision making needs to become more analytic,

rational, and logical. They may be right, but they may also want to establish a niche for their own expertise and values.

A new, young principal enters an elementary school and begins to urge the faculty to move away from traditional models of teaching toward "progressive, child-centered" approaches that "will better serve the children." The principal is probably sincere, but the new approaches may do more to express the principal's ideological commitments and needs to feel effective than to improve children's education.

A political view of organizational change suggests that there is no such thing as permanent improvement: "Happily ever after" exists only in fairy tales. In the real world, there are today's winners and losers, and there will be tomorrow's winners and losers. In such a world, significant change occurs only when there are significant shifts in the balance of power. If the proportion of young people is declining and the proportion of senior citizens is climbing rapidly, public schools are likely to be in trouble, unless they can create a senior citizen market. If the environment of the banking industry becomes more competitive, so that banks have to pursue customers more aggressively, the power of the loan department is likely to decline, while the power of the (newly acquired) marketing people rises rapidly.

The political perspective means that (1) organizations change all the time and (2) they never change. There is constant jockeying for position, and yesterday's elites may be tomorrow's outs. In life, as in football and chess, players come and go, but the game goes on. The political frame says to a change agent: In order to make things different, you need power and you need to be prepared for conflict as a part of the process. The degree, intensity, and form of the conflict will vary with the issues at stake and with the forms of power that you mobilize.

Gamson's distinction between authorities and partisans (see Chapter Seven) implies two directions from which change can occur: bottom-up (relying on the mobilization of interest groups to assert their agendas) and top-down (relying on authorities' capacity to get subordinates to accept the change). Many change efforts involve some mixture of both. Several examples illustrate some of the dynamics.

Bottom-Up Change

The battle over the existence, rights, and responsibilities of labor unions has been fought in the United States and Western Europe from the nineteenth century to the present. In many industries and geographic regions, the battle is essentially over. Labor and management have long since made peace and developed relatively stable working relationships. In others, the battle continues.

Initially, the battle was a classic case of authorities versus partisans. Labor organizers relied mainly on bottom-up influence techniques: building group unity, demonstrations, walkouts, and sitdowns. Managers resisted with a variety of social control mechanisms: legal restrictions, lawsuits, discharge of union sympathizers, and use of police or the military to quell strikers. Management insisted on its right to make binding decisions about conditions of employment and to negotiate individually with each employee. Unions insisted that such a relationship was both unequal and unjust and permitted arbitrary and exploitive behavior by management.

Over time, unions increasingly attempted to combine bottom-up with top-down. They mobilized political power to change the laws governing trade unions—with the end result that the existence of unions is firmly implanted in the legal system. The rights of both unions and employers are now specified through an extensive body of law and regulation.

Throughout the battles over labor unions, both sides argued their positions on grounds of justice and rationality. Employers argued that unions violated the individual's "right to work." Unions responded that individuals had never had a right to work, only a right to ask employers to give them work. Although the battle was argued on rational grounds, the political perspective suggests that power, not ideology, was the decisive factor. Alinsky's statement that people "speak on moral principles but act on power principles" (1971, p. 13) suggests that unions made gains because they obtained enough power. When the auto workers had enough power to shut down the industry, management had to make concessions, regardless of the ideological merits.

What enabled the workers to obtain power? One answer points to a by-product of industrialization—the concentration of workers in large factories and large cities. The scale of the new factories and urban areas was so large as to dwarf the individual, creating an increased sense of powerlessness. But the fact that workers were concentrated in large numbers also provided the conditions under which organization became possible.

A similar argument can be made about the conditions that brought the civil rights movement in the United States to the fore in the 1960s. In the early twentieth century, the majority of blacks lived in rural areas of the South. By 1960 a majority lived in cities and in the North. In that year, there were more than one million black residents in New York and almost as many in Chicago (Bell, 1976). It is difficult for blue-collar workers or black citizens to organize if they are scattered in small numbers across large areas. It is much easier if they are concentrated in large numbers in few places. Industrialization and urbanization made it more necessary but also easier for both groups to organize.

The rise of the consumer movement presents another example of a political change process that evolved from shifts in the balance of power between producers and consumers. Western capitalism traditionally assumed that market mechanisms would solve problems of product quality. If a manufacturer tried to sell a shoddy product, it would be rejected by consumers. The discipline of the market would quickly correct the manufacturer's error. There are many examples of such a process, but they tell only part of the story.

Consumers can reject an inferior product only if they

know it to be inferior. If the product is highly complex (like an automobile or a color television), they may learn that the product is defective only after they have bought it. Moreover, they can choose a superior product the next time only if there is one that is recognizably superior. The trend toward oligopoly in many industries reduced the number of suppliers who might produce genuinely different products. United States auto makers may produce a bewildering array of "models" and "options," but most of them are the same automobile in different packaging. Finally, in an era when consumers buy a number of relatively expensive, durable items (like automobiles, television sets, and automatic washing machines), it is small comfort to the owners of a lemon to know that, next time, they may take their chance on buying a lemon from some other manufacturer. Such factors gradually increased consumers' desire to have other ways of influencing producers. In Hirschman's (1970) terms, they needed to supplement "exit" with "voice."

Historically, it was difficult for consumers to organize for the same reasons that historically blocked blue-collar workers and blacks—they were too widely diffused. A combination of changes made such organization more feasible. Some were technical—the changes in communication and transportation that made it easier for people who were geographically separated to communicate and interact. The mass media made it easier for people with a common problem to become aware of their commonalities. There were also cultural shifts. One was a shift away from a traditional emphasis on individualism and toward an emphasis on the assertion of group rights. Blacks, women, Hispanics, Native Americans, gays, and many other groups became increasingly active in pressing for their rights. A second cultural shift was a decline in confidence in all institutions, including private management. People were less willing to trust that managers made informed, responsible, and unselfish decisions in matters that affected consumers' interests.

All those factors were mobilized by consumer advocates—most notably Ralph Nader—who articulated the concept of consumer rights and developed organizations to advocate and lobby for those rights. The result has been a significant set of changes. The recall of defective products has become a common and legally mandated practice. It was once unheard of. Manufacturers are required by law to conform to mandated standards of product safety. Federal and state governments have established consumer protection agencies, and corporations have responded with consumer affairs departments of their own. Whether these changes have significantly improved the lot of consumers is open to question, but the relative strength of their bargaining position has increased over the past decade.

The examples of trade unions, the civil rights movement, and the rise of consumer activism suggest several generalizations about the process by which political shifts come about in organizations and societies. In all three cases, the precondition for change was a significant disruption in previous patterns. Trade unions developed in a context of the industrial revolution, rapid urbanization, and decline of the family farm. The civil rights movement came to the fore after a period of massive occupational and geographical shifts for black citizens. The consumer movement developed after a period of major shifts in the relationships between producers and consumers. In each case, something was occurring in the larger environment to unfreeze existing patterns and to create dissatisfaction for one group within the larger system. All three movements also had some element of the classic pattern for revolution: a period of rising expectations followed by disappointment.

In each case, the initial vehicle for advocating and promoting change was mobilizing and organizing—the formation of trade unions, of civil rights organizations, of consumer advocacy groups. The establishment contested bitterly the legitimacy of such group activities while using coercive tactics in an attempt to block them. Employers used lawsuits against trade unions, but they also relied on coercion and violence. The civil rights movement, particularly during its early stages, was subject to violent repressive efforts by whites. General Motors hired a private detective in hopes of finding something they could use against Ralph Nader.

In every case, the newly organized group made claims on the policy process. Labor unions fought to have their rights em-

bodied in state and federal legislation. Consumer advocacy organizations made extensive use of the courts and lobbying to
press their claims.

Any of those movements might have failed had they been
weaker or their opposition stronger. Each did, in fact, suffer
many profound setbacks, but each was able to mobilize enough
power to survive and make headway.

The three examples may be misleading in that, by comparison with many efforts at bottom-up change, they have been
relatively successful. There is no accurate census of attempts to
change from below, but many—perhaps most—such efforts fail.
Even the most successful are only relatively so. Union-busting
practices are still widespread, both in the United States and in
other parts of the world (the fate of the Polish Solidarity union
is one example). Discrimination against blacks is still widespread. A new crop of defective and dangerous products rolls
off the assembly lines every year.

For every successful bottom-up change effort, there are
many efforts that fail and many more that were never attempted
because no one believed they could succeed. That experience is
part of the basis for a widespread dictum that "if you want to
change organizations, you have to begin at the top." Yet research on top-down change efforts is mostly a catalogue of failures. The next section discusses the political problems in induc-
ing top-down change.

The Problem of Change from the Top

Deal and Nutt (1980) conducted a revealing study of a
group of local school districts that received federal funding to
develop experimental programs for improving the quality of
education. A typical scenario for such a project had the following set of steps:

1. The central administration learned of the federal funding
    program and investigated program guidelines.
2. A small group of administrators met to develop a proposal
    for improving some aspect of the educational program.

(The process was usually rushed and involved very few people, because time was short for meeting the proposal deadline.)

3. When funding was approved, the administration announced with pride and enthusiasm that the district had been successful in a national competition and would receive substantial federal funding for a new project to improve instruction.

4. The administration was startled and perplexed when teachers greeted the new proposal with resistance, criticism, and anger.

5. The administration felt caught in the middle between the teachers and the funding agency but viewed teacher resistance as a sign of defensiveness and unwillingness to change.

6. The federally funded program became a political football that produced more disharmony, mistrust, and conflict than tangible improvement in the educational program.

The programs studied by Deal and Nutt exemplified top-down change efforts under comparatively favorable circumstances. The districts were not in crisis, and the change effort received both a blessing as a worthy project and financial support from the federal government. Yet the change efforts elicited a political battle, and in many cases the administration was outgunned. In one district the teachers mobilized such intense community opposition to the project that the superintendent of schools was forced out of office.

In most cases the administrators never anticipated the possibility of major political battles. Their proposal called for programs that they viewed as progressive, effective, and good for everyone. They rarely wondered about the risks involved in *administrators'* proposing changes that *teachers* were to carry out. They assumed that most people would applaud their success in creating a new opportunity for the school system and underestimated the possibility that the program would bring to the surface significant differences in political agendas between administrators and faculty.

The patterns described by Deal and Nutt can be seen repeatedly in examples of attempted top-down change. They can be seen in Helen Demarco's case, both in Paul Osborne's strategy for change and in the middle managers' mobilizing their own power to resist change. The patterns can be seen in countless unsuccessful efforts at organizational improvement and change mounted by chief executives, frustrated managers, hopeful study teams, and high-status management consultants. In every case, the mistake is to assume that a combination of the right idea (as perceived by the person trying to make a change) and legitimate authority is sufficient to produce change. That assumption runs afoul of the political agendas and political power of the "lowerarchy"—the individuals and groups in middle- and lower-level positions in the organization who can devise a host of creative and maddening ways to resist, divert, undermine, or ignore change efforts.

The Politics of Organizational Design

Organizational design is the process of shaping and structuring organizations. Most approaches to organizational design are based on a structural perspective. The theory of design that is currently most influential is "contingency theory." Contingency theorists argue that there is no one best way to organize. The best structure depends on the task of an organization and its environment. All contingency theories incorporate the assumption that the right structure is the one that will best achieve the organization's basic goals. For example, Galbraith (1973) builds his theory around the problem of information: What information does an organization need to achieve its task? How much uncertainty is there in the information? How much communication is necessary in order for different parts of the organization to know what the others are doing? The theory argues that organizations operating in a highly uncertain environment will need a more flexible, less bureaucratic structure than those operating in more stable and predictable settings. Similar views appear in Lawrence and Lorsch (1967), Perrow (1970), and Mintzberg (1979).

Pfeffer (1978) has questioned the validity of structural perspectives on design and has offered an explicitly political conception as an alternative: "Since organizations are coalitions, and the different participants have varying interests and preferences, the critical question becomes not how organizations should be designed to maximize effectiveness, but rather, whose preferences and interests are to be served by the organization. . . . What is effective for students may be ineffective for administrators. What is effectiveness as defined by consumers may be ineffectiveness as defined by stockholders. The assessment of organizations is dependent upon one's preferences and one's perspective" (p. 223). Pfeffer argues that the different groups in an organization have conflicting preferences but also have a shared interest in avoiding continual conflict. So the groups agree on ways of dividing up power and resources, and those divisions are reflected in the design of the organization. Organization structures are "the resolution, at a given time, of the contending claims for control, subject to the constraint that the structures permit the organization to survive" (p. 224).

As an example, Pfeffer looks at the process of "participative management." Whereas human resource theory focuses on the use of participation to enhance fulfillment of individual needs, Pfeffer analyzes it as an example of cooptation—a process whereby an organization gives something to individuals so as to induce them to ally with organizational needs and purposes. If women in a university are vocal in demanding equity, the administration might create a "Committee on the Status of Women" and provide it with a secretary, a research assistant, and occasional meetings with top administrators. Administrators might put highly vocal women on the committee and hope that they will focus their energies on the internal problems of the committee rather than on changing the university. If the strategy is successful, the administration can defuse a potential problem while using the committee as public evidence of the university's commitment to equity and fairness. Similarly, when lower-level employees demand more influence, management can let them make decisions but make sure that it controls the information and the alternatives available to them.

Pfeffer does not argue that efficiency is never relevant to organizational design. The most powerful group in a coalition may have a stake in making the organization efficient. In such cases it may appear that efficiency dominates design decisions, but the appearance masks the political reality. If the top group becomes more concerned about its own rewards and "perks" than about the efficiency of the organization (a fairly common historical development in private and public organizations), then efficiency ceases to be the dominant factor.

Stakeholders and Policy Making

Mason and Mitroff (1981) and Mitroff (1983) present a technology for helping managers make policy decisions under conditions of uncertainty and conflict. In such decisions, different stakeholders often form factions that have different views about the problem and about how it should be solved. Mason and Mitroff argue that implicit in those differences are implicit assumptions about the larger set of stakeholders who are relevant to any decision.

Mitroff (1983, chap. 2) gives the example of a drug company facing competitive pressure from generic substitutes for its patented prescription drug. Management had split into three factions: One group wanted to raise the price, one wanted to lower it, and one wanted to keep it the same while cutting internal costs. Each group collected information, constructed models, and developed reports showing that its solution was correct. The process became a frustrating spiral. Mitroff intervened to get each group to indicate who were the major stakeholders in the decision and what assumptions each group made about those stakeholders. It turned out that everyone agreed that the most critical stakeholders were physicians who prescribed the drug. Each group made different assumptions about how physicians would respond to a price change; but no one really knew. The three groups finally agreed to experiment with a price increase in selected markets to test their assumptions about physician behavior.

Three Cases Revisited

It should be clear that the political approach is significantly different from the structural and human resource frames.

We have already presented political analyses of the Helen Demarco case to illustrate game theory and bargaining processes.
It is easy to see political dynamics in the Demarco case. Paul Osborne used his authority as chief executive in an effort to gain
the support of outside constituents and neutralize the potential
opposition of subordinates. Instead of neutralizing, he galvan-
ized partisans, who used a combination of technical expertise
and skillful manipulation to substitute their plan for his. The
situation was rife with conflict, but, like many conflicts, the
issue was not decided by a direct confrontation. The managers
could have leaked the technical flaws of the Osborne plan to the
press, creating a more direct confrontation between authority
and expertise. They chose instead to use behind-the-scenes
manipulation. It is not fully clear who won and who lost—an
ambiguity common in political battles. But the political perspective argues that the decision was based on power and
manipulation more than on organizational goals, technical rationality, or human needs.

     Can the political perspective also be applied to the feud-
ing couple as they stare at each other across the candlelight?
The wife's statement, "This marriage is unfair," can be seen as a
statement about the distribution of power rather than the definition of roles. If she feels less powerful, her statement can be
viewed as a power move—the opening round in a bargaining process. The husband lost some and the wife gained some. Had the
conflict not been negotiated, it might have escalated into a
more bitter power struggle. Either party might have given in—or
given up and left. The bargaining process may not have given
either party everything he or she wanted—bargaining rarely
does—but it produced a new set of agreements acceptable to
both.

     The newspaper reporters' resistance to new technology
can be viewed as a classic battle between partisans and authorities. The editor had the authority to fire reporters who refused
to go along and to reward those who were using the new con-
soles effectively. The reporters might have used their technical
power to damage the newspaper by withholding stories or walking off the job. But they had already sabotaged the change—the
new system was slower and more expensive than the old one.

The editor had spent thousands of dollars for hardware and training but had found no way to stop a subtle work slowdown. The editor and the reporters were at an impasse. The political frame suggests that they needed to negotiate the differences and find a mutually acceptable solution. The alternative was likely to be a damaging showdown in which everyone might wind up a loser.

Conclusion: Strengths and Limits
of the Political Frame

There are many who agree with Alinsky that "political realists see the world as it is: an arena of power politics moved primarily by perceived immediate self-interest" (1971, p. 13). For them, the political frame presents the only realistic portrayal of organizations. The frame captures a number of significant organizational dynamics that are absent or implicit in the structural and human resource views. Neither of those two frames has attended nearly so explicitly to the organizational dynamics of conflict and power politics. The political frame says that power and politics are central to organizations and cannot be swept under the rug. The perspective represents an important antidote to the antiseptic rationality sometimes present in structural analysis and to the excessive optimism that appears in some of the less careful human resource discussions.

But the political perspective can be guilty of its own parochialism. Critics describe two major limitations in the frame: (1) The political perspective is so thoroughly focused on politics that it underestimates the significance of both rational and collaborative processes. (2) The frame is normatively cynical and pessimistic. It overstates the inevitability of conflict and understates the potential for effectiveness and collaboration. Both problems can be seen in Ritti and Funkhouser's *The Ropes to Skip and the Ropes to Know* (1979). The book is clearly and entertainingly written—a rare feat for a textbook in organizational behavior—and purports to offer an inside view of how organizations really function, as opposed to how they pretend to function. It offers tactics and strategies that are intended to help students get ahead. The book presents a view of organizations in which rational decision making is accidental and mostly indeterminate, substantive and technical skills are of no particular significance, and belief in analysis or collaboration mostly shows naiveté. Political savvy and skill in using symbols are what counts. *Doing* a good job is of no great moment, but *appearing* to do a good job is critical. Projects that aim to improve the quality of life in organizations are, at best, harmless vehicles for the expression of political agendas. At worst, they are manipulative nonsense.

A similar example is Caplow's *How to Run Any Organization* (1976). Caplow tries to give practical advice to the new head of any organization. Among the many topics is the "honeymoon" period that occurs right after a newcomer takes office. Should new leaders make sweeping changes right away or wait until they know the organization better? Caplow offers the following advice:

> The outsider following a strong predecessor must establish his authority at once, or he may never be able to do so. The immunity offered by the honeymoon gives him a chance to demonstrate authority by introducing major changes before the old guard has a chance to begin the mutiny it will inevitably attempt. The only thing that limits his role as a new broom sweeping clean is his ignorance of the organization and the danger that some of his innovations will have disastrous results. He can protect himself against this danger by emphasizing changes of style and general policy and avoiding projects that require detailed implementation. His reign of terror, if he conducts one at all, ought to be highly selective and limited to a small number of potential opponents. The other key figures in the organization, having been edified by these examples, should be encouraged and supported in every possible way [p. 16].

In both Ritti and Funkhouser's and Caplow's analyses, the task of an organization and the needs of its members are mostly ignored (except that individuals are expected to look out for their own needs). Both books are thoroughly amoral: It is not important *what* you are trying to accomplish. What counts is whether you play the game well enough to win.

But would Caplow hire an automobile mechanic or a surgeon on the basis of his or her political skills? Would Ritti and Funkhouser fly on an airline whose pilots were trained mainly in creating an *appearance* of competence? Is policy science a contradiction in terms because political power, rather than information and logic, determines every policy decision? Would organizations be viable if most of their members followed the advice they get from the political frame? Could they get anything done? Even if they could, would anyone want to participate in such organizations?

The amorality that often characterizes political perspectives raises questions of values. To what extent does the political perspective, even as it purports to be simply a description of reality, ratify and sanctify some of the least humane and most unsavory aspects of human systems? Argyris and Schön (1974) offer a counterpoint to the political frame. They describe many of the same dynamics that are central to political perspectives. They note that most individuals in organizations do behave as if "maximize winning and minimize losing" were among their dominant values, even though they often espouse a very different set of principles. Argyris and Schön's data suggest that people often behave as they are represented in the political frame. But their data say more:

1. Most people, most of the time, are unaware of the discrepancy between what they intend and what they do.
2. Their behavior helps to create a world in which it is unlikely that they will become aware of the discrepancies.
3. The result is that individuals are often prevented from learning about their own areas of ineffectiveness and persist in self-destructive, self-sealing cycles of behavior. Each new attempt to win often produces more losses.
4. For the organization, the individual win/lose behaviors add up to massive problems of manageability and organizational

learning and to massive frustrations and discontent for participants.

Argyris and Schön's data validate the accuracy of some important elements of the political frame but also raise significant questions about the completeness and the normative implications of the perspective. The political frame says some very important things about organizations much more clearly than either the structural or the human resource frames. Yet it fails to discuss some equally significant issues that those frames capture. Each of the three has much to learn from the others, but no single theory has yet integrated the most important elements of all three.

9

⚜⚜⚜⚜⚜⚜⚜⚜

Cultivating
Organizational Cultures
and Rituals:
The Symbolic Approach

Each of the frames illuminates different aspects of organizations. The structural frame focuses on roles, relationships, and more formal ways of coordinating diverse efforts into common directions. In the human resource frame, individual needs are central, and the basic issue is how to design settings in which individual and organizational needs can be integrated. From a political perspective, organizations are networks of special interests: Coalitions, conflict, and bargaining translate power into action. Groups that win political battles are able to steer the organization in the directions they choose.

The three frames are different, but they have some common assumptions. They assume a world that is relatively *certain*. Goals provide direction. Effectiveness can be seen. Needs can be identified. Power can be understood, developed, and used. Similarly, the three frames also assume a world that is substantially *rational*. Decisions are made by choosing the best alternative. People act rationally, at least as judged by their own needs and beliefs. Groups behave rationally in attempting to further their own self-interests. Finally, the world is relatively *linear*. Goals are established to guide action. People determine what they want and take action to get it. Policies are developed through a sequential process of bargaining and conflict.

The three frames vary in the degree to which the assumptions of certainty, rationality, and linearity are invoked. The structural frame conforms most closely; the political frame probably deviates the most. But in each frame the tenets or scripture of rational thought can be detected and observed. The assumptions color significantly how individuals in organizations define situations, act, and evaluate the consequences of their actions.

Rational assumptions fit well in some organizations—particularly those with clear goals and well-defined technologies. Building a Chrysler is complex, but the basic task is clear. Automobiles are assembled in a well-understood sequence of steps. Once an automobile is assembled, there is a high probability that it will be drivable (despite a certain number of more or less serious production defects). A variety of concrete indicators of sales and profitability provide clear measurements of success.

Even in organizations with unclear goals and weak technologies, some activities conform well to rational logic. A consulting firm may provide a service that is ambiguous, but the firm's accounting and billing systems need to be precise and clear-cut. A school may have trouble proving that students are well taught but may be able to show that its cafeteria services and busing operations are efficient and cost-effective.

The symbolic frame, however, imagines a world that departs significantly from traditional canons of rational thought. The perspective is based on a series of basic assumptions about the nature of organizations and human behavior:

1. What is most important about any event is not what happened but the meaning of what happened.

2. The meaning of an event is determined not simply by what happened but by the ways that humans interpret what happened.

3. Many of the most significant events and processes in organizations are substantially ambiguous or uncertain—it is often difficult or impossible to know what happened, why it happened, or what will happen next.

4. Ambiguity and uncertainty undermine rational approaches to analysis, problem solving, and decision making.

5. When faced with uncertainty and ambiguity, humans create *symbols* to reduce the ambiguity, resolve confusion, increase predictability, and provide direction. Events themselves may remain illogical, random, fluid, and meaningless, but human symbols make them seem otherwise.

The symbolic frame is most applicable in organizations with unclear goals and uncertain technologies. In such organizations, ambiguity is everywhere. Who has power? What is success? Was a decision made? What are the goals? The answers to such questions are often veiled in a fog of uncertainty (Cohen and March, 1974). Serendipity is often more prominent than rationality in organizational events and activities. Connections between cause and effect, activities and goals, are as easily predicted from a table of random numbers or a crystal ball as from technical or systems logic.

The symbolic frame sees the rush of organizational life as more fluid than linear. Organizations function like complex, constantly changing, elastic pinball machines. Decisions, actors, plans, and issues continuously carom through a labyrinth of cushions, barriers, and traps. Managers who turn to Peter Drucker's *The Effective Executive* for guidance might do better to study Lewis Carroll's *Through the Looking-Glass*.

To those who see organizations as basically rational, the outlook of the symbolic frame may seem farfetched or bizarre. But many who have tried to manage or survive in organizations —particularly in the public and human service sectors—will find that the symbolic frame mirrors the reality they have experienced.

The symbolic frame forms a conceptual umbrella for ideas from a variety of disciplines. Symbols and symbolic phenomena have been studied in organization theory and sociology (Selznick, 1957; Blumer, 1969; Clark, 1972; Corwin, 1976; March and Olsen, 1976; Meyer and Rowan, 1978; Weick, 1976b; Davis and others, 1976) and political science (Dittmer, 1977; Edelman, 1977). Freud, Jung, and other psychologists have relied heavily on symbolic concepts to understand human behavior. Anthropologists have traditionally focused on symbols and their place in the culture and lives of human beings (Ortner, 1973). Symbolism cuts across disciplinary boundaries, and the symbolic frame constructs, out of those ideas, a lens for viewing life in collective settings.

The symbolic frame centers on the concepts of meaning, belief, and faith. Historically, humans have found life bewildering. Events often cannot be explained: Loved ones die before their time. Circumstances cannot always be controlled: Tornadoes wipe out towns, and recessions put productive, established firms out of business. Contradictions often cannot be reconciled: Good people do bad, and bad people do good. Dilemmas are everywhere: Can we keep peace without waging war? How can we protect the lives and property of some without impinging on the freedom of others? How can we help people to learn from evaluations that are threatening to them?

To cope with confusion, uncertainty, and chaos, humans create a variety of symbols. *Myths* provide explanations, reconcile contradictions, and resolve dilemmas (Cohen, 1969). *Metaphors* make confusion comprehensible. *Scenarios* provide direction for action in uncharted and seemingly unchartable terrain (Ortner, 1973).

Myths, rituals, and ceremonies are often seen as the province of theologians, anthropologists, mystics, and clergy, but those concepts are now being applied to secular organizations. Indeed, two recent books have applied ideas derived from these diverse sources to modern corporations. *In Search of Excellence* (Peters and Waterman, 1982) focuses on the relationship between a company's culture and its performance. The authors' key argument, supported by studies of excellent companies, is that strong, cohesive cultures produce results. They list eight characteristics that inspire high performance.

In *Corporate Cultures,* Deal and Kennedy (1982) emphasize the same point. Strong cultures produce results. They outline a framework for understanding culture: shared values and beliefs, heroes and heroines, rituals and ceremonies, and a cultural network of priests and priestesses, storytellers, gossips, and spies. In companies where these cultural elements are cohesive, consistent, and widely shared, people know what is expected and what needs to be done and are motivated and committed to doing a good job. Little time is wasted on politics, sabotage, or figuring out how to beat the system. Rather, each individual's identity is fused with the culture. The symbols and symbolic activity give meaning to the workplace and provide opportunities for anyone—from boardroom or executive suite to factory floor—to be a part of a dynamic social institution.

Both books are based on the assumptions and ideas of the symbolic frame. Both illustrate the power of applying old, time-tested ideas to contemporary organizations. The symbolic frame introduces new concepts to the study of organizations and offers alternative ways of interpreting old concepts.

Symbolic Concepts

If managers encounter uncertainty and ambiguity in their work, one thing they can do is to try to understand and control the sources. If sales are dropping for no known reason, management will make efforts to understand the causes of the decline and to develop strategies for improvement. Traditional notions of rational problem solving and decision making will be useful—*unless* the problems are so complex, ambiguous, or uncertain that in fact they cannot be understood or solved.

The symbolic frame assumes that organizations are full of questions that cannot be answered, problems that cannot be solved, and events that cannot be understood or managed. Whenever that is so, humans will create and use symbols to bring meaning out of chaos, clarity out of confusion, and predictability out of mystery. Among the major symbolic forms that humans use are myths, rituals, ceremonies, fairy tales, stories, humor, and play. Are McDonald's' many franchises united by its sophisticated control systems or by golden arches, core values, and the legend of Ray Kroc? Are Harvard professors as autonomous as they appear to be, or are they tightly constrained by the rituals of teaching and the myths and mystique of Harvard? This section explores the many significant roles such symbols play in organizational life.

Myths

The term *myth* is often used pejoratively: "It's only a myth." "That's a myth, not fact." The implication is that there is no truth in myths. Myths may in fact communicate very significant truths, but it is important to understand the difference between myths and theories. Theories are subject to verification or falsification to test their validity. Myths arise to protect people from uncertainty, but they are not intended to be empirically testable. They serve several functions (Cohen, 1969):

1. Myths explain.
2. Myths express.
3. Myths maintain solidarity and cohesion.
4. Myths legitimize.
5. Myths communicate unconscious wishes and conflicts.
6. Myths mediate contradictions.
7. Myths provide narrative to anchor the present in the past.

Myths have two sides. On the one hand, they can blind us to new information and opportunities to learn. The myth that "authority must always equal responsibility," still widely believed by many managers, sets a misleading and unrealistic standard. Consider many of the other myths that managers often live by: the myth of planned organizational change, the myth of the need for change, the myth of organizational rationality, the myth of managerial control, the myth of the objective, neutral expert, and the myth of the one best way (Westerlund and Sjostrand, 1979). All of us have believed in one or more of those myths as we have worked with organizations as participants, managers, or consultants. Many of us still believe, even though we encounter evidence that contradicts the myths. The uncertainty that would accompany the loss of our most cherished myths about organizations is overwhelming. Myths keep us sane —but also dampen our curiosity, distort our images, and misdirect our attention.

On the other hand, despite their potential negative consequences, myths are necessary for meaning, solidarity, stability, and certainty. Manning (1979, pp. 325-327) describes the functions of myths in law enforcement agencies:

> The function of any myth is to arrange themes that are in reality unacceptable or bipolar into integrated or holistic units. . . . Second, myth obviates the concern with the special interest that might be served by a given explanation; it removes the matter from everyday discourse and places it in the realm of the nebulous and mystical. . . . Third, a myth alleviates social crises by providing a verbal explanation for causes, meanings, and consequences of events that might otherwise be considered inexplicable. . . . Because the actual probability that police action will occur to prevent, punish, or obviate the threat of crimes is low, the myth must be maintained. . . . Fourth, the police myth sits apart from the actors in a drama of crime, gives them names and faces, and makes them subject to predictable scenarios with beginnings, middles, and ends. . . . Fifth, myths of police action concentrate public attention upon their force and conserving potential, even in times of rapid change. . . . Sixth, police myths freeze the organization in time and space, giving it a reified authority over the thing it opposes and establish it in timeless Manichean *pas de deux* between the two poles of social life. Law enforcement is no longer seen as mere work, involving decision, discretion, boredom, and unpleasantries; it becomes a sort of creed.

All organizations have myths or sagas (Clark, 1972). But these myths or sagas vary in their strength and intensity (Baldridge, 1975). One of the distinctive characteristics of elite institutions—such as IBM, Ivy League universities, or the United States Marines—is the presence of strong myths and sagas. "Respect for the individual," "Veritas," and "Semper fidelis" are shorthand for the myths that hold these institutions together and infuse activities with passion and meaning. Educational organizations with strong sagas have a strong sense of mission, charismatic leaders at the helm, a committed cadre of strong, influential supporters on the faculty, unique instructional programs, highly committed students, and a strong base of social support from alumni and other significant constituents in the environment (Clark, 1972). Reed, Antioch, Swarthmore, and most "lighthouse" high schools have strong, widely shared myths that are well known to the outside world. The myths support claims of distinctiveness and transform a mere organization into a beloved institution.

Educational organizations with weak sagas are uncertain, embattled, and vulnerable to internal and external pressures. A shared myth makes it easier to develop internal cohesion and sense of direction and to maintain the confidence and support of external constituencies. At the same time, myths can be stubbornly resistant to change and can prevent an organization from adapting when conditions have changed dramatically. Consider the fate of "Ma Bell," the American Telephone and Telegraph Company. For a century, it pursued a goal of "universal service" in a noncompetitive environment. Forced to sever the national system from the local operating companies, the firm must now compete aggressively in a deregulated environment. But in changing, it may lose what has made it successful over the years.

Stories and Fairy Tales

Fairy tales are usually seen as entertainment and moral instruction for small children. Fairy tales suggest to children that a rewarding life can be had if they do not shrink from adversity. Fairy tales comfort, reassure, and offer general directions and hope for the future. They externalize inner conflicts and tensions (Bettelheim, 1977). Stories are often seen as the medium used by those who have nothing more factual to offer: A professor may be accused of doing nothing more than telling "war stories." Such stories are often viewed as a source of entertainment, not truth. Yet stories convey information, morals, values, and myths vividly and convincingly (Mitroff and Kilmann, 1975). Stories and fairy tales both play an important, unappreciated role in modern organizations.

An example of an organizational story comes from Procter & Gamble (Wilkins, 1976). As the story goes, some time before the turn of the century, Harley Procter—a son of one of the founders and an excellent salesman—believed that the company's candle business was in trouble because of a new invention known as the electric light bulb. He was convinced that the company needed to emphasize its soap business. In church one Sunday morning, he experienced a revelation while hearing the minister read about "ivory palaces" in the Forty-fifth Psalm. He described this revelation to his very religious board of directors. He was able to persuade the board to give their "white," or "bath," soap a new name: Ivory. The board later approved a national advertising campaign, and Ivory Soap became a household phrase.

The story has been used within Procter & Gamble to illustrate a number of important ideas and values—the revelation itself, the success of mass advertising, and the importance of science and honesty in establishing Ivory's composition as "$99^{44}/_{100}$% Pure." The tale of Harley Procter illustrates many of the functions that stories serve in organizations. Stories describe events in a way that listeners can easily remember. They summarize vividly, delete distracting details, and present clear, simple messages. They become organizational fairy tales that serve several functions (Westerlund and Sjostrand, 1979):

1. Fairy tales often fulfill a wishful dream—for example, the poor orphaned shepherd boy who becomes a king, or Harley Procter, whose ingenuity and faith built a great business. The memoirs of chief executives often bring that type of fairy tale to mind. Evil powers vainly try to cause the hero's downfall, but he knows and does what is right, and his career becomes a

dream come true. His power is great and everlasting, and he lives happily ever after, at least until retirement.

2. The fairy tale entertains. The fairy tale's excitement is built on the imaginative events and great dangers that life or modern organizations can present. Just as fairy-tale heroes overcome dragons and witches, Harley Procter overcame the threat of the light bulb. When one obstacle is overcome, a new one will appear, but the courageous manager with the right theory can overcome adversity and produce a happy ending: The true and correct organization takes form.

3. The fairy tale gives security. A veteran labor negotiator once described his activity with the following image: It was like a group of people who huddled around a fire in a small clearing in the forest. Surrounding them were many unfriendly and hostile people. Periodically, a member of the group needed to go out and soothe the outsiders with a tale of the perfect future. Meanwhile, the group would sit around the fire murmuring, "One cent, two cents, one cent, two cents." This chant gave them security.

4. The fairy tale gives knowledge. Many fairy tales are based on real events cast in colorful and robust terms. The story of Harley Procter reminds today's managers at Procter & Gamble that faith, ingenuity, and good marketing can turn adversity into great opportunity.

5. The fairy tale is propaganda. It is easily accessible and easy to remember. Since it is enjoyable, it makes the message highly palatable. The story of Harley Procter's revelation takes Ivory Soap beyond the realm of the mundane and the commercial: "99^{44}/$_{100}$% Pure" takes on spiritual overtones and suggests that even God is on the side of Procter & Gamble.

Stories are the medium for communicating an organization's central myth to insiders and outsiders. They establish and perpetuate organizational tradition. They are told and recalled in formal meetings and informal coffee breaks. Stories are used to convey the meaning of the organization to outsiders, thus gaining their confidence and support. A visitor to IBM or Digital Equipment—the two largest computer firms in the United States —is likely to be regaled with stories of the company's history and its unique approach to business. Stories infuse organizational myths into everyday decisions and policies. Stories legitimize existing practice. They provide explanations when things go wrong and assign responsibility when things go right.

Stories and fairy tales help to address problems of morale, security, socialization, legitimacy, and communication. A good story provides a way of responding to an unpleasant fact. A school administrator responded to questions about a new reading program by recounting stories of several children whose ability to read had increased dramatically. As evaluators talked to teachers, parents, and students, the same stories were told repeatedly and new ones were added. Achievement scores became irrelevant data. Stories reflected and reinforced faith and belief in the program. Such stories can be used to communicate the success of a good program. They can also be used defensively to obscure the failure of a bad one. If reading scores decline drastically, a few dramatic success stories might be used to prevent a close look at the program's actual effectiveness. Like myths, stories and fairy tales are double-edged swords, but all are powerful weapons in the arsenal of collective meaning.

Ritual and Ceremony

Outside of churches and social clubs, *ritual* often has negative connotations: "Citizen participation is only a ritual." "Our new president is more ceremony than substance." "Is this just going to be another ritual, or will we really do something?" Such statements carry the message that ritual and ceremony are empty, repetitive, inflexible, and useless. It is easy to cite examples of meaningless rituals, but doing so can obscure the important functions that rituals play in human affairs.

Historically, humans have used ritual and ceremony to create order, clarity, and predictability, particularly in dealing with issues or problems that are too complex, mysterious, or random to be controlled in any other way. Indian rain dances and the Pilgrims' Thanksgiving celebration were both efforts to invoke supernatural assistance in the critical but unpredictable process of raising crops.

Individuals use rituals to reduce uncertainty and anxiety. Anglers and ballplayers wear "lucky" shirts to assist in catching a fish or winning a game. Police officers have coffee with fellow officers before going on duty to control anxiety; they know that they have little control over the events they might encounter in the course of a shift. Soldiers pray and send letters to loved ones before going into battle. Couples may have rituals that bind them together and reduce anxiety—for example, the wife who fears the worst every time her husband takes a business trip and always hides a message somewhere in his suitcase before he leaves.

Rituals and ceremonies are as important to organizations and societies as they are to individuals. They serve four major functions: to socialize, to stabilize, to reduce anxieties and ambiguities, and to convey messages to external constituencies. Some 7,000 women gather at the annual seminar of Mary Kay Cosmetics, Inc. They come to hear personal messages from Mary Kay, to applaud the achievements of star salespeople, to hear success stories from women who turned off the television soap operas to become successful managers, and to celebrate the symbols of their culture. The ceremony brings new members into the fold and maintains uniformity among members of the Mary Kay family long after the seminar ends. It sets failure and obstacles in the "you can do it" spirit symbolized by the bumblebee who can't fly but does anyway. The pageant makes the Mary Kay culture accessible to outsiders—particularly consumers.

Ceremony is equally critical in making decisions of national importance. In the United States, political conventions "select" candidates, even though in recent years there has been little suspense about the outcome. For several months, competing candidates for the presidency trade clichés, invent metaphors, and exchange epithets. The same pageantry unfolds in each election year. The basic issues are almost always the same. The rhetoric and spontaneous demonstrations often seem staged; campaigning is often repetitious and superficial; the act of voting often seems disconnected from the main drama. But the process of electing a president is an important ritual: It provides a sense of social involvement. It is an outlet for the expression of both discontent and enthusiasm. It provides live drama for people to watch and enjoy. It gives millions of people a sense of participation in an exciting adventure. It draws attention to common social ties and the importance of accepting the candidate who wins (Edelman, 1977). It provides an opportunity for candidates to reassure the public that there are clear answers to our most important questions and clear solutions to our most difficult problems.

Even in nations with different political processes, elections can have important symbolic meaning. In Mexico there is only one party, and the candidate of the PRI (the Institutional Revolutionary Party) always wins. Despite the irony of a "revolutionary" party that represents the political establishment, and even though victory is assured, the candidate campaigns relentlessly to communicate the image that "I am of the people." People gather in droves to hear the speeches; there are banners everywhere. The voting process in remote villages unfolds through a ritual like the following (Vogt and Abel, 1977):

1. A crowd gathers and voting booths are set up.
2. A group of literate residents carefully counts the ballots to see that the number exactly equals the official count of voters on the town list.
3. As people watch, an official marks ten ballots with an X for the PRI while one of the literate residents checks off ten names from the list.
4. Another official marks another ten, and so on.
5. Work parties form to deal with the remaining ballots. Two or three literate men mark X's on the ballots. Another group folds the ballots. A third group carries the ballots to the ballot box. Another man puts the ballots in the slot.
6. The process continues until all the ballots are filled out and all the names are checked off.
7. An official signs a paper—fifteen copies—noting that the polls opened at 8:00 A.M. and closed at 5:00 P.M. and that there were no irregularities in voting.
8. The ballot boxes are collected by other officials, and the voting booths are taken down.

The voting process serves purposes other than the formal purpose of electing candidates. The campaign gives everyone a chance to come out for the candidate, declare his or her political position, and bargain with a system that is temporarily flexible. Voting is seen as if it were a transaction with the gods: "We have delivered the votes, now in exchange we want a new bridge built across the river, and the roof of the schoolhouse repaired" (Vogt and Abel, 1977, pp. 185-186).

Despite the significant differences between the electoral systems in Mexico and the United States, both may be viewed primarily as collective rituals: "All times are the times that try men's souls. . . . The age one lives in is always in crisis. . . . Politics is for most of us a parade of abstract symbols which our experience teaches us to be a benevolent or malevolent force that can be close to omnipotent" (Edelman, 1977, p. 13). Elections illustrate many of the basic characteristics of rituals and ceremonies. They are repetitious and occur at fixed intervals (such as the four-year cycle for presidential elections). They involve acting and special, stylized behavior, as in campaign speeches. They are staged (like political conventions), and they follow a predictable order. They have explicit purposes (for example, democratic selection of candidates), but they convey both explicit and implicit symbolic messages. They explain, make things comprehensible, and provide meaning (for example, when a challenger explains how the current problems have been created by the incumbent). They provide connections and order —elections reassure us of both continuity and predictability in the political process. They provide a bridge between order and chaos, and they provide hope. Even though the problems appear to be getting worse, we can select a new candidate who promises to make things better. Rituals both mirror our ideas and shape them: Elections mirror a cultural belief in democracy and shape our beliefs about current political problems and solutions.

Rituals are not confined to politics—they play an equally significant role in organizations. Rituals can communicate meaning from one individual to another or from an organization to its environment. Joseph Wambaugh provides an example of a police officer approaching a tense situation: "I started off with a fancy stick pin. I let the baton go bouncing off the sidewalk back into my hand. Three shoeshine kids were watching me, two Mexican, one Negro. The baton trick impressed the hell out of them. I strung it out like a yo-yo, did some back twirls, and dropped it back into the ring in one smooth motion" (in Manning, 1979, p. 24). Manning writes "The timing of such a movement, its dexterity, speed, and certainty, not only displays a potentially violent weapon (an instrumental message) but contains and makes manifest a set of little signals about the actor. I am a person who uses such weaponry with aplomb, with self-conscious skills, and have indeed used it before, as my facility shows. In this sequence, the policeman not only presents himself, he presents himself as a certain kind of policeman; he expresses a style or character and an aspect of the self" (1979, pp. 24-25).

Some organizational events are clearly ceremonial, such as retirement dinners or welcoming speeches for new employees. But many significant rituals are rarely viewed as such, because they are typically assumed to be rational and instrumental. Consider the following examples:

- *Performance appraisals* rarely produce learning or useful information about employee performance, yet most organizations persist in conducting appraisals every year.
- *Regular meetings* of committees often produce few if any discernible outcomes but do give members another opportunity to make the same speeches and to debate the same perennial issues.
- *Management training programs* often produce little visible improvement in managers' skills, but they do socialize participants into the management culture, and they certify the graduates as having special status.
- *Tests and interviews* for hiring new employees often produce data of doubtful validity, but they may communicate specialness to those who are hired and fairness to those who are not.

The persistence of processes that never accomplish what they are supposed to is one indication of the need for ritual and ceremony in organizations. They provide order and meaning that help to bind an organization together. If the rituals are properly conducted and attuned to the myths that people value, they fire imagination, insight, belief, and emotion. Out of rhythm and out of touch, they become cold, empty forms that people resent and avoid. Countless hours and millions of dollars have been spent trying to change the ritual of teaching. Perhaps it is the ritual of change that provides perennial impetus to make education different. Rituals and ceremonies can release creativity and transform or create meanings, myths, and strategies. They can also cement the status quo and block adaptation and learning. Like other symbols, they can cut both ways.

Metaphor, Humor, and Play

A symbol is something that stands for something else—often something deeper and more complex. Metaphors, humor, and play all illustrate the important "as if" quality that symbols have. They provide ways of grappling with issues that are too complex, mysterious, or threatening to deal with more directly.

Metaphors permit us to imagine something as if it were something else. An excerpt from a conversation between father and daughter in Bateson's (1972) dialogue "Why a swan?" provides an illustration:

Daughter: When a Frenchman calls a man "sort of" camel and I say that a swan is "sort of" human, do we mean the same thing?

Father: All right, let's try to analyze what "sort of" means. Let's take a single sentence and examine it. If I say, "The puppet Petroushka is sort of human," I state a relationship.

Daughter: Between what and what?

Father: Between ideas, I think.

Daughter: Between a puppet and people?

Father: No, between some ideas I have about puppets and some ideas I have about people.

Daughter: Oh. Well, then, what sort of relationship?

Father: I don't know, a metaphoric relationship [pp. 33-37].

Metaphors can be used to make the strange familiar and the familiar strange. They can be used to place the self and others on a social continuum. Candidate A calls his opponent a jellyfish, and the opponent responds by calling A a barracuda. A new chief executive justifies her reorganization as "cleaning up the mess." Others in the organization view it as another example of an outsider putting a feather in her career cap. Metaphors compress complicated issues into understandable images, and they can affect our attitudes, evaluations, and actions. A college president who sees the university as a factory will probably be different from a president who sees the university as a craft guild or a shopping center. Consultants who see themselves as organizational physicians are likely to be different from consultants who see themselves as salesmen or rain dancers.

Humor also serves important "as if" functions. Hansot (1979) argues that it is less important to ask why people are humorous in organizations than to ask why they are so serious. She argues that humor plays a number of important functions in organizations. Humor integrates, expresses skepticism, contributes to flexibility and adaptiveness, and indicates status. Humor is a classic device for distancing, but it can also be used to socialize, include, and convey membership. Humor can establish solidarity and promote face saving. Most importantly, humor is a way of illuminating and breaking frames to indicate that any single definition of the situation is arbitrary (Hansot, 1979).

To illustrate the role of humor in reframing organizational events, consider a story about the late Marcus Foster when he was superintendent of schools in Oakland, California. A panicked high school principal called Foster to ask for help: "Twenty-five armed Black Panthers are standing outside my office!" Foster reportedly responded immediately, "Think of them as pink panthers," and hung up the phone. The humor in the idea of "pink panthers" enabled the principal to handle the situation brilliantly.

Play and humor are linked and can serve some of the same functions. In most work settings, play and work are sharply distinguished: Play is what people do when they are not working. The only images of "play" in common organizational use connote aggression, competition, and struggle (for example, "We've got to beat them at their own game"; "We dropped the ball that time"; "The ball is in his court now"), rather than relaxation and fun.

If play is viewed as a state of mind (Bateson, 1972; Goffman, 1974), any activity can be done playfully. Play permits relaxing the rules in order to explore alternatives. It encourages experimentation, flexibility, and adaptiveness. March (1976) suggests five guidelines for organizational play:

1. Treat goals as hypotheses.
2. Treat intuition as real.
3. Treat hypocrisy as transition.
4. Treat memory as an enemy.
5. Treat experience as a theory.

As another example, organizational effectiveness has typically been associated with productivity, profitability, resources, efficiency, and ability to control the environment. Weick (1981) playfully offers another set of criteria. An effective organization is—

1. Garrulous
2. Clumsy
3. Haphazard
4. Hypocritical
5. Monstrous
6. Octopoid
7. Wondering
8. Grouchy
9. Galumphing

Weick argues that such criteria may be superior to those that have captured the attention of managers and organization theorists in the past. Relaxing the rules to sense new possibilities is something that managers and organizations need to do to survive.

Summary

Against traditional views of organizations as rational and objectively real, the symbolic frame counterposes a set of concepts that emphasize the complexity and ambiguity of organizational phenomena and the extent to which symbols mediate the meaning of organizational events and activities. Myths and stories provide drama, cohesiveness, clarity, and direction to events that are confusing and mysterious. Rituals and ceremonies provide ways of taking action in the face of confusion, unpredictability, and threat. Metaphors, humor, and play provide ways for individuals and organizations to escape the tyranny of facts and logic, to view organizations and their own participation in them *as if* they were something new and different from their appearance, and to find creative alternatives to existing choices.

10

Applying the
Symbolic Approach

Managers and organization theorists usually assume a linear connection between activities, events, and outcomes. Decisions solve problems. Evaluations provide a basis for sanctions. Administrators administer. Structure coordinates activity. Planning shapes the future. Environment affects decision making. Effective decisions shape the environment. Such statements seem so obvious that they are rarely questioned.

Yet these "obvious" connections often fail in the everyday world. Decisions may not decide anything (March and Olsen, 1976). Evaluations rarely accomplish what they are supposed to (Dornbusch and Scott, 1975). Structures may have little to do with activity (Cohen and others, 1979; Weick, 1976a). Differences make leaders (Edelman, 1977). Change efforts produce no change (Baldridge and Deal, 1975; Ross and Deal, 1977). Planning produces no plans or produces plans that have no effect on the future.

The idea that activities may not produce results questions a substantial proportion of human endeavor in organizations.

Such a heresy can undermine the hope and morale of those who want to make a difference. Even while arguing that such connections are often missing, the symbolic frame offers a hopeful interpretation—that organizational structures, activities, and events serve other activities. They serve as myths, stories, ceremonies, rituals, metaphors, and games. They provide meaning, absorb both energy and conflict, and reduce ambiguity.

Structures, activities, and events also signal to the outside world that all is well. If management is making decisions, if plans are being made, if new units are created in response to new problems, if sophisticated evaluation and control systems are in place, then an organization must be well managed and worthy of support. The symbolic function of those activities will be particularly critical in organizations whose outputs are ambiguous and hard to measure.

When external constituencies question the worth of existing practices, organizations promise reform and engage in an activity/ritual called change. If consumers complain about the quality of the current products, the organization creates a consumer affairs department and promises tighter quality standards. If the government questions the fairness of personnel practices, the organization hires an affirmative action officer. If the organization is in a crisis, a new leader is brought in who promises substance, not mere appearance. An example occurred in the crises that rocked Poland beginning in 1980. As the *Boston Globe* reported in the summer of 1980, "Poland's new Communist party leader, Stanislaw Karia, last night promised more democracy and pledged the party would work to regain the confidence of the disquieted Poles. . . . In his first speech as national leader . . . Karia promised less ceremony and more substance and called on the Poles to rally around the party after a summer of labor and political turmoil."

From the vantage point of the symbolic frame, organizational structures, activities, and events are secular myths, rituals, and ceremonies. They express our fears, joys, and expectations. They arouse our affect and kindle our spirit. They reduce our uncertainty and soothe our bewilderment. They provide a shared basis for understanding and for moving ahead. This chapter reexamines organizational structure and process in the light of their symbolic functions.

Structure as Symbol

Traditionally, organizational structure is depicted as a network of interdependent roles and units coordinated through a variety of horizontal and vertical linkages. Since structure needs to be responsive to organizational purposes, the shape of an organization is determined by its goals, technologies, and environment (Woodward, 1970; Perrow, 1972; Lawrence and Lorsch, 1967).

An alternative view is that the belief in the possibility of organizing organizations is a myth. The myth basically holds "that it is possible to break up an organization into certain headings, and that these headings are unequivocal" (Westerlund and Sjostrand, 1979, p. 25). The symbolic view suggests that, at least in some organizations, the structure of organizations may not have much to do with task and technology after all.

Such suspicions are supported by a recent study of the relation between structure and technology in elementary schools. The study found no relation between the structure of a school district and classroom instruction. Policies, efforts, and activities of administrators and specialists had little or no impact on how teachers taught. The research suggested that school districts had three major levels—central administrators, building administrators, and teachers—whose activities were mostly independent of one another. Other research on schools, both public and private, shows similar patterns (Abramowitz and others, 1978). Structure and activity seem to be unrelated, and both are loosely linked with the environment.

The symbolic view suggests a number of noninstrumental purposes that structure can serve. One purpose is to express prevailing values and myths of the society. In many organizations, goals are multiple and elusive, the technology is underdeveloped, the linkages between means and ends is poorly understood, and effectiveness is almost impossible to determine.

Schools, churches, mental health clinics, personnel departments, and management consulting firms all share those characteristics.

One way for such organizations to achieve legitimacy is to maintain an appearance that conforms to the way society *thinks* such organizations should look. A church should have a building, appropriate artifacts, and a member of the clergy. A mental health clinic should have a waiting room, uniformed nurses, and certified mental health professionals.

Meyer and Rowan (1978) apply symbolic logic to the function of structure in public schools. They argue that school will have difficulty sustaining public support unless it gives the right answers to three questions: (1) Does it offer appropriate topics (for example, third-grade English, American history)? (2) Are the topics taught to age-graded students by certified teachers? (3) Does the school look like a school (with classrooms, a gymnasium, a library, and a flag near the front door)? If the school is an institution of higher education, its worth is likely to be measured by the size and beauty of the campus, the number of books in the library, the faculty-student ratio, and the number of professors who received Ph.D.s from high-prestige institutions.

Kamens (1977) carries this theme further by arguing that (1) the major function of colleges and universities is symbolic—to redefine graduates as possessing special qualities or skills, (2) the legitimacy of the transformation must be negotiated with important constituencies, and (3) this is done through legitimizing myths about the quality of education that are validated by the organizational structure of the institution.

The structural form, in Kamens's view, depends on two major features of an institution: whether it is elite or nonelite and whether it allocates students to a particular corporate group in the society. Each type of institution will espouse a different myth and will dramatize different aspects of its structure. Size, complexity, formal curriculum, admissions procedures, and demographics all vary according to the symbolic messages the institution attempts to communicate. An elite school, for example, will—

- dramatize selectivity ("We accept only one out of ten of the highly qualified candidates").
- develop an attractive residential campus ("The residential experience is an essential feature of our total curriculum").
- advertise its high faculty-student ratio ("which provides for ongoing contact and dialogue between individual students and the many dedicated, outstanding faculty members").
- develop a curriculum that restrains specialization ("We seek to educate the whole person, rather than to train narrow specialists").

If an institution or its environment changes, then some adaptation will be necessary to mirror those shifts. Since legitimacy and worth are judged by correspondence between structural characteristics and prevailing myths, organizations are frequently obliged to alter their appearance to produce consonance. In this view, organizational structures are built out of "blocks" of contemporary myth.

Another purpose of organizational structure is to convey a "modern" appearance—to communicate to external audiences that this is not a horse-and-buggy operation but is fully up to date. In response to legal and social pressures, business organizations create affirmative action policies and roles, yet hiring practices change very little. As economics becomes increasingly fashionable, banks hire sophisticated economists but place them in economics departments well away from the mainstream of decision making. As laws are passed mandating education for children with special needs, schools hire psychologists and learning-disabilities specialists, who then perform functions that classroom teachers rarely see or understand. In response to criticism of antiquated management systems, universities adopt sophisticated control systems that produce elaborate printouts but have little effect on ongoing operations. Congress passes laws on occupational safety, and factories create safety units, which post signs that are mostly ignored.

The new structures reflect legal and social expectations and represent a bid for acceptance and support from relevant constituencies. An organization that has no affirmative action program signals nonconformity to prevailing expectations. Nonconformity invites questions, criticism, and inspection. At the same time, it is much easier to appoint an affirmative action officer than to change hiring practices that are deeply embedded in both individual beliefs and organizational culture. Since the presence of the affirmative action officer is much more visible than any given hiring decision, the new role may successfully signal change to the environment, even though little change has occurred. Moreover, a new structure that is mainly symbolic may, in the long run, help to pave the way for more fundamental change in organizational practice.

In government, administrative agencies often serve the same symbolic functions. Agencies are created to encapsulate existing ambivalence or conflicts (Edelman, 1977). Conflict between shippers and railroads led to the formation of the Interstate Commerce Commission. Conflict between labor and management produced the National Labor Relations Board. Conflict between consumers and producers of food and drugs led to the Food and Drug Administration. Concern over pollution led to the Environmental Protection Agency. Yet such agencies often serve mostly political and symbolic functions.

Politically, regulatory agencies are often "captured" by those whom they are supposed to regulate. Major drug companies are far more effective than the public in lobbying and in influencing decisions about drug safety. In practice, the agencies legitimize elite values, reassure the public that "watchdog" agencies are zealously protecting their interests, and struggle for continuing funding from the legislature. They reduce tension and uncertainty and increase the public's sense of confidence and security (Edelman, 1977).

The symbolic perspective on organizational structure is most prominent in organizations with ambiguous goals and technology, but the same logic can be seen even in highly technical organizations. The development of the Polaris missile system was heralded as an example of government activity at its best. One of its distinctive characteristics was the introduction of modern management techniques, such as PERT charts and

PPBS, to the public sector. Those techniques were reflected in several structural forms, such as specialist roles, technical divisions, management meetings, and a "Special Projects Office." Since Polaris was viewed as a highly successful project, it was easy to conclude that the modern management techniques were a major causal factor. The admiral in charge of the project received a plaque recognizing his contribution in bringing modern management to the United States Navy. A visiting team of British experts recommended PERT to the British admiralty. Modern management techniques continued to spread to other organizations.

A later study of the Polaris project suggested a different interpretation of what happened. The activities of the specialists were loosely coupled to other aspects of the project. The technical division produced plans and charts that were mostly ignored. The management meetings served two primary purposes: They were arenas that the admiral used to publicly chide poor performers, and they were revival meetings that reinforced religious fervor around the Polaris project. The Special Project Office served as a briefing area in which members of Congress and other visiting dignitaries were told about the progress of Polaris through an impressive series of diagrams, charts, and forms that often had little to do with the actual status of the project. The team from the British Navy apparently surmised this on their visit and recommended a similar approach to their admiralty (Sapolsky, 1972).

Although the structural forms may not have served their ostensible purposes, they helped to foster a myth that maintained strong external support and kept the "wolves" at bay. The myth provided breathing space so that people could do their work, relying on the basis of informal coordination, and helped to keep spirits and self-confidence high.

From a symbolic perspective, organizations are judged not so much by what they do as by how they appear. The right formal structure provides a ceremonial façade that beams the correct signal of the day to the appropriate audience. The signal provides reassurance, fosters belief, cultivates and maintains faith, and keeps the organization viable. Structures may do little to coordinate activity or dictate relationships among organizational participants, but they do provide internal symbols that help participants to cope, find meaning, and play their roles in the drama without reading the wrong lines, upstaging the lead actors, or responding to a tragedy when it is supposed to be a comedy.

Organizational Processes

Administrative and technical processes are the basic tools that organizations use to get work done. Administrative processes include formal meetings, evaluation systems, planning, accounting systems, management information systems, and labor negotiations.

Technical processes vary with the task to be achieved. In industrial organizations, workers assemble parts into a salable product or conduct operations that result in a batch of something (such as petroleum or industrial chemicals). In people-processing organizations, a variety of technical processes can be observed. Professors give lectures to provide students with knowledge and wisdom that will help them in later life. Physicians diagnose illness and prescribe treatments to help people get well. Social workers write case reports to identify and remedy conditions that entrap individuals in a cycle of poverty.

People who work in organizations spend much of their time engaged in such processes. To justify the time and maintain a sense of productivity and self-worth, it is important to believe that the processes work—that they produce the intended outcomes. But effort does not always lead to effectiveness, and organizational processes often fail to produce what they are supposed to.

Many meetings make no decisions, solve no problems, and lead only to a need for more meetings. Problems sometimes float around without finding solutions while solutions are floating in search of problems (March and Olsen, 1976). Conflict is often ignored rather than resolved or managed (Deal and Nutt, 1980). Planning produces documents that no one uses.

Even at the technical core, particularly in people-processing organizations, there is considerable slippage between processes and intended outcomes. Graduates often wonder why the things they learned at the university seem irrelevant or counterproductive in their new work setting. Patients wonder why symptoms linger after medication and treatment. Poor people see that the same problems persist despite the best efforts of social workers.

Even if processes do not produce results, they are still important. They serve as rituals and ceremonies that provide settings for drama, opportunities for self-expression, forums for airing grievances, and arenas for negotiating new understandings and meanings.

Meetings serve as "garbage cans" into which problems are dumped (March and Olsen, 1976). At any moment in an organization, there are participants looking for places to expend time and energy, problems looking for solutions, and solutions looking for problems. A scheduled meeting attracts all three, and the outcomes depend on a complicated interplay among the inputs that happened to arrive: Who came? What problems, concerns, or needs did participants bring? What solutions were brought? Meanwhile, the garbage can soaks up excess time and energy. It provides an opportunity for new myths to be created and old ones to be renegotiated. It helps individuals become clearer about their roles in the organizational drama and to practice and polish their lines.

A faculty meeting in a distinguished university illustrates the garbage-can logic. The agenda outlined three topics for a two-hour meeting: whether to accept $300,000 to support an annual award for an outstanding woman educator, whether to begin a new doctoral program, and whether to approve a new core curriculum in the school's largest department. The discussion of the $300,000 gift lasted one hour and thirty minutes and covered the following issues: sexism, old conflicts between social science and professions, minority rights, academic freedom, excellence in the school, institutional autonomy, faculty integrity, and declining enrollments. The discussion produced a committee to explore the issue further. The committee members comprised those who had spoken with the greatest feeling and eloquence during the meeting. The discussion of the new doctoral program lasted twenty minutes. The program was approved unanimously. The discussion of the core curriculum lasted about ten minutes. The chairman of the committee that had developed the new curriculum gave a brief speech and answered one question. The curriculum was approved unanimously.

The first item on the agenda—the award for a woman educator—attracted time and energy, old problems, and solutions that were carried by the same faculty members from meeting to meeting. The other two items came late in the meeting after some faculty members had left for other commitments and led to unanimous decisions with little debate or deliberation. Many of the important functions of garbage cans were easily seen and felt in the discussion of the first item. Older professors had opportunities to deliver thoughtful speeches and to be respected. Younger faculty members had a chance to offer new perspectives and to be recognized. The rights of women and minorities were highlighted and reinforced. Academic freedom and institutional autonomy were reaffirmed. The faculty reminded themselves of the school's excellence. The diversity of the faculty was publicly displayed. A new committee gave vocal individuals an additional opportunity to render service. The school's history and ideology were re-created and reinforced.

Garbage cans are particularly likely to form around issues that are emotionally powerful and symbolically visible but technically fuzzy. A discussion of organizational mission is likely to attract a much larger and more diverse set of inputs than a conversation about cost-accounting procedures. Examples of garbage cans in the organizational literature include studies of reorganization (Olsen, 1976b), choosing a new chief administrator (Olsen, 1976a), and conflict over desegregation (Weiner, 1976). Garbage cans may not produce rational discourse, effective problem solving, and improvements in effectiveness, but they serve symbolic functions that help to prevent individual and organizational disintegration.

Planning is an administrative process that has become increasingly prominent as a sign of good management. An organization that does not plan is thought to be reactive, shortsighted, and rudderless. Planning has become a ceremony that an organization must conduct periodically to maintain its legitimacy. A plan is a badge of honor that organizations wear conspicuously and with considerable pride.

Cohen and March (1974) identify four major functions that plans serve in universities:

1. Plans are symbols. Academic organizations provide few "real" feedback data. They have nothing closely analogous to profit or sales figures. How are we doing? Where are we going? An organization that is failing can announce a plan to succeed. An institution that does not have a reactor (or an economics department) can announce a plan to get one and will probably be valued more highly than a university without such a plan.

2. Plans become games. In an organization whose goals and technology are unclear, plans and the insistence on plans become an administrative test of will. If a department wants a new program badly enough, it will spend a substantial amount of effort in "justifying" the expenditure by fitting it into a "plan." If an administrator wishes to avoid saying yes to everything but has no basis for saying no to anything, asking for a plan tests a department's commitment.

3. Plans become excuses for interaction. As several students of planning have noted, the results of the process of planning are usually more important than the plan. Development of a plan forces some discussion and may induce some interest in and commitment to relatively low priorities in departments and schools. Occasionally, that interaction yields results of positive value. But only rarely does it yield anything that would accurately describe the activities of a school or department beyond one or two years into the future. As people engage in discussions of the future, they may modify one another's views about what should be done today, but their conclusions about next year are likely to be altered in the interim by changes in personnel, political climate, foundation policy, or student demand.

4. Plans become advertisements. What is frequently called a "plan" by a university is really an investment brochure,

an attempt to convince private and public donors of the attractiveness of the institution. Such plans are characterized by pictures, by *ex cathedra* pronouncements of excellence, and by the absence of most relevant information.

When Cohen and March (1974) surveyed college presidents, they asked about the linkage between plans and current decisions. The responses fell into four main categories:

1. "Yes, we have a plan. It is used in capital project and physical location decisions."
2. "Yes, we have a plan. Here it is. It was made during the administration of our last president. We are working on a new one."
3. "No, we do not have a plan. We should. We are working on one."
4. "I think there's a plan around here someplace. Miss Jones, do we have a copy of our comprehensive, ten-year plan?" [p. 113].

A study of a large-scale planning project in a suburban school district (Edelfson, Johnson, and Stromquist, 1977) provides another illustration of the symbolic importance of planning. "Project Redesign" was a federally supported five-year planning effort that involved a significant proportion of the district's professionals and citizens in creating a dream for the school district to meet the challenges of the 1980s.

The plan produced no major decisions or changes in the district. But it did provide participants a chance to participate and interact, which they liked. It provided a garbage can that attracted a variety of problems, solutions, and conflicts that might have caused more difficulty if they had surfaced in some other arena. It gave the district another opportunity to present itself as a "lighthouse" district, which everyone appreciated. It renewed faith in the virtues of participation, the merits of grassroots democracy, the value of good ideas, and the efficacy of modern planning techniques.

Planning may not shape the future or inform decisions, but organizations still need to do it. It conveys the impression of foresight and rationality, which encourages outsiders to believe in the organization and to provide support. Planning creates attractive garbage cans and serves as a stage for important rituals and drama.

Evaluation of people, departments, and programs is a major activity in almost any organization. Evaluation efforts often consume substantial time and effort and produce lengthy reports that are presented with considerable ceremony in formal meetings. Yet the results typically disappear into the recesses of people's minds or the shelves of administrators' offices.

Evaluation is something that organizations need to do if they are to be viewed as responsible, serious, and well managed, even though the results of evaluations are rarely used for decision making. Evaluations are used for other purposes. Evaluation data can be used as weapons in political battles or as justification for decisions that would have been made in any event (Weiss, 1980).

In public organizations, Floden and Weiner (1978, p. 17) argue,

> Evaluation is a ritual whose function is to calm the anxieties of the citizenry and to perpetuate an image of government rationality, efficiency, and accountability. The very act of requiring and commissioning evaluations may create the impression that government is seriously committed to the pursuit of publicly espoused goals, such as increasing student achievement or reducing malnutrition. Evaluations lend credence to this image even when programs are created to appease interest groups.
>
> The picture of a committed government serves two functions. First, it improves the image of public officials. In both democratic and authoritarian systems, political leaders must appear to be confident, efficacious, and in control if they hope to produce any changes. . . . The impression of government rationality also promotes a feeling of security of the citizenry. Societal problems are

often magnified by the media to the point where a
crisis seems imminent. The threat of crisis leads to
a widespread sense of helplessness and hopeless-
ness. Evaluations serve to combat this feeling by
fostering the belief that the government is acting
on everyone's behalf to find solutions to pressing
problems. The publicity given to these efforts reduces the level of public anxiety, whether or not
evaluations produce useful information. Evaluations may also serve as a focal point for a reduction
of complex social problems to a choice between
relatively well-defined alternatives. The reduction
of apparent complexity acts both to make the
problems seem more manageable and to give the
citizens the sense that they have a firm understanding of the issues involved.

Evaluation is a process that fosters belief, confidence, and
support from external constituencies and benefactors. Universities convene visiting committees to evaluate schools or departments. The federal government mandates evaluations of many
federal programs. Social service agencies commission studies or
program audits when important problems or issues arise.

Evaluation is often accorded ceremonial status. Prestigious
evaluators are hired. The process receives considerable publicity.
Participants wear "costumes" that are more formal than normal
dress. New roles are enacted: Evaluators ask penetrating questions, and respondents give answers that portray the world as it
is supposed to be. The results are often presented dramatically,
especially when they are favorable. Negative results are often
couched in vacuous language with "Boy Scout" recommendations that no one is likely to take very seriously. Both negative
results and activity to solve the problems disappear after the
ceremony is concluded.

Occasionally an evaluator "blows the whistle" by producing a highly critical report. The drama then becomes a tragedy that is often injurious to both parties. The Coleman Report
argued the thesis that "schools don't make a difference." The

report and the subsequent debate undermined public confidence in the schools, but they also raised questions about the cohesion and maturity of the social sciences.

Evaluation persists because it serves significant symbolic purposes. Without it, we would worry about the efficiency and effectiveness of activities. Evaluation produces "magic numbers" to help us believe that things are working. Evaluation shows that organizations take goals seriously. It demonstrates that an organization cares and wants to improve. Evaluations provide opportunities for participants to share their opinions and have them publicly heard and recognized. Evaluation results help people relabel old practices, provide opportunities for adventure, and foster new beliefs (Rallis, 1980).

Collective bargaining is generally viewed as a necessary process for resolving conflict and achieving workable agreements between labor and management. Through an interplay among players, positions, persuasion, and power, an agreement is reached on wages and working conditions.

But collective bargaining can also be viewed as a ritual and a drama. Two stories illustrate the alternative perspective:

> The first story compares the careers of two union officials. Each had immense potential. But one had a decided advantage in the collective bargaining process: He could not hear well. His contemporary had excellent hearing. On one occasion, hearing a canned management presentation for the third time (even though both sides knew what the settlement would be), he walked out the door and into professional oblivion. The other could turn off his hearing aid and dream of exploits past and future, while pretending to hear the details of the other side's proposals. He is now a very successful union negotiator.

> The second story is about a young executive who took the helm of a firm with the intention of eliminating the bickering and conflict between

management and labor. He commissioned a study
of the company's wage structure and went to the
bargaining table to present his offer. He informed
the union representatives of what he had done and
offered them more than they had expected to get.
The astonished union leaders berated the executive
for undermining the process of collective bargaining and asked for another five cents an hour beyond his offer [Blum, 1961, pp. 63-64].

The stories support the symbolic interpretation of collective bargaining as drama. When some actors fail to follow the
script, others become angry because they cannot deliver their
lines. The drama is played to an audience composed of management, labor, and the public. It expresses a struggle designed
to convince each side that the ending was the result of heroic
battle. The drama, if well acted, conveys the message that the
two opponents fought hard and persistently for what they believed was right (Blum, 1961). The drama conceals the reality
that, in many cases, the actors knew in advance exactly how the
play would end.

Power is usually seen as an attribute that individuals or
systems possess based on resources that they are able to control. Power is discussed as if it were real: Power can be seized,
exercised, or redistributed. The problem is that power, like
many other organizational phenomena, is often ambiguous.
Who has power is not easy to determine. How one might gain
power is often unclear. How and when power is exercised is
hard to assess.

From a symbolic perspective, individuals have power if
others believe they do. Such beliefs are encouraged by events or
outcomes that become linked to particular individuals. The unemployment rate improves, and incumbents take credit. A firm
becomes more profitable, and we attribute that success to the
chief executive. A new program is started at a time when things
are getting better anyway, and the program gets credit.

Myths of leadership generally attribute power to individuals. Individuals cause important events to occur. Whether

things are going well or badly, we like to think that we can legitimately hold someone responsible. Cohen and March (1974, p. 199) conclude about college presidents: "Presidents negotiate with their audiences on the interpretations of their power. As a result, during recent years of campus troubles, many college presidents sought to emphasize the limitations of presidential control. During the more glorious days of conspicuous success, they solicited a recognition of their responsibility for events."

The belief that certain individuals are powerful is also based on observing their interactions. Individuals who have formal status, who talk a lot, who belong to many committees, and who feel close to the action are more likely to be perceived as having power. But there may be little relation between those characteristics and the ability to get what one wants. The relation may even be negative. Those who are dissatisfied may plunge into all sorts of activities in an attempt to change things, yet have no impact (Enerud, 1976).

Individuals are often viewed as powerful because they happen to be in the right place at the right time. Cohen and March (1974, p. 198) conclude: "This is likely to lead to popular impressions of strong presidents during good times and weak presidents during bad times. Persons who are primarily exposed to the symbolic presidency (for example, outsiders) will tend to exaggerate the power of the presidency. Those people who have tried to accomplish something in the institution with presidential support (for example, educational reforms) will tend to underestimate presidential power or presidential will." Edelman (1977, p. 73) makes a similar point:

> *Leadership* is traditionally seen as a set of traits or behaviors which contribute substantially to organizational success or failure. In this view when the profit margin rises, the president of the company gets a raise; when the profit margin dips, we select a new president. Even major league baseball is subject to myths of leadership. By changing pitchers there is an assumption that a hitting streak can be short-circuited. By changing man-

agers, a losing streak can be offset. Leaders lead, followers follow, and organizations prosper. While this logic is pervasive, it is somewhat misleading. Marching one step ahead of a crowd moving in a particular direction may define realistically the connection between leadership and followership. Successful leadership is having followers who believe in the leader. By believing, people are encouraged to link positive events with leadership behaviors. George Gallup once remarked: "People tend to judge a man by his goals, by what he is trying to do, and not necessarily by what he accomplishes or how well he succeeds."

Effective leaders are probably singled out by style, an ability to cope, well-publicized actions on noncontroversial topics, and dramatic performances that emphasize the traits popularly linked to leadership, such as forcefulness, responsibility, courage, and decency. The assumption that leaders can make a real difference is reassuring but often fallacious. Cohen and March (1974, p. 203) compare the college president to the driver of a skidding automobile: "The marginal judgments he makes, his skill, and his luck will probably make some difference to the life prospects of his riders. As a result, his responsibilities are heavy. But whether he is convicted of manslaughter or receives a medal for heroism is largely outside his control."

Leaders make a difference not so much in what they do as in how they appear. If leaders make a difference in a more proactive sense, they may do so by constructing new myths that alter the beliefs of the relevant audience.

Administrative processes are often of more importance for the appearances they convey than for the substance they produce. Appearances are essential for internal meaning and for continued legitimacy and support from external constituencies. The same logic applies to technical processes. Lectures can be viewed as rituals that signify the conveying of knowledge from professors to students. Medical procedures and treatment encourage the belief and expectation that things will get better. They often do, if for no other reason than the hope such procedures have generated. Case writeups and social work visits reduce societal guilt by demonstrating that something concrete is being done to help the poor.

Three Cases Through the Looking-Glass

For each of the frames, we analyzed the same three cases —Helen Demarco, the marital conflict, and the newspaper with the new technology. In each analysis, different questions were posed, new problems framed, and novel strategies suggested or implied. In this final examination of the same three situations, we relax assumptions of rationality and probe the less obvious symbolic dimensions of the three cases.

For Paul Osborne, as the new chief executive of a large organization, the problem was intuitively clear—the organization had become increasingly rigid and inefficient, the financial picture was deteriorating, and new vitality was needed to regain the confidence of major constituents. Under those conditions, the announcement of a bold new plan by the leader conveys hope and optimism to outsiders—a signal that things will be different and, hence, better. But the drama looked very different to insiders. To them the symbol of hope looked more like a Greek tragedy.

Their defense was to fight ritual with ritual. They convened a planning ceremony to study the Osborne plan. Within their ritual, magic numbers and arcane incantations enabled the chickens to outwit the fox (unless the fox was even more cunning than they realized). In any event, the confidence of outsiders probably increased. The technical specialists showed creativity and vitality by coopting rather than overtly fighting the Osborne plan. The new drama altered the identity and the image of the agency—communicating to the outside world signs of new energy and creativity. Paul Osborne's plan may have strengthened the organization both internally and externally. Even though the plan was never implemented as intended, the activity around it might have rejuvenated the organization. Stories of Paul Osborne's success and the manager's technical ingenuity might be told for years to come.

Happy marriages, like productive companies, need strong, symbolic bonds. Those bonds are forged in the mating ritual and celebrated in the marriage ceremony. But they are often weakened by time and the stresses of daily living. The meaning of the marriage is lost in the struggle with old bills and the new house. Stories of the wedding day become repetitious and boring. Old symbols lose their meaning, and old resentments (about former flames or current flirtations) build.

For our married couple, all the above were true. When the wife said, "This marriage is unfair!," she meant, "This relationship has lost its meaning." The ensuing examination of tasks was a revitalization ritual. The ritual realigned roles and redistributed power, but it also provided an opportunity to renew the bonds of marriage. The ritual allowed resentment to be aired, the story of the marriage to be retold, and old symbols to be recalled and renewed. Symbolically, change in the structure of the marriage or the balance of power was less important than renewal and transformation of the couple's symbols. Ten years later, both partners still recount the event to friends. It has become an important benchmark in their marriage and a constant reminder of the need for rituals to sustain symbolic bonds.

The newspaper seemed to be headed for the newsroom equivalent of a shootout. The publisher was extremely frustrated—almost beside himself. He had spent substantial time, energy, and money trying to get reporters to make efficient use of a more efficient system. Training, restructuring, and threats had all failed. By chance, an organization consultant suggested that the root cause of the problem might be symbolic—a reaction to the threat of losing meaning that was invested in old rituals. The consultant conducted a few interviews and observations to check out his hunch. His report to the publisher was brief: "Two questions. Can we have a beer bust for the newsroom two weeks from Friday? And is there anyplace around here that bronzes baby shoes?"

At the Friday beer party, the consultant entered bearing a bronzed Remington typewriter—the symbol of a reporter's art and a key ingredient in the ritual of preparing a story. In appropriate symbolic fashion, he presented it to one of the old hands on the paper, the informal priest of the newsroom. The veteran reporter placed the bronzed Remington on the computer console. In subsequent weeks, the typewriter passed from reporter to reporter. Efficiency improved dramatically. Stories had taken twice as long under the new system because the reporters were secretly typing every story twice—once on their Remingtons and a second time on the new computer system. The old rituals had provided meaning. When they were replaced, they had to be mourned and buried before the new could become part of the culture. The consultant provided the appropriate funeral and resurrection.

Summary

Conventional organizational thought presumes a world in which the connection between structure and activity, activity and outcomes, or events and results is linear and rational. The model can be depicted:

$$\text{Activity} \longrightarrow \text{Outcome}$$

In this view, activities produce desired outcomes, structures coordinate activities, and meetings make decisions. The symbolic frame introduces two variations on this model. The first is that the arrow may be drawn the other way:

$$\text{Activity} \longleftarrow \text{Outcome}$$

In this model, outcomes select activities, meetings attract decisions, and individuals struggle to get attached to the right events. More important, the symbolic frame sees structures, activities, and events as myths, rituals, and ceremonies that foster beliefs, build faith, and create and reinforce meaning. These, in turn, can mediate expectations for outcomes, encourage percep-

tions of connections between activities and outcomes, or actually produce effects. The model can be depicted:

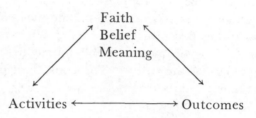

$$\text{Activity} \longrightarrow \begin{array}{c} \text{Faith} \\ \text{Belief} \\ \text{Meaning} \end{array} \longrightarrow \text{Outcome}$$

If we assemble all the possibilities, organizational life
looks like this:

Faith
Belief
Meaning

Activities ⟵——————⟶ Outcomes

Activities can produce outcomes, but outcomes can attract or
select activities. Activities can encourage beliefs. Faith can illu-
minate or interpret outcomes. Outcomes can create or reinforce
beliefs. It is a complicated model of organizations, but it helps to
make chaos comprehensible. It also encourages humility in all
of us who seek to understand, manage, or change organizations.

In a world of chaos, ambiguity, and uncertainty, individuals search for order, predictability, and meaning. Rather than
admit that the ambiguity may not be resolvable and the uncertainty may not be reducible, individuals and societies create
symbolic solutions. Organizational structure and processes then
serve as myths, rituals, and ceremonies that promote cohesion
inside organizations and bond organizations to their environment.

The symbolic frame introduces and elaborates concepts
that have rarely been applied to organizations. Those concepts
sharply redefine organizational dynamics and have significant
implications for managing and changing. In conventional views,
the major questions have been instrumental. We see problems,
develop and implement solutions, and ask, "What did we accomplish?" Often, the answer is "Nothing" or "Not much." We

are often led back to the old expression that the more things change, the more they remain the same. Such a message is disheartening and disillusioning. It often produces a sense of helplessness and a belief that things will never improve significantly.

The symbolic frame sounds a more hopeful note. For a variety of reasons, we try to make things better. It may be that we are restless, or frustrated, or searching for renewed faith in institutions. We engage in a popular ceremony called "change." At the end of the pageant, we can ask three questions:

1. What was expressed?
2. What was attracted?
3. What was legitimized?

The answers are often enormously uplifting. The drama often plays out contradictions and allows us to see a resolution. Old problems, new blood, borrowed expertise, and vital issues are attracted into the arena of change to collide and ferment into new myths and beliefs. Change becomes exciting, uplifting, and vital. The message is heartening and spiritually invigorating. There is always hope. The world is always different. Each day is potentially more exciting and full of meaning than the last. If not, change the symbols, revise the drama, develop new myths, or dance.

11

Classic Tensions: Structure Versus People

Organizational behavior is a young science that studies a complex set of artful phenomena. Humans lived in close contact with the natural world for many centuries before they developed more than a rudimentary science about it. It is easy to imagine that we must understand organizations, since we create them and spend so much time in them. The reality is that human organizations are as complex as anything that scientists have studied. The rise of such organizations is mostly a recent phenomenon, and we know relatively little about them. Even some of the things we are most sure of may turn out to be assumptions of the "flat world" variety.

One would not always sense such humility from reading the existing theory and research. Organization theorists have often written as if they possessed the one truth, which, regrettably, must compete with a variety of pretenders. The field of organizational behavior has long been split into several major intellectual camps. Within each camp, campers share a similar view of the world, study similar problems, use similar methods, and cite one another's accomplishments. Across camps, interchange is limited and mostly combative.

We have grouped the intellectual camps into four major territories, each with its own set of assumptions and approaches, and have called the ideologies of these territories "frames." We believe that each of the four frames represents a significant window on organizations that can be helpful to anyone who tries to cope with the everyday complexity and challenge of organizational life. In this chapter and the next, we go behind the frames to the theory and research on which they are based. We will, in effect, be discussing each of the major subcultures within the larger culture of organization theory. We will identify the main conceptual focus of each perspective, its implications for organizational practice, and its relation to other traditions in the field. For each perspective, we will discuss some of the "classics"—the prototypical examples of theory and research that have been most helpful for us and influential in the field.

Rational Systems Perspectives

The "structural frame" is built on a broader tradition in the field of organizational research to which Gouldner first applied the term *rational systems* in 1959. The rational systems perspective has grown and developed since that time. As we define it, it includes three major conceptual strands:

1. Theories that place particular emphasis on information processing and decision making (for example, Simon, 1947; March and Simon, 1958).
2. Theories that focus primarily on organizational structure (for example, Blau and Scott, 1962; Perrow, 1970, 1972).
3. Theories that focus on the impact of technology and environment on organizational structure and design (for example, Woodward, 1970; Lawrence and Lorsch, 1967).

These three strands are different from one another, but they share a common foundation. That foundation is more or less explicit in different theories but includes the following propositions: (1) Organizations are created and continue to exist in order to achieve (more or less specific) goals. (2) Organizational structure and process are determined mainly by the organization's goals, technology, and environment. (The theories are based on what might be called "telological and technological determinism"). (3) Even though behavior in organizations is not always rational, much of it is governed by "norms of rationality" and is intendedly rational. (4) Goals, tasks, technologies, and structures are the primary determinants of organizational behavior; the needs, capacities, emotions, and self-interests of individuals or groups are less significant.

Decision-Making Theories

The decision-making perspective is represented particularly in the work of Herbert Simon (1957, 1960, 1969) and others of the "Carnegie Tech" school (for example, March and Simon, 1958; Cyert and March, 1963). Simon was the first (and, so far, the only) organization theorist to receive a Nobel Prize, and his contribution to the field is so broad that any attempt at a brief summary will oversimplify. We will discuss several of his most important ideas to illustrate his contribution to the rational systems perspective.

Simon's first major work, *Administrative Behavior,* has as one of its central tenets the proposition that "administrative theory is peculiarly the theory of intended and bounded rationality—of the behavior of human beings who satisfice because they have not the wits to maximize" (1957, p. xxiv). The central preoccupation of the book is the way organizational arrangements and managerial processes control the "premises" on which individuals make decisions.

In *New Science of Management Decisions* (1960), Simon focuses on the distinction between programmed and unprogrammed decisions and on the impact of new information-processing technologies. Organizations face two major classes of problems: routine, repetitive decisions that can be programmed and nonroutine decisions that require human inventiveness. His argument provides an important conceptual underpinning for later research on the relation between task and organizational structure.

In *The Sciences of the Artificial* (1969), Simon offers the argument that humans (at least the "thinking" humans who are prominent in his view of organizations) are relatively simple. It is the environment that makes them complex. He extends that argument (based on limits in human memory and information-processing capacities) into a persuasive exposition of the need for hierarchy in organizations.

Structural Theories

In sociology, "organization theory" has usually meant analysis of the structure of "bureaucracy" or "formal organization" within the context of an intellectual view that traces its origins primarily to the work of Max Weber. Weber (1947) developed a theory of bureaucracy as an ideal type. Bureaucracy was a relatively new organizational form, and Weber saw it as having significant advantages in rationality over previous organizational forms (such as patriarchal organizations). Bureaucracy, as Weber described it, was created to achieve specific, purposive activities. In order to do that, it evolved a number of structural characteristics (rules and regulations, allocation of tasks to offices, hierarchy of authority, selection of officials on the basis of merit, and so forth) that promote rationality.

The structural tradition has generally accepted the basic premise that organizations are purposive, intendedly rational systems. Given such a premise, research and theory have centered on the study of the structural characteristics of organizations, their interrelations, and their relations to other organizational variables.

One outgrowth of the Weberian view is research on the degree to which organizations approximate the Weberian ideal type. Depending on how and where the research was done, studies have reported that there are or there are not substantial consistencies in organizational patterns. Hall (1963) found that organizations vary in their degree of bureaucratization and that different dimensions of the Weberian model are not strongly correlated. Udy (1962) used the Human Relations Area File to study the structural characteristics of work in nonindustrial societies and concluded that there was considerable consistency in the relations among the structural variables that he used (for example, central management, compensatory rewards, task specialization).

The trend in structural research has been to move beyond the specific characteristics of the Weberian pure type and to focus on the relations among a variety of structural features. As one example, Pugh, Hickson, and Hinings (1969) and Pugh and others (1968) collected data on sixty-four structural variables from fifty-two English organizations. Using factor analysis, they identified four "basic dimensions of structure": structuring of activities, concentration of authority, line control of workflow, and size of supportive component.

Another substantial body of structural research focuses on the relation between structure and other organizational variables. Blankenship and Miles (1968) studied the relation between structural features (for example, span of control, organization size, hierarchal position) and managers' approach to decision making. Meyer (1968) studied the relation between formal structure and centralization of decision making. Engel (1970) studied the relation between bureaucratization and professional autonomy, concluding that professionals in moderately bureaucratic settings felt more autonomy than those in high- or low-bureaucracy settings.

Another major strand in structural theory and research has focused on the relation between goals and structure in organizations. The approach has often been a comparative one in which a typology of organizational goals is linked to differences in organizational structure. Parsons (1960) distinguished organizational goals in terms of the societal sector to which an organization contributed. Blau and Scott (1962) used the related question "Who benefits?" to develop a fourfold typology: mutual-benefit associations, business concerns, service organizations, and commonweal organizations. Blau and Scott theorized that each type has a central problem; for example, mutual-benefit organizations have the problem of maintaining internal democracy, while business firms focus on maximizing efficiency (1962, pp. 42-43). Etzioni (1961) distinguished three types of organizational goals: economic (for example, businesses), control (for example, prisons), and cultural (for example, schools). He suggested that organizations will be more effective when their basis for obtaining member compliance is consistent with their goal. The theory suggests that schools should rely on normative controls, while prisons will be more effective with coercive ones.

Such taxonomies have been criticized on a number of grounds: the use of only a single variable for classification, failure to take account of variation *within* organizations, and oversimplified conceptions of organizational goals (Hall, Haas, and Johnson, 1967; Pinder and Moore, 1979). Pinder and Moore's (1979) effort to develop a more sophisticated structural taxonomy based on "the characteristic managerial behaviors employed by the organization to sustain its existence and be effective" retains the basic premises of a rational systems view of organizations.

Environment, Technology, and Structure

The third strand within the rational systems perspective is represented by work on environmental and technological determinants of organizational structure and processes. Variations in task and environment played little role in organizational research until the 1960s. At that time, work began to appear that focused on environmental contingencies.

Burns and Stalker (1961) distinguished between mechanistic and organic organizational forms and suggested that the latter are more appropriate for nonroutine, creative tasks. Woodward (1970) distinguished "small batch," "large batch" or "mass," and "continuous" production technologies and found that differences in technology were related to differences in structure. Lawrence and Lorsch (1967) focused on the relation between environmental uncertainty and internal organizational arrangements. In an argument paralleling Burns and Stalker's, they suggested that high levels of uncertainty in the task environment require more "organic" management systems. They also discussed the importance of internal variation within organizations. Their differentiation/integration hypothesis said that subunits facing different environments need to have different structures but that greater differentiation among subunits adds to problems of coordination. Thompson (1967) developed a series of propositions built particularly on the notion that organizations operating under "norms of rationality" will seek ways to minimize uncertainty and environmental dependence.

Achievements and Limitations of the Rational Systems Perspective

Although there are significant differences among the strands in the rational systems perspective, all of them share a common set of premises. They assume that organizations exist mostly to achieve goals. They usually assume that the goals are set by legitimate authorities, who then differentiate tasks, arrange for coordination of different roles and subunits, and manage the overall effectiveness of the organization. Rational theorists are often very interested in how structures are controlled by goal, task, and technology and how individual behavior is constrained by the demands of organization.

Rational theorists generally acknowledge that organizations are composed of people with wants, needs, capacities, feelings, and so forth. But "personality" (as well as motive, emotion, interpersonal behavior, and the like) is usually treated as relatively unimportant, and the impact of organizations on people, or people on organizations, is treated superficially or not at all. Simon speaks of personality as a "truly magical slogan to charm away the problems that our intellectual tools don't handle" (1957, p. xv). His work focuses very much on how organizations are influenced by limits on human information processing but pays little attention to the meaning of organization in individuals' lives.

Perrow (1972, p. 143) states flatly that "one cannot explain organizations by explaining the attitudes and behavior of the individuals and small groups within them." Thompson

(1967) includes a chapter on the "variable human," but a major point of the chapter is that humans are not all that variable because "the social system provides them with a rather consistent set of aspirations, beliefs about causation, and standards" (p. 115).

Rational systems theorists acknowledge that conflict exists in organizations: Differentiation leads to differences in information, perception, and goals, and those differences lead to conflict. But the perspective emphasizes social control—how does organization channel and bound conflict processes so as to minimize their disruptive consequences? Structuralists tend to emphasize the role of authority and coordinating mechanisms in managing conflict. Lawrence and Lorsch (partly because their theory includes elements from a human resource view) emphasize the need for "problem-solving" approaches to conflict resolution. Rational systems theorists rarely focus on the strategic and tactical aspects of conflict and rarely view conflict from the perspective of partisans as opposed to authorities (Gamson, 1968).

The rational systems perspective has made a number of contributions to our understanding of organizations. No other body of research has contributed so much to our understanding of the relations among organizational goals, organizational tasks and technologies, and organizational structures. No other perspective has provided so much insight into the origins of and constraints on "rational" behavior in organizations. No other perspective has placed so much emphasis on comparative analysis of organizations.

At the same time, the frame has largely ignored the impact of organizations on people and the question of how to make organizations better places for people to live and work. Rational systems theorists have acknowledged the existence of conflict and incompatible goals in organizations but have paid little attention to political processes. Rational systems theorists have focused extensively on the nature and impact of authority but have paid little attention to other forms of power. They have recognized that uncertainty is a critical variable in organizations, but they have usually focused on how uncertainty is managed under conditions of bounded rationality (for example, "problemistic search," "insulation of core technology from environmental influence"). They have rarely noted that uncertainty creates problems of meaning, which may be addressed through symbolic rather than rational solutions.

In addition to asking about the conceptual contributions of rational systems theorists, we can ask about their empirical contributions. How well have the theories been confirmed through empirical investigation? The question is more easily asked than answered. Short of attempting a massive survey of existing literature, we can make a few brief and impressionistic observations. The decision-making school of Simon and others has made a contribution that is more conceptual than empirical. Simon has done empirical work (mostly unstructured observation of decision-making processes either in the laboratory or in the real world), but he is much better known for his ideas than for his data.

Structuralists, however, have contributed a massive amount of data. What is difficult is to assess what it adds up to. Structuralists have used a variety of research methods, but most of the major attempts to test structural propositions have been based either on questionnaire data or on secondary analyses of existing data (for example, economic and census data collected by organizations' internal information systems).

Three major problems complicate the assessment of that body of evidence. One is the problem of the validity of measures. Questionnaires rely on organizational self-reports that are subject to a variety of sources of error. For example, Beyer and Trice (1979) measured "formalization" by asking supervisors to specify what percentage of employees in their unit worked from written rules and how specific those rules were. Supervisors may not know the percentage who work from rules, and even if they do, they might provide distorted data. A supervisor who equates written rules with clear organization might give a different response than one who sees such rules as a symptom of bureaucratic rigidity. Questionnaires can produce very powerful results in the hands of sophisticated researchers who use a variety of techniques to cross-check their results, but such sophistication is more the exception than the rule.

Use of existing data often reduces the likelihood of self-report errors but creates a different problem: a tenuous linkage between theory and measure. Brown and Schneck (1979) used "clerical personnel as a percentage of all administrative staff" as an operational measure of bureaucratization. The logic is that more clerical personnel suggests more filing and processing of information, more rules, and so on. However, the percentage of clerical personnel might also be an index of organizational slack or the complexity of organizational task, neither of which is the same thing as bureaucratization. Such operational definitions can lead to empirical work in which the statistical results may be clear enough, but their meaning is shrouded in ambiguity.

The theory/data-linkage problems are compounded by the pattern of results in much of the structural research. Many studies have never been replicated. Attempts at replication often produce results at variance with the earlier studies. For example, Beyer and Trice (1979) attempted to replicate the study by Blau and Schoenherr (1971); they found more differences than similarities. A similar pattern emerged in Child's (1972) attempt to replicate the work of Pugh, Hickson, and Hinings (1969). In some cases, Child's results were almost identical to those of the earlier study (for example, both found a correlation of .87 between "functional specialization" and "role specialization"), but there were marked differences in others. Child found a correlation of .30 between percentage of clericals and "overall standardization," whereas Pugh and associates had reported a correlation of −.23. Such divergent results are a potent spur to post hoc theorizing but make it difficult to construct an inventory of structural propositions that are consistently supported by empirical data.

There have also been problems in the application of the rational system to practice. A significant emphasis of the frame has been on constraint. Much of the theory tells us what is *not* possible rather than what *is* possible. Rational systems theorists, with some individual differences, tend to articulate a conservative message: There are good reasons for organizations to be the way they are, and there is limited room for creating organizations that are significantly different. Gouldner made this point twenty-nine years ago: "Wrapping themselves in the shrouds of nineteenth-century political economy, some social scientists appear bent on resurrecting a dismal science. Instead of telling man how bureaucracy might be mitigated, they insist that it is inevitable. Instead of explaining how democratic patterns may, to some extent, be fortified and extended, they warn us that democracy cannot be perfect. Instead of controlling the disease, they suggest that we are deluded, or, more politely, incurably romantic, for hoping to control it. Instead of assuming more responsibilities as realistic clinicians, striving to further democratic potentialities wherever they can, many social scientists have become morticians, all too eager to bury men's hopes" (1955, p. 507).

The rational frame has little to say about the relationship of the individual to the organization, a topic of great importance to people who spend an important part of their lives in organizational settings. Whether the question is how to design jobs that fit employees' needs or how individuals can best cope with the politics of surviving and getting ahead, rational systems theorists are largely silent.

There are two primary domains in which the theories have their most specific implications for action. One has to do with the emphasis on organizational rather than individual variables in diagnosing and solving organizational problems. Simon's emphasis on the control of "decision premises" and the structuralists' emphasis on the ways that structure constrains individual behavior lead in the same direction: When an organization is malfunctioning, look to the organizational arrangements rather than to the individuals in searching for a solution. If there is dissatisfaction with the leadership in the organization, the structural frame suggests to look not to the personality and leadership style of the top manager but to the structural relationships between the executive and others in and outside the organization.

A second major application of rational systems theory is in organizational design. Design is still one of the least understood areas in organization theory, but what is known about it stems largely from the rational systems perspective. Galbraith's (1973) and Mintzberg's (1979) work on design draws heavily from all three strands in the rational systems perspective, and much of the existing literature on design draws primarily from scholars within that perspective.

Human Resource Perspectives

Rational systems theorists have focused on how organizations arrange and manage themselves in order to get on with the business of achieving their goals. Human resource theorists focus particularly on the relationship between the individual and the organization—on the way individuals can facilitate or impede organizational effectiveness and the way organizations can create or block human meaning and satisfaction. Human needs, emotions, and abilities rarely play a prominent part in rational systems theories, but they are central to human resource theories.

The human resource perspective is the dominant motif in six related research strands:

1. Person/organization theories that focus on the relationship between people and organizations (for example, Argyris, 1957; McGregor, 1960; Likert, 1967; Herzberg, 1966).
2. Social psychological perspectives that focus on the individual in groups and organizations. Topics include motivation and attitudes (for example, Vroom, 1964; Porter and Lawler, 1968), leadership (for example, Vroom and Yetton, 1973; Fiedler, 1967), and small groups (for example, Collins and Guetzkow, 1964; Hackman and Morris, 1974).
3. Organization development literature that focuses on strategies and technologies for improving human and technical processes in organizations (for example, Schein, 1969; Argyris, 1970; Bennis, 1966; Beckhard, 1969; French and Bell, 1978).
4. Literature on participation and organizational democracy that deals with alterations in organizational power relations (for example, Leitch, 1919; Coch and French, 1948; Marrow, Bowers, and Seashore, 1967; Blumberg, 1969; Jenkins, 1973).

5. Sociotechnical theories that study the interdependence be-
    tween social and technical processes in work settings (for
    example, Trist and Bamforth, 1951; Rice, 1958; Whyte,
    1969).
6. Research on careers and career paths in organizations (for
    example, Hall, 1976; Van Maanen, 1977; Schein, 1978).

All the research strands share a world view, more explicitly in some theories than others, that includes the following
propositions:

1. Organizations exist ultimately to serve human needs rather
    than vice versa.
2. Because organizations are critically dependent on their abil-
    ity to make effective use of human energies and talents, hu-
    mans have a critical impact on organizational processes and
    outcomes.
3. Similarly, humans are critically dependent on organizations
    for many of the most important satisfactions and meanings
    in their lives (because organizations are so large and control
    so many important resources and because work plays such
    a significant role in human lives).
4. When human and organizational needs are poorly synchro-
    nized, one or both will suffer: The organization will be inef-
    fective, or the humans will be exploited, or both. Conversely,
    when human and organizational needs are well synchro-
    nized, both benefit: The organization achieves its goals
    effectively, while humans derive rewards and meaning from
    their participation.

Personality and Organization

Voltaire, Rousseau, Karl Marx, Thorstein Veblen, and
Mary Parker Follett are among many writers of the last three
centuries who have offered perspectives on dislocation between
individual and organization. A group of modern theorists has
taken up the same theme in studying the meaning of work for
the individual. Argyris (1957, 1964) has developed a hypothesis

about the relation between personality and organization that has the following basic postulates: (1) Individual mental health and available "psychological energy" are positively related to the degree of psychological success a person has experienced. (2) Individuals experience psychological success when they are able to define their own goals, determine how to achieve their goals, and evaluate their own effectiveness. (3) On average, opportunities for psychological success lessen as one moves down the hierarchy in formal organizations, as leadership becomes more directive, as management controls increase, and as human relations programs proliferate. (4) The more individuals' aspirations for psychological success are blocked by the conditions of their work, the more they will experience failure, frustration, short time perspective, and internal conflict. Adaptive behaviors will result that include absenteeism, turnover, psychological withdrawal and alienation, "goldbricking," and other reactions that impede organizational effectiveness.

A corollary of the fourth proposition is that the same adaptive activities will occur "if the individual does not desire to experience psychological success and the organization requires an individual to do so" (Argyris, 1964, p. 67). Argyris focuses on the fit between the needs of individuals and the conditions that are created by organizations. Similar theories have been presented by McGregor (1960), Likert (1961, 1967), and Herzberg (1966). Each of the theories contains propositions that relate certain (presumed) characteristics of individuals to certain properties of organizations.

Social Psychological Perspectives

Social psychological theories of organization focus less on the organization than on the individual and the small group within the organization. Topics of particular prominence have included attitudes and motivation, leadership, and group dynamics. Early research in each area was often based on relatively simple and global hypotheses. Gradually, researchers were forced by the empirical evidence to seek more complex explanations for their findings.

A classic example is a long line of research on the relation between satisfaction and productivity. Many researchers attempted to find evidence to support the common-sense proposition that the happy worker is a more productive worker. Vroom (1964) summarized the research on satisfaction and productivity and showed that, on average, there was no relation between the two. He argued persuasively that the relation between satisfaction and productivity depended on what needs were being satisfied, how, and in what context.

Similarly, dozens of studies of leadership tried to isolate the characteristics of a "good" leader. Stogdill's (1974) exhaustive review of this literature shows that the traits of a good leader are surprisingly elusive and that the research shows a complex pattern of interaction between leader and situation.

Small-group research emphasizes the critical role that the group occupies in the relationship between individual and organization. Small groups influence how well individuals perform, how well their needs are met, and how they view their work and the organization. Small-group research has focused on questions like the following:

- Do individuals or groups do better in solving problems and making decisions? (The research shows that it depends on the group and the task.)
- How much influence do groups have on their members? (The influence is often very powerful, but it varies with individuals and groups.)
- Are groups more conservative or more risk-prone than individuals? (Groups are not consistently more conservative or risk taking than individuals, contrary to one common-sense hypothesis. On many tasks, groups consistently make riskier decisions; on others, the reverse is true.)

Organization Development

Organization development, commonly known as OD, is mostly a recent phenomenon. Fifteen years ago there were few managers or organization theorists who had even heard of OD.

Today, at least in North America, there are few who have not. Excellent reviews of the OD literature include Friedlander and Brown (1974) and Alderfer (1977b).

In the United States, OD traces its origins primarily to two related developments in the era following World War II (French and Bell, 1978, chap. 3): (1) the group dynamics efforts inspired by Kurt Lewin that spawned the National Training Laboratories and "laboratory human relations," or "sensitivity," training and (2) the work of the Survey Research Center at the University of Michigan on the use of survey instruments to measure significant human variables in organizations (for example, motivation, communication, leadership styles, climate). Current theory and practice in OD reflect both elements of its parentage. The sensitivity training movement began with an emphasis on experiential learning, small groups as a vehicle for change, and interpersonal openness (Bradford, Gibb, and Benne, 1964). The initial flowering of T-groups in organizations has long since abated, but many of the techniques and values have been transformed into a variety of OD strategies, such as team building, confrontation meetings, intergroup laboratories, grid OD, and process consultation.

When survey research is used as an OD technology, participants in an organization are surveyed for their perceptions of such issues as leadership, organizational climate, decision making, and task effectiveness. The results are tabulated for organizational units, and consultants lead discussions within each unit of the implications of the survey data.

Participation and Organizational Democracy

"Participation" and "organizational democracy" are two forms of efforts to alter traditional, top-down power relations in organizations by giving lower-level participants more influence in decision making. The idea of industrial democracy is an old one. During and after World War I, Leitch (1919) developed an argument for representative democracy in the workplace built along the lines of the United States Constitution. The idea had little impact in an era of Red scares and violent labor/management conflict, but twenty-five years later the idea of "participation" and "participative management" began to attract a following.

Participation, in the United States, has usually referred to changes in managerial practice but not in managerial authority. *Organizational democracy,* in contrast, implies genuine shifts in formal or legal authority for decision making from higher to lower levels of organizations. Reviews of the literature on participation and organizational democracy appear in Blumberg (1969), Jenkins (1973), Katzell and Yankelovich (1975), Katz and Kahn (1978), and Dachler and Wilpert (1978).

The concept of participation was central to a series of studies that contrasted directive and participative methods for introducing changes in work procedures. In directive methods, managers made decisions and announced them to workers. In participative methods, work groups discussed proposed changes and participated in deciding what changes should be made. The results, though not entirely consistent from study to study, usually suggested that resistance was lower and morale was higher under participative approaches.

Organizational democracy has not been a popular concept in the United States or Great Britain but has been tried in varying forms in several European nations. One example is the Yugoslav system of "self-management." In virtually all Yugoslav work organizations, formal power over policy and personnel (roughly equivalent to that of a corporate board of directors) is vested in an elected workers' council. Other experiments with various forms of work democracy have taken place in Norway and Sweden and in Israeli kibbutz work organizations.

Participation has been criticized on two major grounds: that it is ineffective and that it serves mainly as a way for managers to manipulate workers. The first criticism is usually based on the argument that the usefulness of participative methods is heavily dependent on contextual factors (such as workflow, technology, and environment) often ignored in the literature on participation. The second criticism is based on the belief that participation is often a gimmick for giving workers the feeling that they are participating when they have no more power than ever. Many proponents of the latter criticism argue that real changes in power relations can come only with redistribution of formal power.

Conversely, some critics of work democracy have argued that legal redistribution of authority may make little real difference in worker control over the workplace. Particularly in large enterprises, the ability to elect members of a workers' council may make little real difference on the shop floor.

Participation and organizational democracy both concern changes in power relations, but they emphasize different forms of power. To the extent that organization theorists seriously believe that authority is one among several important forms of power in organizations, both can be viewed as significant interventions in work patterns.

Sociotechnical Systems

The sociotechnical concept has focused on the fit between technical and social systems. The classic study by Trist and Bamforth (1951) in coal mining and Rice's (1958) study of organization in a weaving plant both focused on altering technical arrangements so as to produce a better fit with the social patterns and expectations of the work force. In both cases, new technologies had produced a disruption of customary social patterns, and changes were introduced to reintegrate social and technical arrangements. In both cases, there was a movement away from more fractionated work arrangements toward arrangements that resulted in work groups with coherent tasks. The sociotechnical approach overlaps with contingency theory, but contingency theorists usually focus mainly on the need for work arrangements that are appropriate to task and technology. The sociotechnical conception emphasizes the importance of technologies appropriate to social patterns in the work force.

Achievements and Limitations of the
Human Resource Frame

The particular contribution of human resource theorists has been to focus on the question of the meaning of organization for the individual and the possibility that organizations can be designed and managed in ways that are more meaningful and satisfying for human beings. The perspective has raised important questions about the status quo: Must organizations be as they have been? Do the limits of environment, task, and human nature constrain us to continually create organizations that produce the same debilitating problems? Human resource theorists have actively sought social inventions that might improve the quality of life in human systems.

The determination to find a better way has also been the source of many limitations in the human resource perspective. Human resource theorists have rarely looked closely at structural constraints. They have often underplayed those constraints rather than face them head on. They have also been prone to a lopsided view of authority, focusing more on its negative than its positive aspects. They have rarely addressed issues of power and scarce resources directly. Organizational politics has been viewed mostly as a problem to be solved, with little examination of the underlying forces that produce political dynamics in organizations. The role of symbols in organizations has received little attention, at least until recently, even though questions of meaning are appropriate as central concerns of human resource theorists.

The human resource literature has generated a substantial body of empirical research. It is safe to assert that the research is extensive, varied, and methodologically uneven. It is more difficult to make a comprehensive statement about the outcomes of the research.

Human resource theorists have used virtually every social science technique ever developed—anecdotes, case studies, surveys, action research, field experiments, and laboratory experiments. Some studies have been impressive for their methodological sophistication; many have not. One of the most impressive achievements of the human resource frame, however, has been the tremendous amount of experimentation it has generated. The list includes participative management, organizational democracy, T-groups, job enrichment, management by objectives, quality of worklife, survey feedback, flextime, and the many varieties of organization development. Many of those experiments have been scientifically careless, and many have failed to achieve the hoped-for benefits. A few have been, on balance, more harmful than helpful. But learning and evolution of theory have resulted. Even though many of the studies are not very reliable in themselves, the cumulative weight of evidence has produced a gradual increase in understanding of some of the important issues.

An illustration is the use of T-groups as a vehicle for organizational improvement. In the halcyon days of the T-group movement, some proponents of the method expected that it would revolutionize life in organizations, while opponents argued that it would do enormous psychic damage. A large body of research shows that both sides were wrong: Both individuals and organizations are highly resilient, and T-groups are not as potent, positively or negatively, as was first believed (Campbell and Dunnette, 1968). Proponents now have a more realistic, limited view of the benefits of the method. Conversely, although psychic damage can happen, it is very rare (Lieberman, Yalom, and Miles, 1973; Bolman, 1977).

More generally, human resource research has gradually undermined many of the more global and simplistic notions about how to improve organizations. It has forced theorists in the direction of more careful, contingent thinking about the relations between organizational problems and human resource remedies.

12

❦❦❦❦❦❦❦❦

Old Realities
Rediscovered:
Politics and Symbols

Political Perspectives

Even in the field of public administration, organizational politics has sometimes been curiously invisible in the scholarly literature. Many traditional works in the field (for example, Lepawsky, 1955; Mercer and Koester, 1978) focus almost entirely on efficiency and engineering aspects of public organizations, as if the concept of politics were a puzzling embarrassment for scholars, who prefer to emphasize rationality in organizations. Human resource theorists recognize that conflict between individual and organization can lead to processes that are organizationally "irrational," but they focus mostly on collaboration and conflict resolution rather than bargaining and power politics. Rational systems and human resource theorists both tend to view organizational conflict as a sign that something is wrong.

Political perspectives view scarce resources and incompatible preferences as a fundamental reality in any organization. Conflict is a central social process, and organizational decisions and goals emerge from a series of bargains and compromises. The existing political literature falls into two major categories: (1) an emerging body of research focusing on political processes in organizations; (2) a neo-Marxian view that emphasizes class stratification and the power exercised by elites.

Organizational Politics

Political perspectives on organizations are tied together by a common set of assumptions such as the following four propositions: (1) Many of the most important decisions in organizations involve the allocation of scarce resources. (2) Organizations are basically coalitions that comprise a number of individuals and groups. (3) Individuals and groups differ in their values, preferences, beliefs, information, and perceptions of reality. Such differences are enduring and difficult to alter. (4) Organizational goals and decisions emerge from an ongoing process of bargaining and negotiation among major "players" and reflect the relative power that each of the players is able to mobilize.

An early example of a political perspective appears in Selznick's (1949) classic study of the Tennessee Valley Authority. The study focused on how the original aims of the TVA were altered, redirected, and sometimes perverted by "the recalcitrance of the tools in use." As Selznick saw it, the effort to achieve the "end in view" is inevitably limited by a variety of commitments that arise in the process. Some commitments are created by the need to maintain the internal system, some by class interest and belief systems of the personnel, some by "centers of interest generated in the course of action," and so on. Such considerations led Selznick, in a subsequent essay on leadership, to paint the following picture of organization: "In exercising control, leadership has a dual task. It must win the consent of constituent units, in order to maximize voluntary cooperation, and therefore must permit emergent interest blocks a wide degree of representation. At the same time, in order to hold the helm, it must see that a balance of power appropriate to the fulfillment of key commitments will be maintained" (1957, pp. 63-64).

A more recent example of a political analysis appears in Baldridge's (1971) study of decision making in New York University. Baldridge focused particularly on policy-formation processes—the decisions that involved major commitments by the institution. He defined the university as a "configuration of social groups with basically different life-styles and political interests" (p. 23). As he saw it, each of those groups wanted to have an impact on the policy process. To do so, the group had to participate in a multistage process. A group needs to articulate its interests, negotiate with other groups to get those interests translated into institutional policy, and influence the process of policy implementation.

Public agencies and universities are not the only organizations that can be viewed as political systems. Pettigrew (1973) applied the same lens to private firms. He argued that the division of labor in organizations inevitably leads to specialized interest groups: "Wherever there is interdependence among subunits, there will be a need for joint decision making, and there will be 'interest-based' demands" (p. 17).

Another example of the political perspective is Pfeffer's (1978) political conception of organizational design. Pfeffer argued that organizational arrangements are the product of a power struggle whose outcome influences subsequent events in an ongoing contest. Design is not a question of "what purpose" but of "whose purpose." Change in the design occurs when "the distribution of roles, information, tasks, and power implied by the structure is significantly out of line with the distribution of power implied by the relative control over critical resources possessed by the various organizational participants" (pp. 225-226).

A political perspective on organizations is rapidly emerging in the field of public administration and in the study of implementation of social policy. Pressman and Wildavsky (1973) and Bardach (1977) both analyze implementation of social pol-

icy as a complex political process in which there is a low probability that what is implemented will bear much resemblance to
the original purpose of the policy.

Landau and Stout (1979) provide a good example of an
emerging trend in the public administration literature to integrate rational and political variables in the study of bureaucratic
decision making. They note that the federal government has
gone through a long list of new management "improvements"
(PPBS, PERT, zero-based budgeting, and so forth), each of
which promised to make decision making more efficient and rational. Landau and Stout argue that there is virtually no evidence that any of the improvements made much difference, but
the lack of success "has not served to diminish either the expected utility or the normative appeal of the concept" (p. 154).
They argue that decision making in public agencies is inevitably
political and that management control systems have been used
primarily for political purposes, regardless of their espoused
goals.

In a similar vein, Clark and Schrode (1979) present an
empirical study of how public administrators make decisions.
They found that decision opportunities were usually triggered
by "disequilibrium," which was usually caused by pressures
transmitted through a variety of personal contacts. The primary
criteria for evaluating the quality of decisions were feasibility,
acceptability, and defensibility. The prototypical administra
tor, in this analysis, makes decisions that are quick, safe, and
within budget.

The political perspective can also be applied to the question of organization/environment relations. A society (or political economy) is a context within which a number of organizations seek to articulate interests and mobilize power. There has
been little direct research on this issue, but McNeil (1978) argues that a neglected side of Weberian theory can be applied to
the analysis of organizational power, with a focus on five central issues: (1) What are the pressures on managerial elites to
seek dominance of the environment? (2) What strategies are
available for mobilizing power? (3) What mechanisms shape the
actual exercise of power? (4) What are the implications of mod-

els of organizational behavior for the dynamics of their political control? (5) What methodologies can appropriately guide research on power? Presumably, many of the same analytic frameworks are applicable at both the intraorganizational and organization/society levels. For example, using Gamson's distinction between partisans and authorities, the managerial elite of a corporation is an authority in relation to subordinates (and presumably is interested mainly in social control) but a partisan in relation to the larger environment (presumably interested in changing or avoiding social controls that are harmful to the interests of its own organization).

Neo-Marxian Perspectives

Neo-Marxian analysts argue that the design of organizations and the internal processes within them reflect class stratification in the larger society. All the major institutions of a society exist primarily to serve and defend the interests of a relatively small, dominant elite. Schools exist to socialize children in the behaviors and values that will be required in capitalist enterprise, such as the work ethic or obedience to rules and authority (Bowles and Gintis, 1976). Under conditions of capitalist control and class stratification, work organizations inevitably produce worker alienation and fundamental conflicts of interest among different strata. Marghlin (1974) argues that the structural features of modern bureaucracies arise not from considerations of efficiency but from power struggles among different economic groups.

Particularly in the United States, Marxian perspectives have not been a significant influence on organization theory. Parenti (1977) argues that Marxian thinking has been "stigmatized or ignored by American intellectuals and those who pay their salaries: Most often, this evasion is accomplished by labeling any approach which links class, wealth, and capitalism to politics as 'Marxist' " (p. 5). Parenti argues that criticisms of bureaucracy for inefficiency and lethargy describe only half the picture. Bureaus, he argues, are splendidly efficient at doing things that have strong support from political elites (such as building highways and developing weapons) and woefully inadequate in accomplishing tasks that benefit only the poor and powerless (such as reducing minority unemployment or improving low-income housing).

Benson (1977) echoes Parenti's lament over the scarcity of Marxian analysis and the tendency of "conventional" organization theory to accept the legitimacy of existing organizational arrangements. Benson argues the need for a dialectical approach to organizations based on four premises: (1) Humans are continually in the process of constructing the social world. (2) Every structure must always be studied as a part of a larger whole. (3) The social order produces contradictions, internal inconsistencies, and incompatibilities, which make radical changes in the existing order a possibility. (4) The principle of "praxis" calls for "free and creative reconstruction of social arrangements on the basis of a reasoned analysis of both the limits and the potentials of present social forms" (p. 5).

Benson severely criticizes what he sees as the prevailing rationalist bias in organization theory, but his critique is directed almost entirely at works within the rational systems tradition. By ignoring other conceptual strands in organization theory, Benson chooses the easiest target.

Ironically, Marxian analysis of organizations is equally rare in the Soviet Union and Eastern Europe. McManus (1978) suggests that current Soviet thinking about organizations emphasizes engineering and systems views. Political conflict within organizations is ignored because, by definition, it cannot exist in a communist society.

Since Marxian analysis of organizations is rare, little empirical evidence exists, and the theory remains relatively undeveloped. But several topics deserve more attention:

1. The interconnection between the organization and the larger political/economic context in which it is embedded.
2. The importance of historical forces and trends; organization theory is too new to have developed much of a historical tradition, but it needs to do so in the future.
3. Critique of existing social institutions. Whereas many or-

ganization theorists have (implicitly) taken for granted the legitimacy of existing social, economic, and organizational arrangements, the Marxian perspective begins by questioning the established order.

Achievements and Limitations
of the Political Perspective

The political perspective points to the central importance of conflict and political processes in organizations. Alinsky (1971) argues that "political realists see the world as it is: an arena of power politics moved primarily by immediate self-interest" (p. 12). Alinsky is saying, in effect, that the political perspective represents *the* truth about organizations.

The political perspective is an important antidote to the antiseptic rationality that sometimes characterizes rational perspective and the naive optimism that is sometimes present in human resource theories. But political perspectives can be guilty of their own parochialism. They can focus so strongly on politics as to underestimate the significance of both rationality and collaboration in organizations. Political perspectives risk excessive cynicism: overstating the inevitability of conflict, understating the possibilities for effective decisions and meaningful work.

Political perspectives provide a powerful critique of the difficulties of improving organizational decision making through rational or human resource approaches. Landau and Stout (1979) show that "rational" management systems often generate more politics than rationality, and Warwick (1975) shows how human resource applications in the State Department prospered only so long as they had political support at the top.

Thus, the political frame results in two major implications for action: (1) those who increase their power and their political sophistication win more battles than they lose; (2) most efforts to make organizations more rational or humane are likely to fail. Such assumptions are apparently popular among the general public, which eagerly buys books on how to get and keep power or how to win through intimidation. But the inevitability of political processes in organizations remains insufficiently explored.

The data base for political perspectives rests primarily in case studies. Such studies have provided a richly textured and lively account of organizational politics in action. But efforts to develop and test contingent theories of political dynamics have hardly begun. Political theorists have made a strong case for the proposition that power and politics cannot be ignored in organization theory, but they have not yet investigated in detail the complex interplay among rationality, human needs, and politics. How, for example, do norms of rationality bound and constrain political maneuvering, and vice versa? Under what conditions does political pursuit of individual and group self-interest lead to organizations that are wasteful and frustrating for everyone? To say simply that "organizations are political" is true but too easy. What is needed is more differentiated propositions about the variables influencing political processes in organizations.

Symbolic Perspectives

A symbol is something that stands for something else—usually something broader or more complex. A commencement ceremony symbolizes the completion of one phase in an individual's life and the beginning of a new one. A gold watch after twenty-five years of service symbolizes the importance of loyalty and the organization's concern for its people. Symbolic approaches to organizations examine such obvious symbols as the commencement ceremony and the gold-watch ritual, but they go deeper to examine pervasive issues of meaning in organizations.

There has been no review of the "symbolic literature" in organizations, and many scholars whose work falls within this tradition probably do not view themselves as exemplars of a definable symbolic approach to organizations. Nevertheless, we believe that there is a body of related approaches that are compatible with the following set of premises about organizations:

1. What is most important about any event is not what happened but the meaning of what happened.
2. Events and meanings are loosely coupled. The same event may have different meanings depending on the interpretive

framework through which it is viewed, and the same meaning can be expressed through a variety of events.

3. Symbols serve three major functions in organizations: (a) *economy* (symbols respond to the human need for economy in information processing), (b) *elaboration* (symbols resolve ambiguity and give meaning to events), and (c) *valuation and prophesy* (symbols suggest how to feel and how to evaluate events and activities; they provide purpose, faith, and positive myth).

4. Many organizational phenomena that appear dysfunctional when viewed in the light of their ostensible purposes are logical and predictable in view of their symbolic functions.

5. The more ambiguous and uncertain an event or activity, the more it will attract symbolic elaboration, valuation, and prophesy.

*Symbols and Economy: Meyer and Rowan's
Analysis of Public Schools*

Humans are finite information processors who cannot attend to all the data they might find important or useful. One important function of symbols is to summarize large bodies of information into a relatively simple, easily assimilated form. If, for example, a university wishes to hire a new faculty member in organizational behavior, the job description will usually specify that candidates must possess a Ph.D. Not everyone with a Ph.D. is qualified, and it is conceivable that there are strong candidates who do not have a Ph.D. But the degree serves as a symbol of attributes like research training, scholarly interests, persistence, academic socialization, and membership in appropriate social networks. The symbol is an economical way for the institution to communicate to potential candidates and to screen out large numbers of probably unqualified ones.

Meyer and Rowan (1978) argue that three symbols are essential in helping a community to feel confident that education is taking place in its public schools. One symbol is *place*: Education is supposed to take place in a setting that looks like a school. The setting normally will have classrooms, a principal's office, a gym, appropriate grounds, and an American flag. A second symbol is *topic*: The school must have a curriculum that includes such things as third-grade mathematics and sixth-grade social studies. Few parents have the time or inclination to inquire very deeply into what is being taught in third-grade mathematics, but most would become disturbed if they were to learn that it was not being taught to third-graders. A third symbol is *ritual classifications*: Students are assigned to grades, mainly on the basis of chronological age, and are taught by teachers who have been appropriately certified. Few parents know or care what qualifications are necessary for state certification, and few have asked for evidence that certification is demonstrably related to teaching skill. Meyer and Rowan argue that in schools it is the ritual classifications, rather than the core technology, that are tightly controlled.

The symbols serve purposes both of economy and of valuation. While they are in place, they are an economical way for the school to communicate and for parents to satisfy themselves that the school is functioning as it should. They also help to sustain a "logic of confidence" and to minimize scrutiny of the educational process. The logic of confidence serves important functions for the school and for the community. It protects the school from too close examination of processes that are ambiguous, uneven, difficult to assess, and equally difficult to defend. It protects the community from anxiety about its schools and from the need to expend the time and effort that would be required for extensive examination of the reality beyond the symbols.

Meyer and Rowan's analysis suggests that a factor in the high mortality rate of alternative public education programs is that they often violate the customary symbols. Such violation ruptures the logic of confidence and produces intense inspection of what the school is actually doing. The alternative program may stand up to scrutiny as well as or better than the traditional one, but the traditional one is spared the necessity of defending itself.

Ambiguity and Elaboration

One proposition of the symbolic perspective is that symbols will be prominent whenever ambiguity and uncertainty are high. An organization that manufactures computers, metal cans, or organic chemicals operates in an environment where cause/effect relations are relatively well understood and it is fairly easy to determine the quantity and quality of output produced for any given period.

Conversely, human service, educational, and many public-sector organizations operate in an environment where ambiguity is much higher. Such organizations usually have ambiguous goals and weak technology. Cause-and-effect relations are ambiguous and often disputed. There is basic disagreement about the priorities that the institution should follow. It is often very difficult for teachers, psychotherapists, social workers, or clergymen to know or to demonstrate that their efforts in any given situation were efficacious.

It follows that symbols should, in general, be more prominent in such organizations, although there can be cases in which a given activity or function is more ambiguous or uncertain for a manufacturing firm. Public schools have high levels of uncertainty and ambiguity in their core instructional processes but usually have little difficulty predicting who their students will be for the next several years. A computer firm may be very sure about the technical processes involved in producing a particular machine but very uncertain about the number of machines it can sell.

Cohen and March's (1974) study of college presidents is one example of a conceptual framework that emphasizes the central role of ambiguity in determining organizational structures and processes in the particular case of higher education. Cohen and March argue that the best metaphor for describing universities is "organized anarchy" and that decision making in universities is inherently ambiguous: "When we look at universities struggling with the problems of reorganization, reform, choice, and survival, we are struck by one consistent theme: decision opportunities are fundamentally ambiguous stimuli. . . . Although organizations often can be viewed as vehicles for solving well-defined problems and as structures within which conflict is resolved through bargaining, they are also sets of procedures through which organizational participants arrive at interpretations of what they are doing and what they have done while they are doing it. From this point of view, an organization is a collection of choices looking for problems, issues and feelings looking for decision situations in which they might be aired, solutions looking for issues to which they might be the answer, and decision makers looking for work" (p. 81).

Cohen and March suggest that university decision making is determined largely by nearly universal conditions of energy scarcity (there are more problems than the participants can attend to), fluid participation (it is difficult to predict who will participate in any given decision), and ambiguity. In such a situation, problems, solutions, and participants each flow somewhat independently of one another. Any choice opportunity becomes a potential "garbage can" in which a particular mixture of problems, solutions, and participants is stirred around. In such a situation, decisions are more often made through flight or oversight than by resolution of the problem. Any decision can become a garbage can, but those that are more ambiguous and symbolically visible (such as "curricular priorities for the next five years" or "the relationship of teaching and research in faculty promotions") are more attractive than those that are relatively concrete (like "review of accounting procedures"). "It is clear that the garbage can process does not do a particularly good job of resolving problems. But it does enable choices to be made and problems to be resolved even when the organization is plagued with goal ambiguity and conflict, with poorly understood problems that wander in and out of the system, with a variable environment, and with decision makers who may have other things on their minds. This is no mean achievement" (p. 19).

Goffman's (1959) dramaturgical analysis of organizational transactions is another example of a theory that focuses on the ways symbols resolve ambiguity and provide meaning. Goffman views social processes as carefully scripted and highly ritualized. So long as participants enact their roles according to the script, "face-work" can take place: Participants avoid situations that produce uncertainty, anxiety, or loss of face for themselves or others. Goffman's distinction between "on-stage" and "back-stage" performances implies that performances are intendedly symbolic. Waiters in a restaurant, for example, go on stage when they enter the public dining room and must play their role accordingly if the drama is to sustain its meaning for all concerned. Because certain performances have acquired consensual, ritualistic meaning, waiters and diners alike avoid unpredictability and discomfort. Mangham (1978) has applied the same dramaturgical metaphor to the analysis of organizational intervention.

Ethnomethodological approaches (Gephart, 1978; Van Maanen, 1979) combine an approach to research that emphasizes observational and anthropological methods with a set of theories about behaviors and meanings. Those theories view meaning as continually in the process of being socially constructed and elaborated. In Gephart's (1978) terms, "Actors must manage appearances and constantly *ad lib* essentially vague social roles in an emergent stream of existential being and awareness" (p. 556). An organization is "a linguistic device and resource constructed during human sense-making activities. We cannot assume therefore, that conceptions of organizations are stable or that all participants share them" (Gephart, 1978, p. 557). A related view is contained in Weick's (1976b, p. 2) definition of an organization as "a body of thought by thinking thinkers" in which management is equivalent to managing myths, images, symbols, and labels.

Valuation and Prophesy

The functions of valuation and prophesy are distinctly symbolic. They go beyond questions of "what is" to questions of "what should be" or "what can be hoped for." Meyer and Rowan's work was cited earlier as an example of a theory that discusses both the summarizing and valuational functions of symbols. Clark (1972) discusses the prophetic function of symbols in his analysis of organizational sagas. Clark defines a saga as a unified set of publicly expressed beliefs that is rooted in history (that is, an organizational story), focuses on the unique accomplishments of the institution, and is held with conviction and emotional attachment by participants.

Clark gives examples of sagas at three private colleges:

Reed, Antioch, and Swarthmore. In each case, the saga began with the arrival of a heroic figure. The hero held a vision of the unique contribution the institution could make and worked zealously to implant the vision in the institution. A saga became strongly rooted when it attracted a number of influential adherents and when it was institutionalized in both the structure and the symbols of the organization.

Once established, a saga serves a prophetic function by linking past, present, and future in an inspirational story that gives participants the sense that they are taking part in a special process that is distinctly different from the mundane or corrupt world outside. For the organization, the saga enlists loyalty and energy that would be difficult to evoke in an institution without a saga. For the individual, the saga lends meaning and purpose to activities that might otherwise seem mundane and directionless. There are potential negative consequences as well. The saga can become so strongly entrenched that it insulates the organization from its environment and can seduce individuals into cultlike submission of their own interests to those of the system.

Achievements and Limitations of Symbolic Perspectives

Of the four major organizational perspectives, the symbolic is the newest, least developed, and least mapped. For these reasons, it is too early to make a definitive evaluation. Very few extensive empirical investigations have used symbolic theories of organization as a conceptual base. It is already clear that investigation of symbolic phenomena is unlikely to employ traditional conceptions of "rigorous" social science research methods. Easily quantified questionnaires and highly structured experimental investigations are ill suited to the subtle shades of meaning and affect that are so critical in symbolic analysis. If symbolic perspectives grow and prosper (as we believe they will), they are likely to bring with them a revival of traditional fieldwork methods from anthropology and sociology and to promote the current interest in qualitative methods and ethnography.

Symbolic perspectives have already made a significant conceptual contribution, and that contribution is likely to grow. They question traditional views that the "substantive" is somehow better or more rational than the "merely" symbolic. They suggest that if we try to drive ritual, ceremony, and myth out of organizations, we may destroy them rather than improve them. Symbolic perspectives ask that we reexamine many organizational phenomena that have traditionally been viewed as dysfunctional or ineffective. Those activities may be very functional in terms of their symbolic or expressive purposes.

No conceptual perspective is completely value-neutral, and symbolic perspectives raise a knotty question about the two faces of symbols. One face is symbol as camouflage and distortion. Symbols can serve dishonest, cynical, or repressive functions. The myth that a certified teacher is a good teacher may protect incompetence and insulate repressive educational institutions from needed change. The other face is symbol as embodiment and expression of meaning. Humans live in a world that is fundamentally ambiguous and uncertain. An earthquake, a fire, or a sudden reversal in the business cycle can destroy even the most careful and thoughtful of lives or institutions. No amount of reason or resources can provide completely satisfactory insurance against uncertainty, anomie, and meaninglessness. We develop rituals that provide order and predictability. We create sagas that reassure us about the worthy past of our institution and myths that give us something to believe in. Both faces of symbol are significant, and both are easy to illustrate in existing organizations. Recognition and exploration of that duality may be one of the most significant contributions that symbolic analysis of organizations can make.

Structural and political views often focus on the immutability of existing organizational structure and processes. Structural views derive the inevitability from goals and technologies, while political views see it as the product of scarcity and interest-group structures. Symbolic views suggest, instead, that the "facts" of the social world are the facts that humans have chosen to construct. That view can become a basis for optimism about the possibilities of organizational change: "We all create worlds. The more we are able to create worlds that are morally cogent and politically viable, the more we are able, as workers and citizens, to manage or to resist" (Brown, 1978, p. 378).

13

Integrating
Organizational Theories

The rational, human resource, political, and symbolic collectively encompass much of the existing theory and research on human organizations. The major exception includes theories that trace their ancestry primarily to two intellectual antecedents: von Bertalanffy's (1949) development of the idea of a "general theory of systems" and Wiener's (1967) conception of cybernetics as the "science of control and communication in animals and machines." Von Bertalanffy's proposal was the development of a general theory of systems that would cut across disciplines and systems so that the theory would be applicable to the cell, the person, the group, and the society. The general systems approach has spawned such efforts as Miller's (1978) attempt to develop a general theory of living systems and Boulding's (1977) admittedly ambitious proposal to develop a "general theory of practically everything." Combining ideas from systems theory and cybernetics leads to a view of organizations that can be represented in the following propositions:

1. A system is a set of interacting and interrelated units.

2. Human organizations are appropriately viewed as open systems: Their boundaries are permeable, and they are continually engaged in importing, transforming, and exporting matter, energy, information, and people.
3. Human organizations are capable of negative entropy: They are able to maintain and to increase their supply of energy and their level of organization.
4. In order to attain negative entropy—that is, to survive and grow, rather than decay and die—an organization must provide tangible and intangible outputs to its environment that enable it to receive the inputs necessary for its survival.
5. Systems are arranged hierarchally, so that every system is a supersystem for systems contained within it and a subsystem for systems containing it.
6. A system is more than the sum of its parts: Its properties emerge from the relations among the parts and from the system's relation to its environment.
7. Organizations tend to maintain steady states—dynamic equilibriums in which diverse forces are approximately balanced. Such steady states have the property of ultrastability: The more pressures the system experiences to disrupt its equilibrium, the more resources it will use to restore it.
8. Open systems, in order to maintain a steady state, need adaptive processes, including feedback loops, that enable the system to sense relevant changes in the internal or external environment and to adjust the system's properties accordingly.

Two closely related versions of systems theory can be distinguished: open-systems theory (for example, Katz and Kahn, 1978) and sociotechnical systems theory (for example, Rice, 1963).

Open-Systems Theory

Katz and Kahn (1966, 1978) have attempted to develop an open-systems framework to analyze the social psychology of organizations. They conceptualize systems as "cycles of events":

A system imports inputs from the environment, transforms them, and exports outputs back to the environment, and the cycle repeats itself. Systems maintain a dynamic equilibrium (steady state) such that the basic "character" of the organization (manifested in recurring cycles of events) is highly stable, even though the organization evolves over time in response to internal or environmental changes. Systems survive to the degree that they can achieve negentropy. A particularly critical aspect of system functioning is information processing. Systems cannot survive in the absence of negative feedback—information that enables them to detect deviations from course. Inevitably, all information inputs undergo a coding process, which filters some information and transforms other information into categories to which the system is attuned.

Katz and Kahn make few efforts to derive predictions from open-systems theory. Their primary direction is to try to encompass existing knowledge of organizations within an open-systems framework. Their success varies. They make effective use of their framework in dealing with topics to which it is well adapted, such as organization/environment relations and communication. For other issues, such as leadership, motivation, and decision making, the open-systems model recedes into the background. The difficulty stems from two sources: On the one hand, much of the existing theory and research is coded in language that is not easily translated into systems concepts. On the other hand, the systems concepts are so general as to lead to few specific predictions about *human* systems, as opposed to open systems generally.

Thompson (1967) presents a theory that views organizations as open systems continually trying to become less so. Thompson assumes that, under "norms of rationality," organizations seek ways to minimize uncertainty, which is the enemy of rational choice. Since uncertainty cannot be eliminated from the environment, he hypothesizes that organizations seek to insulate their "technical core" from environmental turbulence through the use of boundary-spanning mechanisms that serve as input and output buffers. For example, variable inventories buffer production processes against continual fluctuations in demand, and vertical integration can insulate the core technology from variability in inputs.

Why do organizations operate under norms of rationality? Thompson specifies the goals of an organization as equivalent to the domains in which the organization aspires to operate—the niche that an organization attempts to occupy. Those domains are specified by the "dominant coalition." Since organizational power is based on the ability to manage uncertainty, the dominant coalition is presumably that group best able to reduce uncertainty for the organization. Once the coalition chooses a domain (for example, we will sell boys' shirts to large retailers; we will educate all children within the city limits), the domain generates environmental and technological constraints on organizational rationality. Although the conception of dominant coalition suggests a political view of organizations, most of Thompson's causal propositions assume that organizations make rational responses to environmental and technological constraints. The theory has both open-system and political concepts but is predominantly a rational view of organization.

Weick (1969) presents a very sophisticated systems/cybernetic view of "organizing," but his theory is resolutely abstract. Its limited impact on subsequent research suggests that few people have understood it and known what to make of it. Weick offers an almost forbiddingly terse definition of organizing: "the resolving of equivocality in an enacted environment by means of interlocked behaviors embedded in conditionally related processes" (1969, p. 91).

In translation: Humans and human systems exist in an enacted environment. That is, the system's behavior continually influences the environment that it experiences. (We experience ourselves in a particular place only because our behavior led us there. Our own and others' past and present behavior influences the nature of the place that we experience.) There is always equivocality, or uncertainty, in the enacted environment, since the outside world is always complex and always changing. Organizing occurs whenever relationships (that is, patterns of interlocked behavior) form and begin to reduce some of the uncertainty in the environment. If A and B decide to marry or start a business or work on a joint task to reduce equivocality in both their lives, they are engaging in an organizing process. Weick objects to the static concept "organization" on the ground that organizing is an ongoing process. If the processes stop, entropy sets in and organization collapses. Organization, in this view, is information that has been produced by processes that reduce equivocality. The central motive of living systems is the reduction of equivocality in the enacted environment: Humans and systems are continually in the process of trying to increase their certainty about the world in which they reside.

There are important similarities among Katz and Kahn, Thompson, and Weick. All focus on organization/environment interfaces, and all emphasize the importance of information for organizations. Thompson and Weick focus particularly on uncertainty and the organization's efforts to reduce it. Thompson's theory provides much more specific predictions than does Katz and Kahn's or Weick's, but the theory's predictions are premised on the assumption of "norms of rationality." In effect, Thompson's theory makes specific predictions so long as it remains within a rational systems perspective. Katz and Kahn and Weick all aspire to a much higher level of generality. The price they pay is a high level of abstraction and a dearth of specific predictions.

Sociotechnical Systems Theory

The sociotechnical view is associated with a group of researchers most of whom have been affiliated with the Tavistock Institute in London. The group is best known for microanalysis of work groups and technology, but its theoretical framework makes explicit use of concepts from systems theory.

The classic study in the sociotechnical tradition is Trist and Bamforth's (1951) study of changes in British coal mining. Their work documented the interpenetration of technological systems (the methods by which coal is mined) and social systems (the pattern of social relationships among the miners). When changes in the technical system disrupted the social system, the miners responded with intense resistance. When the new technology was subsequently modified so as to be more consistent with the miners' preferred social arrangements, the resistance declined.

Rice (1963) developed a comprehensive view of organizations as open, sociotechnical systems. His theory combines elements from systems, human resource, and rational theories. Rice posits that every system has a primary task—the task it must perform in order to survive. The concept of primary task provides a vehicle for importing norms of rationality into systems theory, but Rice never fully resolved some of the attendant ambiguities. Is the primary task of a government agency to perform a service or to maximize its budget? The latter is probably more critical to survival, but it does not fit Rice's conception of the kind of organizational task that humans need: "Work, more than any other human activity, relates men and women to reality. It absorbs so large a part of living that it is, or should be, a major source of social and psychological satisfaction. But work, if it is to have this effect, must be meaningful, and the task to which it contributes must be acceptable. So far as human behavior is mature and reality-based, the performance of an accepted task is supported by powerful social and psychological forces that ensure that a considerable capacity for cooperation is evoked among the members of an organization created to perform it. In other words, there is, among the members of most enterprises, a need, whether latent or manifest, to get on with the job" (1963, p. 252).

In Rice's theory, the primary task provides a basis for rational choice, but the task and the way the enterprise is organized to achieve it must respond to human needs. Conversely, human needs cannot be permitted to distort the organization so as to block performance of the primary task. One task of leadership is to manage boundary relations so that the task and social systems are optimally adjusted. Rice's conception of leadership as a boundary function implies that the primary task of a leader is to manage the system's relationship to its environment. Leaders of any system—regardless of size, level, or task—are responsible for ensuring that the system can attain needed inputs from the environment and provide appropriate outputs to the environment. That notion also has an implication for the primary task of organization research: Organization theory becomes the science of boundary relations between system and environment.

Achievements and Limitations of Systems/Cybernetic Perspectives

The strengths and limitations of systems approaches are captured in an evaluation by Katz and Kahn (1978, p. 752) of their theory: "In some respects open-system theory is not a theory at all; it does not pretend to the specific sequences of cause and effect, the specific hypotheses and tests of hypotheses that are the basic elements of theory. Open-system theory is rather a framework, a metatheory, a model in the broadest sense of that overused term. Open-system theory is an approach and a conceptual language for understanding and describing many kinds and levels of phenomena. It is used to describe and explain the behavior of electronic equipment, living organisms, and combinations of organisms. The open-system approach and the major concepts of open-system theory are applicable to any dynamic, recurring process, any cyclical pattern of events that occurs in some larger context."

Generality and parsimony are two of the most significant tests of a scientific theory, and systems theory comes closer to achieving both than any other perspective on organizations. But another test of theory is its fertility in generating interesting, testable predictions. Open-system theory has been notably unsuccessful against that criterion. Systems theory is sufficiently general that it can encompass almost any organizational phenomenon but not sufficiently concrete to produce specific hypotheses for researchers or managers.

Systems theory does point to certain issues as worthy of study. It specifies that organization/environment linkages are critical in organization theory, and systems theory has undoubtedly played a major role in spawning research attention to that interface. Systems theory also suggests the critical importance of boundary-spanning processes and roles, thus stimulating a growing body of theory and research (for example, Kahn and others, 1964; Leifer and Huber, 1977; Tushman, 1977). Systems theory also points to the search for isomorphisms: If we understand something about small groups, it is worth investigating whether parallel phenomena operate at the level of smaller and larger systems.

In sum, systems theory has demonstrated that it has significant, though nonspecific, heuristic value, and it comes closer than any other body of theory to becoming a general theory of systems. In the very long run, a general theory is the likely direction for research and theory. In the nearer term, however, it is unlikely that other theorists will necessarily do better to reconceptualize their theories in systems terms. Systems theory, because it aspires to encompass *all* systems, has not developed concepts that are specific to *human* systems. The approach is attractively systematic and general, but it loses much of the richness contained in the four frames for understanding human organizations. We suspect that the short-term payoff will be greater if rational, human resource, political, and symbolic theorists simply import concepts from systems theory when they are useful.

Integrating the Frames

Each of the major conceptual perspectives is conceptually coherent and supported (at least in part) by available empirical evidence. In fact, we can assert, for each perspective, a set of propositions that we believe are conceptually, empirically, and intuitively reasonable. It is surprising that conversations across the different perspectives have been so heavily characterized by polarization and mutual acrimony. Alderfer's (1977a) observation that such conversations are influenced as much by the dynamics of intergroup conflict as by intellectual differences seems accurate.

The problem in organization theory is not that the one true theory is being lost among a crowd of pretenders. The problem is more difficult: There are several valid perspectives. Each is interesting and significant, but each gets at only part of the truth. Much time and energy has been invested in trying to demonstrate that "micro is better than macro" or "organization theory is superior to organizational behavior." The micro/macro dichotomy, in particular, oversimplifies the pluralism of the field and suggests that one or the other must be incorrect.

We have focused mainly on organizational theory and behavior that fall fairly neatly into one of the four frames or into systems theory. But we have acknowledged along the way that some work makes use of conceptions from more than one of the five major lenses. Such work is still a minority, but Table 2 pre-

Table 2. Examples of Dual-Perspective Research.

Perspectives	Authors	Salient Concepts
Rational/Human resource	Lawrence and Lorsch (1967)	"Differentiation and integration"
Rational/Political	Cyert and March (1963)	"Sequential attention to goals"
	Lipsky (1980)	"Street-level bureaucrat"
Human resource/ Political	Alderfer and Smith (1980)	"Embedded intergroups"
Human resource/ Symbolic	Argyris and Schön (1978)	"Theories for action"
Human resource/ Systems	Trist and Bamforth (1951)	"Socio-technical systems"
Political/Symbolic	Ranson, Hinings, and Greenwood (1980)	"Provinces of meaning"
	Cohen and March (1974)	"Organized anarchy"

sents illustrations for several combinations of two frames. We have identified few published examples that utilize three or more perspectives, but one example is Kanter's (1977) analysis of men and women in the corporation. Her theory incorporates aspects of the rational, human resource, and political perspectives.

The relative scarcity of work that comprehends multiple perspectives corresponds to our view that pluralism is the current state of organization research. That is where the field is, but that is not where it needs to remain. In this section we present a series of propositions that represent an effort to summarize where the field is and where it needs to go.

1. *The current pluralism impedes research by impeding communication among different perspectives.* Differentiation, as Lawrence and Lorsch (1967) argued, produces problems of integration. Communication is impeded for two reasons: (1) people do not try to communicate (for example, scholars read only the literature that conforms to their own theoretical predilections); (2) when they do try, they misunderstand one another.

To illustrate the first problem, consider two works that say very similar things but in different language and with little apparent recognition of complementarity. Argyris and Schön (1974, 1978) argue that individuals and organizations are often ineffective because they do not do what they intend, they are unaware of the discrepancy, and their "theory of action" prevents them from learning. Argyris and Schön's concepts of "espoused theory" and "theory in use" combine elements of human resource and symbolic perspectives on organizations. Beer (1981), in a stimulating essay on the equifinality of death, argues that systems fail to do what they are constructed to do because their models of reality lack "requisite variety" but the models prevent recognition of their own errors. Beer uses systems theory and cybernetics to say something remarkably parallel to Argyris and Schön's message. Is he saying the same thing? Would he agree with Argyris and Schön's prescriptions for improving organizational learning? It is difficult to be sure, because of the very different language used in the two theories. There may be instructive parallels between "requisite variety" (Beer) and "single-loop learning" (Argyris and Schön), but translation problems impede the effort to tease them out.

An example of the second problem—mutual understanding—appears in a published dialogue between Salancik and Pfeffer (1977, 1978) and Alderfer (1977a). Salancik and Pfeffer (1977) presented a critique of need-satisfaction theories. Alderfer (1977a), the author of a need-satisfaction theory, responded with a critique of Salancik and Pfeffer, who responded (1978) with a further critique of need satisfaction and a proposal for "social information processing" theories. The need-satisfaction theories that Alderfer defends are central to the human resource perspective. Social construction of reality, which Salancik and Pfeffer defend, is central to the symbolic perspective. There is significant validity in both views. They are more complementary than conflicting. But in the heat of debate, the complementarity was lost. Alderfer (1977a, p. 666) misinterprets Salancik and Pfeffer's conception of "redefining the situation" as being equivalent to "defensive coping." In effect, he takes a symbolic concept and translates it into a human resource concept (in this case, a concept from psychoanalytic theory), but the translation radically alters the meaning.

Conversely, Salancik and Pfeffer (1977, p. 441) concede the existence of physiological needs and argue implicitly that humans have a need for social acceptance (Pfeffer and Salancik, 1978, p. 235). Yet they make a sweeping attack on the concept of psychological needs. The concepts "need" and "interpretation of the situation" are so interconnected that neither can be studied adequately without considering the other. But that will not happen if scholars on both sides treat the issue as a win/lose proposition.

2. *Each perspective has a unique, comparative advantage.* Each of the four frames describes a set of phenomena that are present in any human system but are more visible or prominent under some conditions and more likely to recede into the background under other conditions. Table 3 presents a set of hypothesized linkages between the four perspectives and five contextual variables. The table suggests, for example, that structural systems phenomena will be in the foreground under conditions of high consensus, low rates of change, high certainty, and relatively young organizations. Human resource phenomena will be particularly prominent under high abundance, high consensus, and rapid change and in relatively old organizations. Political processes are likely to be most prominent when resources are declining or scarce, dissensus is widespread, change is rapid, uncertainty is high, and the organization is older. Symbolic processes will be most visible under conditions of dissensus, rapid change, and high uncertainty.

We are not asserting that each frame is valid only under certain conditions. Symbolic processes are not irrelevant under

Table 3. Context and the Salience of the Organizational Frames.

| Contextual Variables | Frame | | | |
	Struc-tural	Human Resource	Politi-cal	Sym-bolic
Abundance (slack)	0	+	−	0
Cultural homogeneity	+	+	−	−
Rate of change	−	+	+	+
Certainty	+	0	−	−
Age of Organization	−	+	+	+

Explanation of symbols:

+   The hypothesized relation between the salience of the perspective and the contextual variable is positive (for example, the structural perspective is more salient as abundance increases).

−   The hypothesized relation is negative (for example, the political frame is less salient as abundance increases).

0   No relation is predicted, or the variables are uncorrelated.

conditions of consensus and certainty; they are very much present. But they are much less obvious when everyone is clear about the job to be done and everyone agrees on the best way to do it.

It is likely that not all the linkages suggested in Table 3 are empirically valid. Those linkages represent a series of hypotheses that have not been explicitly tested. But it is important for theorists to be aware of the range of conditions that they are implicitly assuming. Salancik and Pfeffer (1978, p. 235) note that, in experiments on the phenomenon of "insufficient justification," it is to be expected that the individual will redefine the more ambiguous phenomenon (job satisfaction) rather than the more explicit one (hourly wage), but they miss a larger implication. Their view that humans cognitively redefine a situation to make it more satisfying is particularly appropriate for situations and for needs that are relatively ambiguous. Students were found to rate a boring task as more interesting when they were underpaid than when they were overpaid. Those results are consistent with the symbolic-frame proposition that redefinition is likely to occur under conditions of ambiguity.

But the study does not use different tasks to test the proposition that some tasks are more responsive to human needs than other tasks. Suppose the experiment had included two tasks—for example, reading nonsense syllables and watching *Star Wars*—as well as two pay conditions. It is likely that under-paid students would rate the boring task as more interesting, but it is also likely that the *Star Wars* group would rate their task as more interesting, regardless of what they were paid. Al-derfer and Salancik and Pfeffer are both partly correct, but each is emphasizing a different aspect of the organizational situation.

3. *Each perspective enacts a different image of organiza-tion.* Pondy and Mitroff (1979, p. 28) describe what they see as a troublesome paradox: "What we teach now to practitioners will create the very phenomena that we have available to study in the future." The statement is valid but not paradoxical. It recognizes a truth that is dawning in all the social sciences. Any science of human social behavior is a science of the artificial—a science about the worlds that humans and human cultures have chosen to create. In the social sciences, there is no ultimate way to distinguish between valid prediction and effective self-fulfill-ing prophecy. Consider the following model of the causal rela-tion between organization theories and organizational phenom-ena:

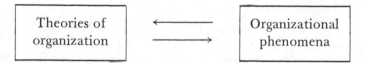

Traditional models of social science have assumed that the significant causal arrow is from the phenomena to the the-ory. The assumption is that there is an objective reality that exists independent of human theories about it and simply waits for us to understand it. Symbolic perspectives, taken to their extreme, imply the opposite—that reality is solely the product of our theories about it. Both views oversimplify and mislead. Neither organizations nor humans are infinitely malleable, but students can be taught to believe a variety of theories about or-ganizations, and organizations can be significantly influenced by the theories of their participants.

Our theories and our methods influence the world that we perceive and the world that we enact as scientists and as managers. Any perspective can be self-fulfilling. Organizational research is likely to be a slow and stolid process, so long as most of us continue to defend passionately our current intellectual preferences. Much more exciting and creative possibilities emerge if we can begin to work at the intersections.

4. *Each perspective contains ingredients that are essential to an integrative science of organization.* The rational systems or structural approach reminds us that most humans and human institutions, regardless of how badly they do in practice, are *intendedly and subjectively* rational. Structuralists correctly insist on the crucial importance of structure and context in influencing the premises on which people make choices.

The human resource frame reminds us that the participants in human systems are indeed humans, in all their exquisite complexity—with their reasoning and their feelings, their conscious and their unconscious, their capacity to learn and their skill in defense, their abilities and their deficiencies. It reminds us that humans are adaptable but not infinitely so: They persist in behaving like people, and organizations have to come to grips with that.

The political frame correctly asserts that scarce resources are a factor in every human system and that there are enduring differences among individuals and groups in how those resources should be allocated. Conflict may result from misunderstanding, skill deficiencies, or failure in will, but some conflict is deeply embedded in organization and society. The two ps about which we are so often ambivalent—power and politics—will not go away and cannot be ignored.

The symbolic frame reminds us of the enormous extent to which reality is socially constructed and symbolically mediated. "Meaning" is what is most important about any human event, but meaning is not objectively given; it exists only as the event is interpreted through one belief system or another. Particularly in situations where multiple cultures intersect and the important issues or tasks are fraught with ambiguity, symbolic processes will be central to any science of organization.

Systems theory and cybernetics remind us that all systems are embedded in larger systems and contain smaller ones. They encourage us to search for concepts and hypotheses that will link and help to explain systems at every level. Organization theory may never achieve propositions with the generality, parsimony, and elegance of the general theory of relativity, but systems theory encourages researchers to keep trying.

A morality tale borrowed from Stafford Beer (1981, p. 187) aptly summarizes where the field is and what it needs to do:

> Here we are in the countryside, surrounded by all the intricate, multicolored, ever-changing complexities of the natural environment. A specialist comes along to the fallen tree trunk on which we are sitting. "Can you understand it all, then?" he asks. No, we agree, it is all a great mystery. "What you need," says the specialist, "is a pair of my truth spectacles." We buy them for a small sum —though it is more than they are worth because (did we but know it) the truth spectacles are simply dark, red-tinted glasses.
>
> "What do you see?" asks the specialist. We tell him that we see everything is red. What is more, we cannot any longer see a lot of the complicated details that we saw before. "Exactly! That is our triumph," says the specialist. "What you are seeing is the truth that underlies all the confusion. The world is *really* red. And the rules that govern it are *actually* quite simple."

Organization theorists have spent much time arguing among themselves whether organizations are really a cheery orange, a dull gray, a murky brown, or whatever color the beholder favors. We need theories that bring order out of confusion without dulling and filtering important organizational realities. We need to try on a variety of spectacles and spend more time dealing with the complexity of human organizations before we can safely conclude that they are *actually* as simple as existing models make them out to be.

14

Matching Management
Approaches to the
Organizational Situation

The frames provide four unique windows for "organization watchers"—those who want to understand the day-to-day pageantry in social systems. But managers—most of them, anyway—are more than system spectators. They need tools that will enable them to act more intelligently. An action orientation leads naturally to the question, "What do you do with four frames?" The next two chapters provide several answers to that question. In this chapter we discuss "reframing"—switching across frames to generate new insights and options for managerial action. Reframing leads to greater freedom of choice: It avoids the knee-jerk reactions and repetitious solutions that lead managers into mistakes and organizational traps. Reframing encourages a more flexible and playful approach to the more vexing problems of organizational life.

Each frame provides a different way of interpreting events,

and each implies a very different approach to effective management. Together, they offer a comprehensive view. You may wonder whether four theories, with their differences, tensions, and contradictions, are too complicated and cumbersome to be of any use in the hectic and turbulent world of modern organizations. We think not. Even though managers do not have unlimited time to sit in their offices and ponder the application of four distinct perspectives, organizations are too complicated for easy answers or cookbook solutions. Nothing is more practical than a good theory, even a complicated theory, *if* it helps managers to understand what is happening and what they can do about it. To be helpful, a theory needs to reflect life as managers experience it.

Life as Managers Know It

Much of the prevailing mythology of management depicts managers as rational actors who spend most of their time planning, organizing, coordinating, and controlling the activities of subordinates. Periodicals, books, and business schools often convey the image of the modern manager: unruffled, three-piece suit, well-organized desk, calling the shots with the help of loyal subordinates and sophisticated information systems. The manager develops strategic plans, which are communicated through a well-defined structure to produce predictable and effective responses. It sounds good, but it is mostly fantasy.

Social scientists (Mintzberg, 1973; Kotter, 1982) have provided a fascinating glimpse of what managerial life is really like. It is a hectic existence. Managers spend most of their time shifting rapidly from one meeting with one set of problems to another meeting where they encounter a completely different blend of challenges. Kotter spent months observing senior managers and rarely observed them really making a decision. Decisions emerged from a fluid and sometimes confusing series of conversations, meetings, and memos. Managers often have sophisticated information systems, but the systems tend to assure an overload of detailed information about what happened last month or last year. Even more important than what happened yesterday is what might happen tomorrow. The information systems offer surprisingly little information to help managers decide what to do next. For such decisions, they operate mostly on the basis of intuition, hunch, and "judgment"—derived from long experience in their organization and its successes or failures. They are far too busy to spend time thinking or reading; they get most of their information orally—in meetings or over the telephone. They are hassled priests, modern muddlers, and corporate wheeler-dealers.

How does one reconcile the actual work of managers with the epic imagery? What does the discrepancy mean to people who often feel deep down that what they really do has little relation to what they should be doing? What happens if managers aspire to an unattainable ideal? One common consequence is frustration and feelings of inadequacy: "There must be something wrong with me!" Managers believe that they should be rational and in control, yet they often find themselves surprised and bewildered. They believe that they are supposed to plan, organize, delegate, and control, yet they find themselves meeting, muddling, and playing catch-up. They want to see themselves as problem solvers and decision makers, but the problems are so ill defined and the decisions so murky that they often find today's decision in yesterday's action or get swept into decision by the ongoing flow of events.

Prevailing mythology leads managers to see their organizations as more rational than they are and to see themselves with more power to control organizational events than they have. The perceptions are incomplete and misleading. The myths are reinforced by much of the management literature and the multitude of courses, seminars, and workshops that managers attend. They need a way to separate myth from reality, to create better myths, and to critique the advice they are given. Reframing provides a promising avenue.

Reframing and Critique

Too often, managers are given the message, "It really is pretty easy, if you just do it right." Blanchard and Johnson (1982) tell managers in only 100 pages how to be a "one-minute manager" who uses one-minute meetings and memos to solve problems, resolve conflicts, and motivate subordinates. It is an important message to ponder, but suppose that you have read the book, and you stop to ask, "Which of the frames are embedded in the description of the one-minute manager?" You will find that the one-minute manager operates almost entirely from the human resource frame. In effect, Blanchard and Johnson imply that the same set of management techniques will work in any situation, regardless of differences in structure, politics, or culture. Managers who follow their advice will be aware of potential pitfalls if they remember that three of the four frames have been ignored. Blanchard and Johnson present a helpful discussion but leave three fourths of an organization's terrain uncharted.

Tregoe and Zimmerman's (1980) book on corporate strategy provides another example. It requires only 125 pages to tell managers how to define their organization's "driving force" in order to have a unified corporate strategy. But the book falls almost completely within the structural frame. People, politics, and symbols are not seen as relevant to the problem of developing a corporate strategy. Much of the literature on planning and corporate strategy makes the same assumption, which helps to explain why so few organizations do it the way the literature says they should.

We did not choose those two books because they are bad examples. Both contain useful and provocative insights. But we think they are among countless examples that ultimately deceive the reader: They suggest that managing is easy when it is not. They focus on only a narrow slice of a more complex reality. They suggest that a little more clear thinking or interpersonal skill will produce quantum leaps forward. There is an interesting parallel between management and losing weight: The endless stream of books, articles, and courses suggests that a lot of people want to do it, but no one has figured out how to make it easy.

Any book, article, seminar, or advice on management can be critically reframed. The first step is to ask which frame(s) it uses and which it ignores. The second is to expand the horizon by applying each of the other frames. The same process can be applied to any organizational situation, problem, strategy, or contemplated action. As one example, remember our old friend Helen Demarco. When we first met her in Chapter One, she was feeling regret and remorse. She had participated in a wasteful charade, because she knew no other way to save the organization from a disastrous project wanted only by Paul Osborne.

If reframing can be freeing, how might Helen have altered her approach? We can start by asking, "What frame(s) did Helen use?" Her analysis was based on three critical assumptions: (1) Paul Osborne's plan was wrong. (2) Osborne was too committed to it and too suspicious of middle managers to listen to reason. (3) The only option was to manipulate Osborne into accepting an alternative plan.

The first assumption is a technical one and might fit loosely in the structural frame, but Helen never seriously asked whether the problem might in part stem from structural factors —such as vague goals or ill-defined roles. The second and third assumptions fit best under the political frame. Helen has made an interpretation about Osborne's interests—and his power. She sees an enduring difference that is unlikely to be resolved. She chooses a political strategy, exploiting a major source of middle-management power: control over the information that top management receives.

The first step in the reframing process leads to the conclusion that Helen largely ignored the structural, human resource, and symbolic frames. She saw the problem politically and acted accordingly. But what were her options? The next step is to reframe Helen's situation, using each of the frames. In earlier chapters, we did this separately. Here we use all four in sequence to focus on the same case.

How could Helen have approached the problem as one of structure? She might have noted that there appeared to be a problem of linkage or coordination between the chief executive and senior management. That might mean that one or both roles were inadequately or incorrectly defined. It might mean that a need existed for a coordinating device such as a committee that included both Osborne and some of the technical specialists in the organization. Perhaps the difference occurred because Osborne and the middle managers were responding to very different parts of the organization's task environment: Osborne to pressures from outsiders, the middle managers to technical imperatives.

Flip the frame from structure to human resource. This view suggests that conflict and misunderstanding often reflect issues of management style, interpersonal skills, and poor communications. Osborne's "Theory X" style is producing the predicted resentment and resistance. But middle managers make things predictably worse with strategies of manipulation and concealment. Much of the problem might be communications: Perhaps Osborne does not fully understand the technical issues, and Helen does not fully understand what Osborne has in mind. Such an insight might lead Helen to ask what could be done to improve communications and enable both sides to test the assumptions they are making.

Reframe one more time. What is happening symbolically? Helen and Paul Osborne are using different interpretive frameworks that emphasize different symbols. Helen is emphasizing technical symbols that embody rationality, expertise, and accuracy. Osborne appears to find meaning in symbols of progress, change, and improvement. Reframing might help Helen to see something she had previously missed—that she and Paul Osborne both care about symbols that are positively valued and important to the organization. Rationality is not necessarily inconsistent with progress, and technical accuracy is potentially compatible with improvement. The fact that she and Paul care about different symbols is not automatically a problem, since symbols can be attached to multiple realities, combined through shared values, and transformed by joint rituals. Reframing might lead Helen to ask, "What could we do collectively that would embrace and communicate both sets of symbols?"

Each recasting of the problem immediately suggests new questions to ask and new options for action. For any given situation, one or two of the frames may be much more useful than the others. But deliberate and critical reframing can be a powerful way to break out of our "psychic prisons"—the automatic assumptions that limit what we see, how we think, and what we do.

Understanding and Managing Organizations

Across the Frames:
Organizations as Multiple Realities

For some people, the concept of choice in defining problems and selecting alternatives seems unnatural. They tend to see one frame as right and others as wrong; some as useful, others as silly or unrealistic; one or two as appealing but the others as repellent. Their own common-sense personal theory of organizations is well defined and well defended. When another frame confirms their predictions, they are happy to embrace its message. When it challenges their assumptions, they want to deny or attack its message.

But all organizations are multiple realities. Every event can be interpreted in a number of ways. To demonstrate that point, Table 4 examines a number of organizational processes through each of the frames. The comparison across the frames helps to clarify many cases of confusion and conflict. When people interpret events through different frames, disagreement and conflict are inevitable. But we usually do not think of these as differences in perspectives. We label those who see things differently as wrong—irrational, power-hungry, insensitive, or frivolous. Exploration of the plausibility of different interpretations helps to penetrate below the surface of conflict and pinpoint its origins.

Consider the implications of these diverse interpretations for organizational life. What people see and do is strongly determined by their personal theories of organizational events. Take any meeting. Suppose that Mary is trying to reach a decision, Mark wants to make sure everyone has a chance to participate, Linda is there to prove herself and score points, and Sam sees himself as attending a ritual to celebrate an important cultural event. It is easy to anticipate the confusion: Each individual will see the others as puzzling, or confused, or ineffective. Depending on their frame, participants may lament the lack of clarity, or warmth, or victory, or substance.

The potential problems are well illustrated in the following newspaper account:

Table 4. Four Interpretations of Organizational Processes.

| Process | Frame | | | |
	Structural	Human Resource	Political	Symbolic
Planning	Strategies to set objectives and coordinate resources	Gatherings to promote participation	Arenas to air conflicts and realign power	Ritual to signal responsibility, produce a symbol, and negotiate meaning
Decision making	Rational sequence to produce right decision	Open process to produce commitment	Opportunity to gain or exercise power	Ritual to provide comfort and support until decision happens
Reorganizing	Realign roles and responsibilities to fit tasks and environment	Maintain a balance between human needs and formal roles	Redistribute power and form new coalitions	Maintain an image of accountability and responsiveness; negotiate new social order
Evaluating	Basis for distributing rewards or penalties to control performance	Basis for helping individuals grow and improve	Opportunity to exercise power	Occasion to play roles in a shared ritual
Approaching conflict	Maintain organizational goals by having authorities resolve conflict	Develop relationships by having individuals confront conflict	Develop power by bargaining, forcing, or manipulating to win	Develop shared values and use conflict to negotiate meaning
Goal setting	Keep organization headed in a direction	Keep people involved and communication open	Provide opportunity for individuals or groups to make interests known	Develop symbols and shared values
Communication	Transmit facts and information	Exchange information, needs, feelings	Vehicle for influencing or manipulating others	Telling stories
Meeting	Formalized place to make decisions	Informal place to be involved, share feelings	Competitive place to win points	Sacred place to celebrate and transform the culture
Motivating	Monetary rewards	Growth, self-actualization	Coercion, manipulation, seduction	Symbols—plaques—perks—T-shirts

Doctor Fights Order to Quit Maine Island

Dr. Gregory O'Keefe found himself the focus of a fierce battle between the 1,200 year-round
residents of Vinalhaven, Maine (an island fishing
community), and the National Health Service Corps
(NHSC), which pays his salary and is insisting he
take a promotion to an administrator's desk in
Rockville, Md.

O'Keefe doesn't want to go, and his patients
don't want him to either. The islanders are so upset that, much to the surprise of NHSC officials,
they have enlisted the aid of Sen. William Cohen
(R.-Maine) and U.S. Health and Human Services
Secretary Margaret Heckler to keep him here.

It's certainly not the prestige or glamour of
the job that is holding O'Keefe, who drives the
town's only ambulance and, as often as twice a
week, takes critically ill patients to mainland hospitals via an emergency ferry run or a Coast Guard
cutter, private plane, or even lobster boat.

Apparently unyielding in their insistence
that O'Keefe accept the promotion or resign,
NHSC officials seemed startled last week by the
spate of protests from angry islanders, which
prompted nationwide media attention and inquiries
from the Maine Congressional delegation. NHSC
says it probably would not replace O'Keefe on the
island, which, in the agency's view, is now able to
support a private medical practice.

Cohen described himself as "frustrated by
the lack of responsiveness of lower-level bureaucrats." . . . But to the NHSC, O'Keefe is a foot soldier in a military organization of more than 1,600
physicians assigned to isolated, medically needy
communities. And he's had the audacity to question the orders of a superior officer.

"It's like a soldier who wanted to stay at Ft.
Myers and jumped on TV and called the Defense

Secretary a rat for wanting him to move," Shirley
Barth, press officer for the federal Public Health
Service, said in a telephone interview Thursday
[*Boston Globe,* October 15, 1983, p. 1].

The NHSC officials apparently had trouble seeing beyond
the structural frame—they had a task to do and a structure for
achieving it; the opposition was illegitimate. O'Keefe saw it in
human resource terms—he felt the work he was doing was meaningful and satisfying, and the islanders needed him. For Senator
Cohen, it was a political issue—could minor bureaucrats be allowed to abuse their power in a way that was insensitive and
harmful to his constituents? For the hardy residents of Vinalhaven, O'Keefe was a heroic figure of mythic dimensions—"If
he gets one night's sleep out of twenty, he's lucky, but he's always up there smiling and working." The islanders were full of
stories about Dr. O'Keefe's humility, skill, humanness, dedication, wit, confidence, and caring.

With everyone using different frames, confusion and conflict were predictable. The inability of NHSC officials to understand and acknowledge the existence of other frames is a good
example of the costs of clinging to a single view of a situation.
In their minds, they were doing exactly what they should, but
to everyone else they became another symbol of mindless bureaucracy.

The example illustrates another important use of reframing. In many situations the hardest thing to understand is why
other people are reacting as they are. Whenever others' actions
seem to make no sense, it is worth asking whether you and they
are using different frames. Even if their frame is inappropriate
or misguided, it helps to know what it is. It makes sense to
them, and their frame—not yours—determines how they will act.

Choosing a Frame

The four frames can be applied to most organizational situations, and each will usually suggest different questions and
options. If the frames suggest different directions, how does a
manager decide which route to follow? Table 5 outlines a series

Table 5. Characteristics of Situations in Which
Each of the Frames Is a Good Fit.

	Frame			
Question	Structural	Human Resource	Political	Symbolic
Objective or subjective	Objective	Subjective	Objective and subjective	Subjective
Technical or distributive	Technical	Technical or distributive	Distributive	Distributive
Level of ambiguity	Low	Moderate	Moderate to high	High
Resources	Scarce to moderate	Moderate to abundant	Scarce	Scarce to abundant
Level of conflict	Low to moderate	Moderate	Moderate to high	Moderate to high
Top-down or bottom-up	Top-down	Top-down	Bottom-up	Top-down or bottom-up

of questions that can be used to define situations in which each of the frames is most likely to be appropriate and useful.

1. *Are the goals or the results to be achieved mainly objective or subjective?* By *objective* we mean observable events, activities, and resources. *Subjective* refers to the values, perceptions, feelings, and reactions of individuals and groups. An issue is objective when the primary concern is getting something to happen, regardless of how people feel about it. An issue is subjective if the primary concern is people's reactions and feelings. Objective problems include designing a production process, making budget decisions, and buying a computer. Subjective problems include improving morale, building loyalty and confidence, or changing attitudes.

The world is not so neat that all problems are cleanly packaged into one category or the other. Suppose that the problem is to increase sales. Improving the product is an objective problem. Changing customer attitudes is a subjective problem. Improving the product in a way that will change customer attitudes combines elements of both. Asking the question may help to separate the objective and subjective elements of the problem, and it may be necessary to apply different frames to each.

Table 5 suggests that the human resource and the symbolic frames are more likely to apply to "subjective" problems (such as problems of morale, attitude, loyalty, confidence, or commitment). The structural frame is more likely to fit objective problems, and the political frame may fit problems that include both objective and subjective elements.

2. *Is the problem mainly technical or distributive?* A problem is technical if the primary question is: What is the best way to do something? A problem is distributive if the question is: Who gets what? Developing a cost-effective artificial kidney machine is a technical problem. Deciding who gets such a machine if there are not enough to go around is a distributive question.

The structural frame is likely to apply to problems that are technical, such as the best layout for a warehouse. The political and symbolic frames are more likely to be appropriate for distributive problems (such as the problem of who gets the artificial kidney machine). The human resource frame may apply to situations that combine technical and distributive elements (such as designing an incentive system for hourly workers).

3. *How much ambiguity?* We have argued that uncertainty is a pervasive reality in organizations, so that completely unambiguous problems rarely occur. But some situations are a lot more ambiguous than others. Ambiguity is relatively low when the assumptions of the structural frame are met: Goals are reasonably clear, the technology is well understood, and people's behavior is mostly rational. The human resource frame anticipates moderate levels of ambiguity because it assumes that human behavior is complex and often "irrational."

As ambiguity gets higher, the political and symbolic frames become increasingly relevant. The political frame assumes that actors generally seek to act rationally in pursuit of their self-interest, but the resulting battles among individuals and interest groups may be confused and chaotic. The symbolic frame assumes that symbols are a way of creating a perception of order, meaning, and "truth" in situations that are too complex, uncertain, or mysterious to be susceptible to rational analysis.

4. *Are resources scarce or abundant?* The human resource frame fits situations of relative abundance because its
relatively optimistic assumptions about human capacity for
growth and collaboration are most likely to be valid in firms
that are profitable and growing or public agencies that are
strongly supported and well funded. At the other extreme, the
political frame is particularly appropriate when resources are extremely tight. In those conditions, self-interest and self-protection are likely to give rise to the dynamics of power and conflict
that are central to the political frame.

The structural frame is likely to fit situations in the middle. The idea of structure implies limits on available options,
implying conditions of moderate scarcity. Extreme scarcity
often fosters levels of conflict that exceed the capacity of existing authority systems.

Since symbols seem to play a part in every culture and
every social class, from the very poor to the very wealthy, the
relevance of the symbolic frame is not significantly affected by
scarcity or abundance of resources.

5. *How much conflict exists around this issue?* Since
high conflict tends to undermine authority and existing institutions, the structural frame is likely to fit best when conflict is
low enough to be managed and contained within existing structures. The human resource frame is relevant to situations of
moderate conflict. It postulates conflict between individual and
organization and provides suggestions for how to manage and
reduce that conflict. Beyond a certain point, though, conflict is
so deep and powerful that it exceeds the capacity of human resource options. In those situations, the political and symbolic
frames are most likely to be useful.

6. *Is the manager operating top-down or bottom-up?* The
structural frame assumes that revising the structure is the major
solution to organizational problems, and the option of structural change is an option that is open primarily to people with
authority, who can make changes from the top down. Similarly,
the human resource frame has developed a series of approaches
to organizational improvement that usually require change or
support from the top in order to be successful. The political

frame, in contrast, is particularly appropriate for change from the bottom up. Bottom-up change agents rarely use authority, so that they need to find some other base of power.

To illustrate the use of the questions in Table 5, consider the following case:

> *Case A:* You are the manager of a large branch office for an insurance company. The branch has had chronic problems of low motivation, absenteeism, and turnover among its hourly employees. You believe that improving morale for those employees would make a very significant impact on productivity and expenses in the branch.

What frame would best apply? Before reading further, use the questions in Table 5 to analyze this case.

The long-run objective is greater productivity, but the immediate problem is "morale," which makes it a subjective problem. Since the problem focuses on making things better, it is a technical rather than a distributive issue. The level of ambiguity is probably moderate, since a fair amount is known about what affects worker morale and what can be done about it. The problem gives no direct indication of level of resources or conflict, but it seems reasonable to assume that both are moderate in the typical insurance company branch office. Since you have authority over the department, you are working top-down.

The analysis shows that the case fits the human resource frame best and the political frame least (the problem is primarily technical rather than distributive, resources are not scarce, and the manager is working top-down). If you reframed the problem to focus on production rather than morale, the structural frame would fit well.

> *Case B:* You are still the manager of the insurance branch, but this time you face a different problem. In your city, your major competitors have larger marketing staffs than you do. They can devote more time cultivating the insurance agents

who sell your company's products. The insurance
business has been relatively unprofitable for the
past few years, and your company is engaged in a
major effort to cut costs. Even so, you feel you can
remain competitive only if you add two more marketing representatives to your branch. Your problem is to make this case persuasively to your boss.

This time, you might want to think about politics and
symbols. Conflict is high, resources are scarce, and you will be
working from the bottom up trying to persuade your boss to
give you a larger share of a shrinking pie.

As a third example, consider once again the Helen Demarco case. In some ways, Helen's situation fits the political frame:
There are both objective elements (designing a plan that is technically sound) and subjective ones (influencing the director).
There is conflict between Helen and the director, and she is
working from the bottom up. The technical problem may or
may not be ambiguous, but the more important problem of influencing Osborne is both subjective and ambiguous. The case is
a poor candidate for the structural frame, and Helen might have
an uphill battle using a human resource approach. The tide in
the Demarco case is moving toward politics and symbols, and
Helen chooses to go with the flow.

Finally, consider the contrast between McDonald's and
Harvard University that we discussed earlier. If we seek to design a role structure for McDonald's outlets, we are dealing with
a problem that is largely objective and technical, with reasonable resources, low ambiguity and conflict, and top-down decision making. At Harvard, though, the tasks of teaching and
doing research are much more subjective and ambiguous, and
conflict over goals and means is much higher. The six questions
suggest that the structural frame will be more helpful in understanding the managerial problems at McDonald's, while the symbolic frame will fit better for Harvard.

The questions in Table 5 are suggested as a set of helpful
guides to thinking about which frame to choose. We are not
suggesting that they can be followed mechanically to the one

correct answer for every situation. In some cases, the questions might tell you to use the same frame that you and everyone else have always used. If the old frame shows signs of inadequacy, it may be time to try a new perspective. In other cases, the analysis might lead you to a perspective completely different from the way anyone else in your organization thinks. You may have discovered an exciting and creative new option, but you will have to face the problem of how to communicate to those who see a different reality.

Summary

Reframing—the sequential application of each frame to the same event or issue—can be applied in a number of ways to clarify what is happening and generate options. Reframing can be used as a way to evaluate strategies or advice by asking: What frames have been considered, and which have been ignored?

A third use of reframing is to diagnose the multiple realities of the people with whom we interact daily. When their behavior is strange, puzzling, or wrong, it is worth asking whether we and they are "in different worlds" because we are seeing through different lenses.

Finally, we need to know how to fit frames to situations. The mix of objective or subjective elements, the level of ambiguity, the conflict and availability of resources, and the role of the actor all can influence the usefulness of each frame.

15

⁘⁘⁘⁘⁘⁘⁘⁘⁘⁘⁘⁘⁘⁘⁘

Learning to Use
Different Leadership Styles

Critique is one application of the process of reframing. A second is the use of frames to generate "scripts"—implicit or explicit instructions for approaching the tasks of management. Many managers tacitly embrace or lean toward one frame or another, which limits them to action scripts that are consistent with their preferred frame. Use of other frames can generate a very different set of options. To illustrate the process, we will use the frames to generate scripts for four leadership styles and apply those styles to a case, Robert F. Kennedy High School.

ROBERT F. KENNEDY HIGH SCHOOL

On July 15, 1970, David King became principal of the Robert F. Kennedy High School, the newest of the six high

9-474-183 Robert F. Kennedy High School. Copyright © 1974 by the President and Fellows of Harvard College.

The case was prepared by John J. Gabarro as a basis for class discussion rather than to illustrate either effective or ineffective handling of an administrative situation. Reprinted by permission of the Harvard Business School.

schools in Great Ridge, Illinois. The school had opened in the fall of 1968 amid national acclaim for being one of the first schools in the country to be designed and constructed for the "house system" concept. Kennedy High's organization was broken down into four "houses," each of which contained 300 students, a faculty of 18, and a housemaster. The Kennedy complex was specially designed so that each house was in a separate building connected to the "core facilities"* and other houses by an enclosed outside passageway. Each house had its own entrance, classrooms, toilets, conference rooms, and housemaster's office.

King knew that Kennedy High was not intended to be an ordinary school when it was first conceived. It had been hailed as a major innovation in inner-city education, and a Chicago television station had made a documentary on it in 1968. Kennedy High had opened with a carefully selected staff of teachers, many of whom were chosen from other Great Ridge schools and at least a dozen of whom had been specially recruited from out of state. Indeed, King knew his faculty included graduates from several elite East and West Coast schools, such as Stanford, Yale, and Princeton, as well as several of the very best Midwestern schools. Even the racial mix of students had been carefully balanced so that blacks, whites, and Puerto Ricans each comprised a third of the student body (although King also knew—perhaps better than its planners—that Kennedy's students were drawn from the toughest and poorest areas of town). The building itself was also widely admired for its beauty and functionality and had won several national architectural awards.

Despite these careful and elaborate preparations, Kennedy High School was in serious difficulty by July of 1970. It had been racked by violence the preceding year, having been twice closed by student disturbances and once by a teacher walkout. It was also widely reported (although King did not know for sure) that achievement scores of its ninth- and tenth-grade students had actually declined during the last two years,

---

*The core facilities included the cafeteria, nurse's room, guidance offices, the boys' and girls' gyms, the offices, the shops, and the auditorium.

while no significant improvement could be found in the scores of the eleventh- and twelfth-graders' tests. Thus, the Kennedy High School for which King was taking over as principal had fallen far short of its planners' hopes and expectations.

David King

David King was born and raised in Great Ridge, Illinois. His father was one of the city's first black principals, and thus King was not only familiar with the city but with its school system as well. After two years of military service, King decided to follow his father's footsteps and went to Great Ridge State Teachers College, from which he received his B.Ed. in 1955 and his M.Ed. in 1960. King was certified in elementary and secondary school administration, English, and physical education. King had taught English and coached in a predominantly black middle school until 1960, when he was asked to become the school's assistant principal. He remained in that post until 1965, when he was asked to take over the George Thibeault Middle School, a large middle school of 900 pupils which at the time was reputed to be the most "difficult" middle school in the city. While at Thibeault, King gained a citywide reputation for being a gifted and popular administrator and was credited with changing Thibeault from the worst middle school in the system to one of the best. He had been very effective in building community support, recruiting new faculty, and raising academic standards. He was also credited with turning out basketball and baseball teams which had won state and country middle school championships. King knew that he had been selected for the Kennedy job over several more senior candidates because of his ability to handle tough situations. The superintendent had made that clear when he told King why he had been selected for the job.

The superintendent had also told him that he would need every bit of skill and luck he could muster. King knew of the formidable credentials of Jack Weis, his predecessor at Kennedy High. Weis, a white, had been the superintendent of a small, local township school system before becoming Kennedy's first principal. He had also written a book on the "house system" concept, as well as a second book on inner-city education. Weis had earned a Ph.D. from the University of Chicago and a divinity degree from Harvard. Yet, despite his impressive background and obvious ability, Weis had resigned in disillusionment and was described by many as a "broken man." In fact, King remembered seeing the physical change which Weis had undergone over that two-year period. Weis's appearance had become progressively more fatigued and strained until he developed what appeared to be permanent black rings under his eyes and a perpetual stoop. King remembered how he had pitied the man and wondered how Weis could find the job worth the obvious personal toll it was taking on him.

History of the School

1968-1969: The school's troubles began to manifest themselves in the school's first year of operation. Rumors of conflicts between the housemasters and the six subject-area department heads were widespread throughout the system by the middle of the first year. The conflicts stemmed from differences in interpretations of curriculum policy on required learning and course content. In response to these conflicts, Dr. Weis had instituted a "free market" policy by which subject-area department heads were supposed to convince housemasters of why they should offer certain courses, while housemasters were supposed to convince department heads of which teachers they wanted assigned to their houses and why they wanted those teachers. Many observers in the school system felt that this policy exacerbated the conflicts.

To add to this climate of conflict, a teacher was assaulted in her classroom in February of 1969. The beating frightened many of the staff, particularly some of the older teachers. A delegation of eight teachers asked Weis to hire security guards a week after the assault. The request precipitated a debate within the faculty about the desirability of having guards in the school. One group felt that the guards would instill a sense of safety within the school and thus promote a better learning climate, while the other group felt that the presence of guards in the school would be repressive and would destroy the sense of community and trust which was developing within the school. Dr. Weis refused the request for security guards because he believed that symbolically they would represent everything the school was trying to change. In April a second teacher was robbed and beaten in her classroom after school hours and the debate was rekindled, except that this time a group of Spanish-speaking parents threatened to boycott the school unless better security measures were instituted. Again Dr. Weis refused the request for security guards.

1969-1970: The second year of the school's existence was even more troubled than the first. Because of cutbacks ordered during the summer of 1969, Dr. Weis was not able to replace eight teachers who resigned during the summer, and it was no longer possible for each house to staff all of its courses with its own faculty. Dr. Weis therefore instituted a "flexible staffing" policy whereby some teachers were asked to teach a course outside of their assigned house and students in the eleventh and twelfth grades were able to take some elective and required courses in other houses. During this period, Chauncey Carver, one of the housemasters, publicly attacked the move as a step toward destroying the house system. In a letter to the *Great Ridge Times,* he accused the board of education of trying to subvert the house concept by cutting back funds.

The debate over the flexible staffing policy was heightened when two of the other housemasters joined a group of faculty and department chairmen in opposing Chauncey Carver's criticisms. This group argued that the individual house faculties of fifteen to eighteen teachers could never offer their students the breadth of courses that a schoolwide faculty of sixty-five to seventy teachers could offer and that interhouse cross-registration should be encouraged for that reason.

Further expansion of a cross-registration or flexible staffing policy was halted, however, because of difficulties encountered in the scheduling of classes in the fall of 1969. Several errors were found in the master schedule which had been pre-

planned during the preceding summer. Various schedule difficulties persisted until November of 1969, when the vice-principal responsible for the scheduling of classes resigned. Mr. Burtram Perkins, a Kennedy housemaster who had formerly planned
the schedule at Central High, assumed the scheduling function
in addition to his duties as housemaster. The scheduling activity
took most of Perkins' time until February.

Security again became an issue when three sophomores
were assaulted because they refused to give up their lunch money
during a "shakedown." It was believed that the assailants were
from outside the school and were not students. Several teachers approached Dr. Weis and asked him to request security
guards from the board of education. Again, Dr. Weis declined,
but he asked Bill Smith, a vice-principal at the school, to secure
all doors except for the entrances to each of the four houses,
the main entrance to the school, and the cafeteria. This move
appeared to reduce the number of outsiders in the school.

In May of 1970 a disturbance occurred in the cafeteria
which appeared to grow out of a fight between two boys. The
fight spread and resulted in considerable damage to the school,
including the breaking of classroom windows and desks. The
disturbance was severe enough for Dr. Weis to close the school.
A number of teachers and students reported that outsiders were
involved in the fight and in damaging the classrooms. Several
students were taken to the hospital for minor injuries, but all
were released. A similar disturbance occurred two weeks later,
and again the school was closed. The board of education then
ordered a temporary detail of municipal police to the school
despite Dr. Weis's advice to the contrary. In protest to the as-
signment of the police detail, thirty of Kennedy's sixty-eight
teachers staged a walkout, which was joined by over half the
student body. The police detail was removed from the school,
and an agreement was worked out by an ad hoc subcommittee
of the board of education with informal representatives of
teachers who were for and against assigning a police detail. The
compromise called for the temporary stationing of a police
cruiser near the school.

King's First Week at Kennedy High

Mr. King arrived at Kennedy High on Monday, July 15th, and spent most of his first week individually interviewing the school's key administrators (see Exhibit 1 for a listing of Kennedy's administrative staff as of July 15th). He also had a meeting with all of his administrators and department heads on Friday of that week. Mr. King's purpose in these meetings was to familiarize himself with the school, its problems, and its key people.

His first interview was with Bill Smith, who was one of his vice-principals. Mr. Smith was black and had worked as a counselor and as a vice-principal of a middle school prior to coming to Kennedy. King knew that Smith had a reputation for being a tough disciplinarian and was very much disliked among many of the younger faculty and students. However, King had also heard from several teachers, whose judgment he respected, that Smith had been instrumental in keeping the school from "blowing apart" the preceding year. It became clear early in the interview that Smith felt that more stringent steps were needed to keep outsiders from wandering into the buildings. In particular, Smith urged King to consider locking all of the school's thirty doors except for the front entrance so that everyone would enter and leave through one set of doors only. Smith also told him that many of the teachers and pupils had become fearful of living and working in the building and that "no learning will ever begin to take place until we make it so people don't have to be afraid anymore." At the end of the interview, Smith told King that he had been approached by a nearby school system to become its director of counseling but that he had not yet made up his mind. He said that he was committed enough to Kennedy High that he did not want to leave but that his decision depended on how hopeful he felt about its future.

As King talked with others, he discovered that the "door question" was one of considerable controversy within the faculty and that feelings ran high, both in favor of the idea of locking all the doors and against it. Two of the housemasters in particular, Chauncey Carver, a black, and Frank Czepak, a white, were strongly against closing the house entrances. The two men felt that such an action would symbolically reduce house "autonomy" and the feeling of distinctness that was a central aspect of the house concept.

Chauncey Carver, master of "C" House, was particularly vehement on this issue as well as on the question of whether students of one house should be allowed to take classes in another house. Carver said that the flexible staffing program introduced the preceding year had nearly destroyed the house concept and that he, Carver, would resign if King intended to expand the cross-house enrollment of students. Carver also complained about what he described as "interference" from department heads in his teachers' autonomy.

Carver appeared to be an outstanding housemaster from everything that King had heard about him—even from his many enemies. Carver had an abrasive personality but seemed to have the best-operating house in the school and was well liked by most of his teachers and pupils. His program also appeared to be the most innovative of all. However, it was also the program which was most frequently attacked by the department heads for lacking substance and not covering the requirements outlined in the system's curriculum guide. Even with these criticisms, King imagined how much easier it would be if he had four housemasters like Chauncey Carver.

During his interviews with the other three housemasters, King discovered that they all felt infringed upon by the department heads but that only Carver and Czepak were strongly against "locking the doors" and that two other housemasters actively favored cross-house course enrollments. King's fourth interview was with Burtram Perkins, who was also a housemaster. Perkins was a black in his late forties who had been an assistant to the principal of Central High before coming to Kennedy. Perkins spent most of the interview discussing how schedule pressures could be relieved. Perkins was currently involved in developing the schedule for the 1970–1971 school year until a vice-principal was appointed to perform that job (Kennedy High had allocations for two vice-principals and two assistants in addition to the housemasters. See Exhibit 1).

Exhibit 1

Administrative Organization
Robert F. Kennedy High School
Great Ridge, Illinois

Principal:	David King, 42 (black) B.Ed., M.Ed., Great Ridge State College
Vice-Principal:	William Smith, 44 (black) B.Ed., Breakwater State College M.Ed., (Counseling) Great Ridge State College
Vice-Principal:	vacant—to be filled
Housemaster, A House:	Burtram Perkins, 47 (black) B.S., M.Ed., Univ. of Illinois
Housemaster, B House:	Frank Czepak, 36 (white) B.S., Univ. of Illinois M.Ed., Great Ridge State College
Housemaster, C House:	Chauncey Carver, 32 (black) A.B., Wesleyan Univ. B.F.A., Pratt Institute M.A.T., Yale University
Housemaster, D House:	John Bonavota, 26 (white) B.Ed., Great Ridge State College M.Ed., Ohio State University
Assistant to the Principal:	vacant—to be filled
Assistant to the Principal: (for Community Affairs)	vacant—to be filled

Two pieces of information concerning Perkins came to King's attention during his first week there. The first was that several teachers were circulating a letter requesting Perkins' removal as a housemaster because they felt he could not control the house or direct the faculty. This surprised King because he had heard that Perkins was widely respected within the faculty and had earned a reputation for supporting high academic standards and for working tirelessly with new teachers. However, as King inquired further, he discovered that Perkins was greatly liked within the faculty but was also generally recognized as a poor housemaster. The second piece of information concerned how Perkins' house compared with the others. Although students had been randomly assigned to each house, Perkins' house had the largest absence rate and the greatest number of disciplinary problems in the school. Smith had also told him that Perkins' dropout rate for 1969-1970 was three times that of any other house.

While King was in the process of interviewing his staff, he was called on by Mr. David Crimmins, chairman of the history department. Crimmins was a native of Great Ridge, white, and in his late forties. Crimmins was scheduled for an appointment the following week but asked King if he could see him immediately. Crimmins said he wanted to talk with King because he had heard that a letter was being circulated asking for Perkins' removal and he wanted to present the other side of the argument. Crimmins became very emotional during the conversation and said that Perkins was viewed by many of the teachers and department chairmen as the only housemaster who was making an effort to maintain high academic standards and that his transfer would be seen as a blow to those concerned with quality education. He also described in detail Perkins' devotion and commitment to the school and the fact that Perkins was the only administrator with the ability to straighten out the schedule and that he had done this in addition to all of his other duties. Crimmins ended by saying that if Perkins were transferred, he, Crimmins, would personally write a letter to the regional accreditation council telling them how badly standards had sunk at Kennedy. King assured him that it would not be necessary to take such a drastic measure and that a cooperative resolution would be found. King was aware of the accreditation review that Kennedy High faced the following April, and he did not wish to complicate the process unnecessarily in any way.

Within twenty minutes of Crimmins' departure, King was visited by a young white teacher named Tim Shea who said that he had heard that Crimmins had come in to see him. Shea said that he was one of the teachers who organized the movement to get rid of Perkins. Shea said that he liked and admired Perkins very much because of his devotion to the school but that Perkins' house was so disorganized and discipline so bad that it was nearly impossible to do any good teaching. Shea added that it was "a shame to lock the school up when stronger leadership is all that's needed."

King's impressions of his administrators generally matched what he had heard about them before arriving at the school. Carver seemed to be a very bright, innovative, and charismatic leader whose mere presence generated excitement. Czepak seemed to be a highly competent, though not very imaginative, administrator who had earned the respect of his faculty and students. Bonavota, who was only twenty-six, seemed very bright and earnest but unseasoned and unsure of himself. King felt that with a little guidance and training Bonavota might have the greatest promise of all. At the moment, however, he appeared to be a very uncertain and somewhat confused person who had difficulty simply coping. Perkins seemed to be a very sincere and devoted person who had a good mind for administrative details but an almost total incapacity for leadership.

King knew that he would have the opportunity to make several administrative appointments because of the three vacancies which existed. Indeed, should Smith resign as vice-principal, King would be in the position of filling both vice-principalships. He knew that his recommendations for these positions would carry a great deal of weight with the central office. The only constraint that King felt in making these appointments was the need to achieve some kind of racial balance among the Kennedy administrative group. With his own appointment as principal, the number of black administrators exceeded the number of white administrators by a ratio of two to one, and as yet Kennedy did not have a single Puerto Rican administrator even though a third of its pupils had Spanish surnames.

The Friday Afternoon Meeting

In contrast to the individual interviews, King was surprised to find how quiet and conflict-free these same people were in the staff meeting that he called on Friday. He was amazed at how slow, polite, and friendly the conversation appeared to be among people who had so vehemently expressed negative opinions of each other in private. After about forty-five minutes of discussion about the upcoming accreditation review, King broached the subject of housemaster–department head relations. The ensuing silence was finally broken by a joke which Czepak made about the uselessness of discussing that topic. King probed further by asking whether everyone was happy with the current practices. Crimmins suggested that this was a topic that might be better discussed in a smaller group. Everyone in the room seemed to agree with Crimmins except for Betsy Dula, a young white woman in her late twenties who was chairman of the English department. She said that one of the problems with the school was that no one was willing to tackle tough issues until they exploded. She said that relations between housemasters and department heads were terrible and it made her job very difficult. She then attacked Chauncey Carver for impeding her evaluation of a nontenured teacher in Carver's house. The two argued for several minutes about the teacher and the quality of the experimental sophomore English course that the teacher was giving. Finally, Carver, who by now was quite angry, coldly warned Mrs. Dula that he would "break her neck" if she stepped into his house again. King intervened in an attempt to cool both their tempers, and the meeting ended shortly thereafter.

The following morning, Mrs. Dula called King at home and told him that unless Chauncey Carver publicly apologized for his threat, she would file a grievance with the teachers' union and take it to court if necessary. King assured Mrs. Dula that he would talk with Carver on Monday. King then called Eleanor Debbs, one of the school's math teachers whom he had known well for many years and whose judgment he respected. Mrs. Debbs was a close friend of both Carver and Mrs. Dula and was also vice-president of the city's teachers' union. He learned from her that both had been long-term adversaries but that she felt both were excellent professionals.

She also reported that Mrs. Dula would be a formidable opponent and could muster considerable support among the faculty. Mrs. Debbs, who was herself black, feared that a confrontation between Dula and Carver might create tensions along race lines within the school even though both Dula and Carver were generally quite popular with students of all races. Mrs. Debbs strongly urged King not to let the matter drop. Mrs. Debbs also told him that she had overheard Bill Smith, the vice-principal, say at a party the preceding night that he felt that King didn't have either the stomach or the forcefulness necessary to survive at Kennedy. Smith further stated that the only reason he was staying was that he did not expect King to last the year. Should that prove to be the case, Smith felt that he would be appointed principal.

David King, the new principal of Kennedy High School, faces a formidable set of leadership problems. The school is in disarray. The previous principal left "a broken man." The staff is fiercely divided. How might reframing help David King face these problems? We will begin by using each frame to write a script—really, a description of a management style—for David King.

Exhibit A contains a description of a David King who is basically committed to a structural approach. The description provides only a very brief and general description of David King's orientation to organizations, but we have found that managers can take the script and apply it to the case.

Exhibit A

A Structural Script for David King

Over the course of his career as an administrator, Mr. King has developed a clear philosophy of leadership that has been effective for him and that fits his own personal style.

Mr. King believes that the primary function of a leader is to clarify the goals of a school and to provide people with a clear structure within which they can work. When people are not sure what they are supposed to be doing, confusion, frustration, and conflict are likely. An effective school is one in which each individual is clear about his or her responsibility and contribution and in which there are clearly established policies and lines of authority. "The key thing is the structure," says Mr. King. "Once you've got the right structure, and the people understand it, a school can function the way people want it to."

People who know Mr. King credit much of his success to his hard work, his clarity about where he wants to go, and his ability to create structures and procedures that enable people to do what they need and what the school needs. "Dave King doesn't get caught up in personalities or a lot of emotional baggage. He knows his job is to create a school where kids can learn and teachers can teach, and he never loses sight of his goal."

We have given both students and managers the following instructions: "Assume that you are David King. It is Sunday, and you have completed your first week at RFK. You promised Mrs. Dula that you would have a meeting Monday with Chauncey Carver. How will you approach your meeting with Mr. Carver?"

In seminars and classes, we have then asked volunteers to roleplay David King in the meeting with Chauncey Carver. (The rest of the group observes the group roleplay and comments on it at the end.) The following is a representative example of a manager roleplaying King following the guidelines of the structural script:

(King calls the meeting in his office. He is seated behind his desk, working on some papers, when Chauncey arrives.)
David: Chauncey, thanks for coming by. I wanted to talk to you about some of the ideas I'm developing about how to go to work on some of the problems at Robert F. Kennedy. I'd like to get the benefit of your thinking.
Chauncey: Sure.

David: It seems to me that we have some serious organizational problems, particularly around the role of the housemaster and the department chair. One of the first tasks we need to work on is how to clarify that role relationship and reduce the kind of conflict that we've been having.

Chauncey: The problem is that the department chairs don't understand the house concept. Their minds are still in a traditional high school.

David: That may mean that the role of the department head needs to be reexamined. Department chairs and housemasters both have to be clear about their own jobs and how they interface with each other.

Chauncey: That's fine with me. I'm pretty clear about my job.

David: Another thing I wanted to talk about is the incident that occurred in Friday's meeting between you and Betsy Dula. Would you agree that your response to Betsy was not a professional way to talk to a colleague?

Chauncey: No, I wouldn't. Betsy publicly attacked me in that meeting, and I had a right to defend myself. She knows I'm exaggerating when I say I'll break her neck, but I wanted to be clear that I'm tired of her interference.

David: That may be, Chauncey, but I think you owe her an apology in order to clear the air. We need to create a climate where the professionals can work together.

Chauncey: She attacks me and I'm supposed to apologize to her? The answer is no!

In this example, David King opened with a discussion of structural issues. Observers felt that David was effective and that the meeting moved along well *until* he tried to pressure Chauncey to apologize. Many managers interpret the description of the structural role to mean that David's style is autocratic, although nothing in the script requires such an interpretation. Such a David King often creates a major explosion when he tries to force an apology. But an apology is not a structural solution to a structural problem; it is a personal solution to an interpersonal problem.

The more successful "structural" David Kings typically stay on course in searching for a structural solution to the role conflict. An example is the creation of a task force to examine the structure of the school, chaired by the principal and including both Chauncey and Betsy in its membership.

Exhibit B describes a David King whose leadership focuses on human resource considerations.

Exhibit B

A Human Resource Script for David King

Over the course of his career as an administrator, Mr. King has developed a clear philosophy of leadership that has been effective for him and that fits his own personal style.

Mr. King believes that a school is basically people. When people feel the school is responsive to their needs and supportive of their goals, you can count on their commitment and loyalty. Administrators who are authoritarian and insensitive, who don't communicate effectively, can never be effective leaders in a school. "I want every teacher, parent, and kid to know that the administration listens, that we care, and that we want to involve them in building a school we can all be proud of."

People who know Mr. King credit much of his success to his personal warmth, his openness, and his sensitivity to the feelings of both students and staff. "Dave King is one of the most genuine, caring people I've ever known. He has an amazing combination of gentleness and underlying strength. When you talk to him, you always feel he's really interested in you and what you have to say. He's not wishy-washy—he'll tell it like it is. But you always get the sense that people come first with Dave King."

In the following script, Chauncey is played by the same

individual, but a different volunteer plays David King and tries to follow the human resource script.

(David sets up a meeting informally in Chauncey's office.)

David: Chauncey, I really appreciate your finding time to meet on such short notice. You are a key person in this school, and I called this meeting because I really need your help.

Chauncey: What kind of help are you looking for?

David: Here's what I'm concerned about. Betsy called me yesterday, and she's very upset about the exchange you and she had in Friday's meeting. She threatened to file a grievance unless she got a public apology from you.

Chauncey: There's no way I'm going to apologize to her! She should consider apologizing to me.

David: I'm not saying an apology is the right answer. I am saying that this kind of dissension is a problem for the whole school. What can we do to resolve the tension between you and Betsy?

Chauncey: She'll calm down. We've had fights before.

David: I'm still worried. How would it be if the three of us got together to talk about what happened and what we can do about it?

Chauncey: It won't accomplish anything.

David: You don't think it will work?

Chauncey: We'll just rehash the same old battles.

David: I understand your concern, but I'm more optimistic that you and Betsy are both professionals and that you can work this out.

David King, operating with a human resource script, rarely generates significant anger or conflict. He leads with friendliness and warmth and frequently wins agreement from Chauncey to attend a meeting (though rarely agreement for more than that). Observers credited King with effectiveness in building a working relationship with Chauncey but questioned whether he is making progress on the problems in the high school.

Exhibit C presents a David King who takes a political view of organizations and leadership.

Exhibit C

A Political Script for David King

Over the course of his career as an administrator, Mr. King has developed a clear philosophy of leadership that has been effective for him and that fits his own personal style.

"The only school administrator who's going to survive in urban schools these days is someone who recognizes political reality and knows how to deal with it" summarizes Mr. King's philosophy. He believes that a school and its community include a variety of interest groups, each with its own agenda. There are not enough resources to give every group what it wants, and there is bound to be conflict. The job of the leader is to recognize the major constituencies, develop ties to their leadership, and manage conflict so that it is as productive as possible. "You can't give every group everything it wants. You can try to create arenas where the groups can negotiate their differences and come up with reasonable compromises. Even more important, a building leader has to work at articulating what everyone in the school has in common. The message I try to get across is: Let's not waste our energies fighting with each other when we have plenty of enemies outside that we can all fight together. If we don't get our act together internally, we're going to get creamed by the folks outside who have their own agendas."

People who know Dave King credit his success to a combination of diplomacy, negotiation skills, and toughness. "When you first meet Dave, you might get the impression that he's not all that tough, but don't be fooled. He's too smart to get out on limbs if he doesn't have to, and he won't lead a charge until he's sure he's got people behind him. But he can be a street fighter any time he needs to be."

A meeting between Chauncey and the political David King might go as follows:

(David drops in on Chauncey in Chauncey's office.)

David: Chauncey, have you got a couple of minutes?

Chauncey: Sure, what's up?

David: I see a problem, and I'd like to get your input. Have you talked to Betsy Dula since Friday's meeting?

Chauncey: No. Why?

David: Hey, she called me yesterday, and she was steaming. Remember when you told her to stay out of your house? How did you think she reacted to that?

Chauncey: She didn't like it, but I didn't like her jumping on me in that meeting.

David: Understood. Anyway, she says she's ready to go all the way on this one: file a grievance, make it a public battle, the whole thing. What'll it mean if she does that?

Chauncey: She may be bluffing. We've had battles before. I think she'll calm down.

David: I'm worried about what if she doesn't. The school is under a lot of pressure from the parents and the board. We've got accreditation coming up. How's it going to play in the newspaper if we have a major public battle between two administrators, particularly when a white woman claims a black man threatened to attack her?

Chauncey: You're right, we don't need that.

David: That's why I wanted your advice. What's it going to take to get this one calmed down?

In the example, the political David King is mindful of the political dynamics both in and outside the school. He knows he wants Chauncey to work on solving the problem with Betsy, but he moves in gradually, never appearing to take sides or to push Chauncey into a corner. Observers of this David King felt he was extremely skillful in maneuvering Chauncey but wondered whether he could get away with using the same approach repeatedly. Would people begin to wonder where he really stood and whether he could be trusted?

Exhibit D presents a symbolic frame script for David King—a script that emphasizes personal charisma and explicit attention to symbols and to organizational culture.

Exhibit D

A Symbolic Script for David King

Over the course of his career as an administrator, Mr. King has developed a clear philosophy of leadership that has been effective for him and that fits his own personal style.

Mr. King believes that the most important part of a leader's job is inspiration—giving people something they can believe in. "Who's going to get excited about a school that everyone says is a mess? What you get excited about is a place that's special, a place with a unique identity, a place where you can feel that what you do is really important. I believe, and I want everyone in this school to believe, that if we work together, we can build the best high school in the state. That's something that you can't prove with test scores and attendance records. You have to build an idea of what makes this place special, and it helps to have a flair for drama."

Mr. King believes in looking for dramatic, visible symbols that can get people excited and give them a sense of the mission of the school. He joins students at lunch in the cafeteria and asks them what school is like for them. He makes appearances in classrooms and challenges students to dare to be great. He rides on school buses in the morning and leads cheers at basketball games.

People who know Mr. King credit his success to his commitment to education, his flair for drama, and his personal charisma. "The man's a dynamo. You walk into his office—the door is open to anyone—and you feel the energy. You only have to spend ten minutes with him, and you feel like you'd follow him anywhere."

The same individual played Chauncey a fourth time, this time with a volunteer playing a symbolic David King.

(David has invited Chauncey to his office.)

David: Chauncey! Hey, come on in. It's great that we can get together! You know, you're one of the real leaders in this school. We're going to need that kind of leadership as we work to make this the best high school in Great Ridge.

Chauncey: I'll do what I can.

David: I knew I could count on you, because I know that you're as excited as I am about the potential in this school!

Chauncey: Well, yeah, but this school's got a lot of problems.

David: Hell, yes, we've got problems, and we have to do something about them. But you could spend all your time worrying about problems and never get around to the important thing: What kind of school do we all want to build here? Do we want it to be one more worn-out urban high school, or do we want a place that's special, that really shows what you can do when everyone really works at it? This may sound corny, but I never forget what Dr. King said, "I have a dream!" That's how I feel about this school, and I want everyone to share in that dream.

Chauncey: I'm with you, but we got a lot of folks here who don't really believe in the house system. They really want to tear down what we've been trying to build.

David: Chauncey, there are conflicts here, but frankly, that's part of what makes it a challenge. Now, take that meeting Friday, that was really exciting! Sure, you and Betsy had a tug of war, but what it showed me is that you're both professionals, you both care about the school, and you're both willing to stand up and fight for what you believe in. If you and I and Betsy and the whole staff really care about making this school a real lighthouse, we can do it. We'll have some battles along the way, but that's how we learn.

Observers of the symbolic David King were impressed with his enthusiasm and optimism, and even Chauncey felt more hopeful than he had before the meeting. At the same time, observers worried whether David was so caught up in symbols and the big picture that he would never solve more pressing matters, such as Betsy's grievance.

As the examples illustrate, the different scripts produce significant differences in David King's approach and in Chauncey's response. In the preceding roleplays, for example, the structural approach led to polarization and unresolved conflict, but the symbolic approach enlisted even Chauncey's enthusiasm. In other runs of the same scripts, the structural version has led to agreement while the symbolic approach left Chauncey suspicious and cynical. No one of the scripts is consistently more effective than the others; all four frames can be implemented well or badly in this situation.

We have used these scripts for roleplays with a number of students and practicing managers. Many individuals are not equally comfortable with all four scripts, but most are able to play at least two or three. A number of people have been surprised to find that they could roleplay effectively with an approach they saw as "not me."

Watching all four roleplays has often been powerful for individuals who approach the class believing that "there's only one way to deal with someone like Chauncey." After watching four different David Kings, they usually see that there are at least four different ways, each illustrating a different set of possibilities.

16

Practices of
Successful Managers
and Organizations

One step beyond reframing, we arrive at the nagging question: How can the frames be integrated? No fully comprehensive theory yet exists that encompasses all four frames. In this chapter we take an interim step toward that goal by examining the practices of successful organizations and successful managers. If each frame describes a critical organizational domain, then it is reasonable to expect that effective practice must somehow respond to all the frames.

Managers who understand and use only one or two of the frames are like a highly specialized species: They may be well adapted to a very narrow environment but extremely vulnerable to changes in climate or competition. Like the dinosaur, such specialized managers were able to dominate the world in stable and protected environments. They were the dominant breed of an earlier era when technology changed more slowly, government and industry were more insulated from each other, and the major economic forces were local or regional rather than national and global. It is still possible for single-frame managers to find a protected niche where they *might* be very effective for five or ten years, possibly longer. But the turbulent managerial world of the next few decades will belong to the managers and the organizations with a more comprehensive understanding of the phenomena of each of the four frames.

This chapter begins with an exploration of current theories of effective practice. We examine two major recent studies that focus on organizational excellence (Peters and Waterman, 1982) and on the characteristics of effective senior managers (Kotter, 1982). We will explore the ways outstanding companies and outstanding managers address (or fail to address) the issues of the four frames. We then turn to a discussion of "alignment"—the process of matching structure, people, politics, and symbols to one another—and discuss ways to diagnose the fit among those four elements.

Two Studies of Effectiveness

"In Search of Excellence"

Peters and Waterman (1982) explored the question: What do high-performing corporations have in common? They studied sixty-two large companies in six major industries: high technology (Digital Equipment and IBM, for example), consumer products (including Kodak and Procter & Gamble), manufacturing (including 3M and Caterpillar Tractor), service (for example, McDonald's and Delta Air Lines), project management (companies like Boeing and Bechtel), and natural resources (Exxon, Du Pont). The companies were chosen on the basis of both objective performance indicators (such as long-term growth and profitability) and the judgments of knowledgeable observers.

It is important to note that the companies were not wholly representative of American business. More than two thirds were in high technology or consumer goods. A number of industries were either absent or underrepresented (including banks, insurance companies, and manufacturers of consumer durable goods). Companies in slow, mature industries had little chance of making the list: There were no railroads, steel companies, utilities, or coal mining firms.

Peters and Waterman based their study on interviews, observations, and literature about the companies. The bulk of their book is a series of stories and anecdotes about how the high-performing companies manage to be effective, but the authors summarize their results with a list of eight characteristics that they found to be characteristic of nearly all the high-performing companies (Peters and Waterman, 1982, pp. 13–16). We list the eight in Table 6, along with our sense of which of the organizational frames are relevant to each.

Table 6. Frames Relevant to the Eight Characteristics Found for High-Performing Companies by Peters and Waterman (1982).

Characteristic	Relevant Frame(s)
1. Bias for action	Structural
	Symbolic
2. Close to the customer	Human resource
3. Autonomy and entrepreneurship	Human resource
	Structural
4. Productivity through people	Human resource
	Symbolic
5. Hands-on, value-driven	Symbolic
6. Stick to the knitting	Human resource
	Symbolic
7. Simple form, lean staff	Structural
8. Simultaneous loose/tight properties	Human resource
	Structural
	Symbolic

Let's look at each of the eight properties. A "bias for action" means that the effective companies did not get bogged down in endless paperwork and bureaucratic entanglements. When they were not sure something would work, they conducted a quick, small experiment rather than a two-year research project. The motto seemed to be, "Act first and learn from the results," rather than trying to anticipate and solve every problem before doing anything. An action tendency is a potential antidote to two constant dangers: the constraining and dulling effects of the "dead hand of structure" and the pervasiveness of uncertainty and ambiguity. An organization that requires everyone to fully justify every course of action before doing anything is likely to be an organization that never does anything new or different. That much certainty takes so much time and energy that a new initiative is dated and irrelevant by the time the organization is ready to pursue it. "Bias for action" becomes a symbol of a culture that supports creativity and risk taking.

The second characteristic of high performers, "close to the customer," fits under the human resource frame, if we view customers as part of an organization's human resources. In high-performing companies, close contact with the customer was often an obsession at every level of the organization.

The third characteristic was that effective companies encouraged and rewarded innovative entrepreneurial actions by employees. In large companies, innovation is often stifled by bureaucracy and the fear of making mistakes. The excellent companies encouraged risks and tolerated occasional failures as a necessary price. Methods for promoting autonomy combined structural and human resource approaches. Structures were highly decentralized, even fractionated into large numbers of relatively independent subunits. Communications, norms, and incentive systems were designed to provide protection and rewards for innovators and security for those who might fail in their efforts.

The fourth characteristic, "productivity through people," restates a central premise of the human resource frame. Peters and Waterman acknowledge that most companies give lip service to "people," but the excellent companies really mean it. In the excellent companies they studied, they saw several consistent signs of a concern for people: extensive use of language that underscored the importance of each individual, a tendency for the organization to view itself as an extended family, an informality in the chain of command, and intensive activities to train and socialize employees.

In regard to the fifth characteristic, "hands-on, value-driven," Peters and Waterman say: "If we were asked for one all-purpose bit of advice for management, . . . we might be tempted to reply, 'Figure out your value system. Decide what your company *stands for*'" (p. 279). Every excellent company they studied "is clear on what it stands for and takes the process of value shaping seriously" (p. 279). The values are rarely transmitted formally or in writing. Instead, they move through an organization in the form of "stories, myths, legends, and metaphors"—the very things that are central to the symbolic frame. "The excellent companies are unashamed collectors and tellers of stories, of legends and myths in support of their basic beliefs. Frito-Lay tells service stories. Johnson & Johnson tells quality stories. 3M tells innovation stories" (p. 282).

The sixth characteristic, "stick to the knitting," means that the successful corporations explicitly avoid becoming conglomerates. IBM stays out of the toothpaste business, and Procter & Gamble doesn't try to sell computers. The companies usually grew through spinning off new businesses that were closely related to what they knew best. They rarely participated in the currently popular "merger mania." Acquisition of unrelated businesses creates two problems. One is a human resource issue—the senior managers in the acquirer do not know how to run the new business, but they believe that they do. The business press is filled with stories of profitable acquired firms that were mismanaged and sometimes ruined by the new owners' well-meaning but misguided attempts to make the subsidiary fit the old corporate mold. There is also a cultural problem. The symbols and cultural glue that will work in one industry will not be portable into a very different one. Procter & Gamble's marketing-driven culture and 3M's technology-driven culture have both been very successful, but neither culture would work for the other company.

"Simple form, lean staff" is a structural rule of thumb. As organizations get bigger, their structure becomes more and more complicated. Organization charts become too large and complicated to fit on anything less than a large wall. Even small decisions may have to be routed through dozens of departments and myriad meetings to ensure that "all the bases are covered."

The excellent companies generally tried to minimize those trends. A prototypical example is Johnson & Johnson, a $5 billion company that is split into some 150 $30 million "companies," each a member of one of eight product groups. The corporate staff is relatively small, and each division is buffered from excessive intrusions by corporate staffers. The same basic rule was followed in many of the other companies: Keep the headquarters relatively small, and split the company into loosely coupled, manageable chunks. This strategy reduces complexity and increases flexibility for each of the separate units to accomplish its own mission as effectively as possible, free of constant worry about how its actions affect all the other units.

The final characteristic, "simultaneous loose/tight properties," is a summary characteristic. According to Peters and Waterman, the high performers are able to combine high levels of central control with substantial decentralization, autonomy, and entrepreneurship. They are able to "have their cake and eat it too." How can they do this? Primarily they control mostly through the values and culture rather than through procedures and control systems. If a company has a widely shared culture, if its people are relatively homogeneous (most 3M managers are chemical engineers, but most Procter & Gamble managers came up through marketing), and if everyone is committed to the same basic mission, then the company can afford to give individuals substantial leeway, knowing that they are not likely to get too far out of bounds.

If it works for the companies that Peters and Waterman studied, will it work for everyone? Probably not. Reframe their analysis by asking what frames were considered and which were ignored. The eight properties of effective companies include every frame but one—politics are nowhere to be seen. Might it be that a secret weapon of effective organizations is that they eliminate politics? Or is there a bias in Peters and Waterman's analysis that might frustrate other organizations that try to fall into line with the eight marks of excellence?

Recall that the sample included only companies with strong records of growth and profitability over a number of years. These are companies with relatively abundant resources, a condition under which political dynamics are less likely to be prominent. When the company is growing and profitable, there are lots of new, high-level jobs to go around and plenty of resources to distribute to everyone. Organizational slack is high and can be used to buy off conflict. Recall too that the strong culture produced a condition of homogeneity rather than pluralism. Almost everyone shared the same values, beliefs, and myths. A unifying culture is one way to reduce conflict and the political processes that go with it.

By definition, the sample excluded companies that had not been doing well—where resources would be tighter and conflict higher. The sample also excluded public organizations, which are inevitably embedded in and responsible to the political processes of government. The excellent companies were "close to the customer," but none of them was dependent on the whims of Congressional committees for its annual budget.

Even in the successful companies, it is likely that politics are more important than Peters and Waterman's analysis suggests. If you ask a manager, "What makes your organization successful?," you will probably not be told about coalitions, conflict, and jockeying for position, even if they exist. In most organizations politics are kept in the closet—secrets known to every insider but rarely on public display.

It is reassuring that Peters and Waterman's "lessons from America's best-run companies" capture important elements of the structural, human resource, and symbolic frames, but the absence of political considerations may be important for managers to consider. What would happen, for example, when an excellent company hit a weakening or a reversal in the business cycle? The political frame suggests that resources would become scarcer, conflict would increase, and political dynamics would become more prominent. In fact, at least one of the companies that they studied—Digital Equipment—encountered such a period during the recession of 1982-1983, and the newspapers soon carried accounts of top management conflict and the departures of numerous senior executives. Similarly, any sophisticated public-sector manager knows that politics have to be addressed because they cannot be ignored, swept under the rug, or made to disappear.

"The General Managers"

Kotter (1982) took a different approach from Peters and Waterman. Instead of focusing on excellent companies, he focused on very successful managers in a variety of companies. Over a five-year period (1976-1981), he studied fifteen "general managers," defined as "individuals who hold positions with some multifunctional responsibility for a business" (Kotter, 1982, p. 2). Kotter's sample averaged $150,000 in annual salary (in 1978) and managed organizations with at least several hundred employees. Some ran organizations with more than 10,000 employees and budgets over $1 billion annually.

Kotter noted that the most striking feature of the general managers' (GM) jobs was the enormous complexity and uncertainty they faced and their dependence on networks of people whose support and effort were necessary for them to do their jobs. "As a result of these demands, the typical GM faced significant obstacles in both figuring out what to do and . . . getting things done" (p. 122). Table 7 lists six major challenges or dilemmas that Kotter found to characterize management jobs, along with the frames that are relevant to each.

Table 7. Frames Relevant to Challenges in General Managers' Jobs Found by Kotter (1982).

Challenge	Relevant Frame
Set goals and policies under conditions of uncertainty	Structural
	Symbolic
Achieve "delicate balance" in allocation of scarce resources across different businesses or functions	Structural
	Political
Keep on top of large, complex set of activities	Structural
	Human resource
Get support from bosses	Human resource
	Political
Get support from corporate staff and other constituents	Human resource
	Political
Motivate, coordinate, and control large, diverse group of subordinates	Structural
	Human resource
	Symbolic

The table shows parallels with the four frames. General managers need to set a general direction—an agenda—for their organizations. Partly, that is a technical problem (what is the right goal?), but the high uncertainty in GM jobs means that agenda setting is in part an act of faith. Allocating scarce resources combines structural and political considerations—deciding where resources will best further the mission but finding ways to satisfy important constituents at the same time. Keeping on top of a large and complicated set of activities requires an effective structure to contain chaos but also requires an effective network of relations with the many people who can provide key information.

The last three challenges relate to getting the support and resources of three critical groups: superiors, subordinates, and other key stakeholders (including corporate staffs, customers, suppliers, other functions in the organization). Successful GMs were notable for high levels of interpersonal skills and comfort with the use of power—basic tools of the human resource and political frames, respectively.

Kotter found many differences among the general managers. Some were attributable to differences in background and personal characteristics, and many were attributable to differences in their jobs. All the general managers had spent most of their careers in the same industry, many in the same company. Most of them believed that their skills were general and they could manage almost anything. The evidence, however, suggested the opposite. A major component of the general managers' success derived from long experience and extensive knowledge of their organization, its task, and its people.

Despite the many differences, Kotter also found significant similarities among the more successful GMs. The similarities arose from three basic tasks of the job—setting agendas, building a network, and using the network to get things done. The more successful GMs were more aggressive and strategic in setting agendas and more active and aggressive in building a network. They often spent less time getting the network to perform because their network did not need much prodding. The GMs' success depended on the efforts and cooperation of hundreds or even thousands of other people. To be successful, they needed to define an agenda that others could understand and support, and they needed to get others on their side. "These effective executives did not approach their jobs by planning, organizing, motivating, and controlling in a very formal sense. Instead, they relied on more continuous, more informal, and more subtle methods to cope with their large and complex job demands. The most important products of their approach were agendas and networks, not formal plans and organizational charts. . . . They typically spent the vast majority of their time with other people, discussing a wide variety of topics. . . . [They] asked numerous questions, yet they rarely could be seen making big decisions. These conversations often included a considerable amount of joking and non-work-related issues. . . . The GMs rarely gave orders, but often tried to influence others. Their time was seldom planned in advance in any detail and was usually characterized by brief and disjointed conversations" (p. 127). Kotter acknowledges that, on the surface, the GMs' behavior does not seem very "professional" in the light of current mythology about good management. But he argues that such behavior is the necessary response to the diversity, complexity, and uncertainty that senior managers face.

Similarities and Differences

Comparing Kotter's results with those of Peters and Waterman, we see both similarities and differences. The two studies give roughly equal emphasis to the importance of structural and human resource considerations. But Kotter puts much greater emphasis on political issues and less on symbolic ones than Peters and Waterman. We suggested earlier that the absence of the political element in Peters and Waterman results from the sample and from their focus on "What makes your company work well?" Differences in methodology are another factor. Peters and Waterman's research consisted mostly of informal interviews and casual observations. Kotter's research was more intensive and systematic: He interviewed each GM for several hours and observed each over the course of several full workdays. A senior manager might not mention politics in a single interview, but it would be much harder to keep that topic in the closet over the course of several days. It is not surprising that issues of power, dependence, and scarce resources were much more prominent in Kotter's more intensive study.

In Kotter's sample, only a few managers actively managed their organization's culture, although the few included one of the two top performers in the sample. Many others did not—including most of the less outstanding GMs. There may be two reasons that many GMs focused less on symbolic issues. They came from a broader range of companies than Peters and Waterman's sample, some with relatively weak cultures. Moreover, most of the GMs were not chief executives; they had responsibility for a major unit within a larger corporation. They may have operated within the context of a culture that was largely defined and managed by their superiors.

Organizational Change and Alignment

Our examination of research on effective organizations and effective managers confirms that the four frames are vital tools for management. Each of the four frames corresponds to a basic organizational domain:

- *Structural frame*—goal direction, structural clarity, and task accomplishment.
- *Human resource frame*—effective response to human needs and use of human resources.
- *Political frame*—coalitions, conflicts, and problems of resource allocation.
- *Symbolic frame*—shared values, symbols, and cohesion.

In healthy, high-performing organizations, the four domains need to be aligned with one another in such a way that they are mutually supporting. An example discussed earlier is Johnson & Johnson, a diversified producer of health care products (ranging from BAND-AIDS to headache remedies). The company's highly decentralized structure provides autonomy and flexibility to operating divisions but is aligned with a strong philosophy and credo that unifies the different divisions and bonds individual employees to the company. Johnson & Johnson attracts individuals who are compatible with its structure and philosophy and works hard to maintain morale and long-term employment for its work force. Like any large, diversified company, Johnson & Johnson faces political issues of competition among subsidiaries and between subsidiaries and corporate headquarters, but the conflicts remain manageable because of a shared sense of mission.

One test of an organization's alignment is its ability to survive a major crisis. Johnson & Johnson faced such a crisis when one of its most important products, Tylenol, was linked to deaths in Chicago. Even though it was quickly shown that Johnson & Johnson was not responsible for the poisoned capsules, many analysts predicted that the Tylenol brand could never recover from the damage to consumer confidence. In many organizations, crises breed bickering, division, blame, or "That's not my problem." But Johnson & Johnson's subunits pulled together, and the company emerged from the crisis as strong as before, or stronger.

Problems arise when one domain changes but others do not. The emergence of teachers' unions, for example, produced dramatic changes in the political climate of school districts. Before unions, school districts had been relatively placid, often run by patriarchal superintendents who specialized in benevolent paternalism. Teachers focused largely on "professionalism" and left much of the decision making to administrators. A variety of economic, social, and political changes in the larger environment exacerbated the conflict between teachers and administrators. Benevolent paternalism was shattered by labor/management wars, with each side willing to go to almost any length to win. The new shifts required a realignment of other major organizational domains. Old myths of "we are all professionals with the same interests" had to be abandoned. Administrators needed different skills and understandings to be effective in managing under the new conditions. Many lacked the political savvy and fortitude to survive unionization. Structures had to be modified by developing evaluation and control systems to cope with the newly adversarial relationships between teachers and administrators.

Similarly, changes in people can create strains in structure, politics, or culture. Trends in the American work force have created a group of workers in many industries who are more educated, autonomous, and skilled than their predecessors. Such workers respond much better to discretion and involvement than to authoritarian routine. They resist centralized structures and mechanized workflows. Often they are also more politically active and knowledgeable. They know more about the rules of the game and the power of numbers. Internal politics in many organizations have become more animated and acrimonious than in the days when employees—assembly line workers, nurses, teachers, or social workers—quietly did what they were told. Finally, workers are more likely to question what has always been taken for granted—the values, rituals, and symbols that were once unquestioned in the workplace. The demise of the Horatio Alger myth has had a profound impact on the way workers think about their jobs and their leisure. Comparable questions about legitimate authority have undermined much of the cohesion that once characterized many public and private organizations. The United States Army once used patriotic messages on post office billboards as its primary recruiting vehicle. Now it uses slick advertising in television and magazines to promise college scholarships and guaranteed training in the technical specialty of one's choice.

Changes in structure may arise from changes in goals or technology, shifts in managerial ideology, or legal pressures. In any event, they can disrupt the alignment of major organizational domains. The profound changes in American Telephone & Telegraph are a dramatic case in point. As a result of a government antitrust suit, "Ma Bell" was forced to exit from the local telephone business. The new structure was dramatically out of line with the human, political, and cultural dimensions of the old AT&T. Historically, the company had dominated the telephone business in the United States, enjoying a monopoly on most long-distance and local service. The work force was well adapted to working in a relatively stable, noncompetitive environment. For nearly a century, the company had built a culture around universal service, one centralized system, and lifetime security for employees. Universal service is now an ana-chronism, with each of the local companies off on its own and crowds of competitors moving into the telephone company's traditional markets. The old culture has lost both relevance and meaning. New skills and attitudes are required to meet a dra-matically different set of conditions. Frustration and apprehen-sion have increased among employees, and many have left the company rather than try to adapt to the new circumstances. Po-litical squabbling and bickering have erupted as the old culture has weakened. Even the stockholders are worried. AT&T was al-ways viewed as the bluest of blue-chip stocks, the ideal vehicle for cautious investors desiring security and income. Suddenly many stock analysts are telling conservative investors to sell be-cause the stock has become too speculative.

Using the frames to project the impact of change gives managers a strategic way to think about planned innovations or unplanned shifts in the environment. By anticipating how changes in one dimension might affect the others, managers may be able to mount initiatives to reduce the disruption and chaos that accompany organizational change. In the case of AT&T, the structural change has become a given, and manage-ment now needs to address questions like these: What kind of work force will we need, and how can we retrain existing em-ployees or bring in new ones? Since conflict is inevitable in a period of dramatic change, how can we identify the major inter-ests and create arenas in which the differences can be effectively addressed? How can we begin to adapt or redefine the old values, shared meanings, and rituals to develop a culture that is appropriate to the new circumstances?

The environment of most organizations will continue to change rapidly during the coming years. Such changes inevitably create possibilities for misalignment of the domains represented by the four frames. Individual resistance to change and organi-zational inertia can be powerful forces leading to rigidity and defensiveness in the face of new conditions. In the financial services industry, for example, the old, clear-cut distinctions among banks, insurance companies, and investment firms are blurring rapidly. In the face of bewildering changes, some financial institutions are standing pat and running the risk of extinction. Others are moving aggressively to realign their goals, human resources, political dynamics, and culture. Those that succeed will be the successful organizations of the future.

Summary

Integration of the frames is a problem for individual managers and for their organizations. Managers in stable environments or narrow jobs may be able to survive if they use only one or two of the frames, but they are the exceptions. Each frame addresses a critical task of management. Kotter's research on general managers underscores the importance of structural, human, and political dimensions. Peters and Waterman's study of high-performing corporations omits politics but emphasizes structure, people, and symbols. Together, the two studies suggest ways to integrate the four frames in order to produce alignment of all four dimensions.

Epilogue:
Leadership Qualities
for Meeting Complex
New Challenges

Throughout the book, we have addressed our primary audience as "managers." We are quite aware that those who read the book will include hospital administrators, school principals or superintendents, agency heads, chief executives, and area supervisors. We have used the term *manager* as an umbrella label since its use is so common and since it seems to capture the essence of what a variety of people do to manage organizations.

But our message is intended to inspire leadership—among both managers and those who consider themselves leaders rather than managers of organizations. Although we realize the distinction between management and leadership is elusive, we also know that the differences spark actual intellectual debates and

293

form the basis for real behavior patterns. Some of our colleagues like to think they study management and actually reside in schools with that title. Others claim to be scholars of leadership and, in style and rhetoric, they actively set themselves apart from management types. In the business world, some practitioners we know refer to themselves as managers; others see themselves as leaders and avoid the manager label as much as they can. These differences are part of the culture of each group and serve as a basis for their respective identities.

To us, the major difference between managers and leaders is how they view organizations. Managers tend to think rationally or humanistically—sometimes resorting to politics as a last resort. Leaders, on the other hand, are able to see all dimensions of social collectives—including oft-neglected political and symbolic levels of human behavior. They are leading managers, managerial leaders, something more in any event than custodians of the status quo. They are able to see things differently—to have visions of new strategies or patterns in everyday thought and deed. Their flexibility of thinking fosters flexibility in their behavior. They are able to act inconsistently when consistency fails to work, tenderly when emotions are raw, nonrationally when situations make no sense, politically when reason falls to parochial self-interest, playfully when goals and purposes seem counterproductive. These are the kind of people that will lead (or manage) the organizations of tomorrow.

Challenges That Lie Ahead

Leaders (or managers) of organizations are warned each year of the impending difficulties or doom the future holds. No theorist, publisher, or futurist with presence of mind would ever tell managers that they could expect a decade or year of easy sledding. No leader of wisdom and virtue would ever accept a sinecure or caretaker position. There is something about both management and leadership that continues to make those acts more complex, turbulent, demanding, and draining today and tomorrow than they were the month, year, or decade before.

Part of the escalation of turmoil and headaches of management and leadership may be ritualistic. Each generation of practitioners may need bigger problems to face; along the same lines, each generation of theorists may require more complexity and conflict to explain and interpret. But some signs suggest that leading and managing may be more difficult in modern times—on the way to even greater challenges in the future. Hospitals, for example, will undoubtedly wrestle with the major revolutions in health care. Elementary and high schools, just past the disruptions of desegregation, school closings, and major cutbacks, are experiencing a widespread crisis of confidence. Across society, questions about the capabilities of schools are hotly contested. Government agencies are grappling with budget cuts and queries about the benefits of national or state control. Witness the private sector: Banks and insurance companies are trying to move large-scale operations away from managing details toward a sales-driven, marketing focus. Automobile manufacturers are trying to regain markets lost to foreign competition. Many airlines are teetering on the verge of bankruptcy. Computer companies are contending with both growth and glut. As noted earlier, the telephone company is trying to survive changes of magnitude unparalleled in human experience.

If one gives credence to the prophesies of *Megatrends,* what we are witnessing now is just the tip of what the future holds. Revolutions in technology and in information production and the accelerating pace of change will transform most sectors of work radically. As in the past, the form and function of human organization will struggle to keep up, but they will lag well behind the other changes. And unless leaders (or leading managers) arise to help us close the gap, to create complex organizations to equal complex technologies, productivity and morale will sag. Work for many people will lose its meaning.

Something even more basic is at risk as well. Interorganizational relations—especially among nation states—have become tense and strained. We now have the technological capability to destroy the world. Unless we can develop more profound ways to understand complex relationships among countries, we stand to lose the human race as we know it. Once again, leaders who understand how social collectives work, who can think and act imaginatively while dealing with enormous human, structural, political, and cultural differences, are needed to help us avoid catastrophe, as well as to improve productivity. The fundamental issues are organizational; the challenges are becoming more difficult. The leadership paradox of the organization's future is how to balance flexibility and commitment, how to maintain integrity without encouraging rigid and intractable human organizations.

Sidestepping Pitfalls of Inflexibility

When faced with formidable challenges, managers (even leaders) tend to become inflexible. We define new problems in familiar terms, such as "communication difficulties." We redouble our energies using strategies that served us in the past— "Planning didn't help much with those changes before. This time we'll try strategic planning, and we'll involve the entire management team." Staying with the "same" problems, and employing the "same" solutions makes us feel comfortable and in control—the value of management rituals. But unless the problems are defined accurately and the strategies mesh with organizational realities, situations will not improve. Usually they will get worse.

In coping with problems of declining resources, for example, most managers decided to cut back people, programs, and units the same way they were added; others tried to develop a rationale for making cuts even though there was never really one for making the additions in the first place. Both strategies got managers into trouble—mainly because they ignored the fact that no one likes to lose anything and that people, programs, and units finally became symbols, a basis for meaning and belief. At a time when flexibility in thought and deeds might have helped, most managers became even more rigid—and so did their organizations. The leaders of the future will need to sidestep this tendency, to find opportunities in organizational crises. A school closing, for example, may be the ideal event for redistributing power in a local community. The end of a financial quarter marked by poor performance may be the perfect time to re-examine the values of an automotive manufacturer. Even the devastating changes mandated for AT&T may provide an opportunity to revitalize and transform a rich tradition of service into formidable competition for new companies without an equivalent legacy of experience. But these opportunities can only be seized by leaders who see the possibilities through a sensitive, complicated scheme of how and why organizations behave as they do.

Avoiding Traps of Overresponsiveness

The flip side of managerial inflexibility is the tendency to overrespond. Often this tendency follows inflexibility. In the face of severe problems, managers employ the tried and true. When that doesn't work, managers try to appease everyone and in the process give up control. When control goes, an organization loses its core. Particularly in times of scarce resources, there is not enough for everyone to get what they want. When this becomes obvious, anarchy erupts—until the fittest prevail. Once that happens, the manager can return to managing—but in a totally different organization.

This pattern was evident in the turmoil of universities in the 1960s. College and university presidents first tried to quell the student revolt—relying on the same strategies and tactics they had always used. When these maneuvers did not work, most institutions tried to respond to student demands. Although these gestures often *did* work, they worked at the expense of long-standing scholastic values and faculty prerogatives. Many universities never fully recovered from the overresponse; many college presidents soon found that their management task had taken on an entirely new complexion.

Leaders need to be flexible, much as a backbone needs to give when we bend to pick up an object from the floor. By looking at an event or issue from four perspectives, a leader is able to see how far he or she can bend without losing an important battle or reducing the potency of a powerful symbol.

Core Beliefs, Flexible Thinking,
and Elastic Strategies

Walking the tightrope between rigidity and spinelessness is an activity that every manager experiences. Those that lean toward inflexibility know the results of pushing even a good idea too far, too fast, at the wrong time. Those who are overly responsive feel the frustration of organizational inertia. Successful managers are able to create and sustain a tension-filled balance between the two extremes. They are able to get things done without getting done in. They know what they stand for and what they want. But they are able to think creatively about how to make things happen and can develop strategies with enough give to respond to organizational realities. Philosopher-poets, playful thinkers, negotiators who can give and take with other actors and other interests in shaping a shared direction—that is the profile of the successful manager or leader of the future.

Commitment to Core Beliefs

At the present time, philosophy and poetry fall outside the jurisdiction of training for managers, which contributes to the common portrait of the manager as a chameleon who can adapt to most any setting or as a dispassionate maneuverer whose activities are shaped by a rational assessment of whatever is currently expedient. We believe that today's managers as leaders must be actively thoughtful and dramatically explicit about their core values and beliefs. Many of America's legendary corporate heroes—Tom Watson, Walt Disney, Adolphous Busch, David Packard—articulated their own philosophy or values in such a striking way that they are still observable in the behavior and operations of their respective companies. Whether one agrees or not with Ronald Reagan or Franklin Delano Roosevelt, each has espoused a different, but stable and cohesive, set of values and beliefs. In turn, these have served as a formulation for their commitment and a vision for the direction America might take.

Flexible, Comprehensive View of Organizations

Having a core set of values or a vision is only one side of management. Commitment can lead to inflexibility, which ultimately threatens the vision. Managers need to be able to think flexibly about organizations, to see them from several angles, to adapt their style to fit emerging issues. Dwight Eisenhower's predisposition to structure and rational discourse blinded him to many political and symbolic issues within his administration. Jimmy Carter's preoccupation with details and rationality made it hard for him to marshall support for his programs or to capture the spirit of most Americans. Theodore Roosevelt's flair for the dramatic served him well for a while. But his symbolic dash and genius was not sufficient to make his third party bid for the presidency a successful one. Even FDR's multifaceted approach to the presidency—a superb observer of human needs, a charming persuader, a solid administrator, a political manipulator, and a master of ritual and ceremony—failed when he underestimated the reaction to his plan to enlarge the Supreme Court.

Managers need to be committed to values. They need to cultivate a style that suits their own personality, training, and predispositions. But they also need to develop the ability to see organizations as organic forms with needs, roles, power, and symbols chemically mixing in order to provide direction and shape behavior. Our contribution to the manager of the future is to introduce the concept of frame-flipping—the ability to see an organization through four different lenses. Flexibility in thought encourages flexibility in action, the ability to play a necessary role in a situation without sacrificing core values. FDR's recognized ability as lion and fox, Mao's reputation as tiger and monkey are not necessarily contradictions that indicate weak values. Rather they are signs that each knew intuitively the various dimensions of social collection and could act flexibly to achieve their vision in complex organizations. Through play, they were able to deal with the leadership paradox of commitment and flexibility.

Development of Elastic Strategies

Flexible thinking in action produces elastic strategies. Elastic strategies can give and be shaped by organizational dynamics. But they also create tension within an organization that alters the shape in the direction of the pull. The history of organizational reform depicts a dismal record of trying to change organizations. But as managers are able to develop elastic strategies and create the formal or informal occasions where these can shape and be reshaped, the ability to produce change should increase. It is through negotiation that shared values and goals are formed. Successful managers or leaders of the future will create the elasticity and encourage the give and take that keeps organizations evolving and changing.

Future Leaders:
Philosopher-Poets, Players, and Negotiators

We have sketched a formidable challenge for organizations of the future, as well as for those who will manage them. The management approaches of the present will not stand the tests of the future; we doubt whether they have really worked in the past. We see future managers or leaders as poets and philosophers, with skills that come from experience and attention to the fundamental values of human experience. We see future managers as playful theorists able to see organizations through a complex prism—a basic framework that we have tried to introduce. We see future managers as negotiators able to design elastic strategies that shape and can be shaped—a task that can be accomplished only through a sound understanding of how human organizations work. Maybe they are managers, maybe leaders. But the fundamental requirements are a commitment to values and a flexible approach to complex organizations.

References

Abramowitz, S., and others. *High School, 1977.* Washington, D.C.: National Institute of Education, 1978.

Alderfer, C. P. *Existence, Relatedness, and Growth.* New York: Free Press, 1972.

Alderfer, C. P. "A Critique of Salancik and Pfeffer's Examination of Need-Satisfaction Theories." *Administrative Science Quarterly,* 1977a, *22,* 658-669.

Alderfer, C. P. "Organization Development." *Annual Review of Psychology,* 1977b, *28,* 197-223.

Alderfer, C. P., and Smith, K. K. "Studying Intergroup Relations Embedded in Organizations." Unpublished manuscript, Yale School of Organization and Management, 1980.

Aldrich, H., and Pfeffer, J. "Environments of Organizations." In A. Inkeles (Ed.), *Annual Review of Sociology, 1976.* Palo Alto, Calif.: Annual Reviews, 1976.

Alinsky, S. *Rules for Radicals.* New York: Vintage, 1971.

Argyris, C. *Personality and Organization.* New York: Harper & Row, 1957.

Argyris, C. *Interpersonal Competence and Organizational Effectiveness.* Homewood, Ill.: Irwin, 1962.

Argyris, C. *Integrating the Individual and the Organization.* New York: Wiley, 1964.

Argyris, C. *Intervention Theory and Method*. Reading, Mass.: Addison-Wesley, 1970.

Argyris, C., and Schön, D. A. *Theory in Practice: Increasing Professional Effectiveness*. San Francisco: Jossey-Bass, 1974.

Argyris, C., and Schön, D. A. *Organizational Learning: A Theory of Action Perspective*. Reading, Mass.: Addison-Wesley, 1978.

Baldridge, J. V. *Power and Conflict in the University*. New York: Wiley, 1971.

Baldridge, J. V. "Organizational Change: Institutional Sagas, External Challenges, and Internal Politics." In J. V. Baldridge and T. E. Deal, *Managing Change in Educational Organizations*. Berkeley, Calif.: McCutchan, 1975.

Baldridge, J. V., and Deal, T. E. *Managing Change in Educational Organizations*. Berkeley, Calif.: McCutchan, 1975.

Bardach, E. *The Implementation Game: What Happens After a Bill Becomes Law*. Cambridge, Mass.: M.I.T. Press, 1977.

Bateson, G. *Steps to an Ecology of Mind*. New York: Ballantine Books, 1972.

Beckhard, R. *Organizational Development*. Reading, Mass.: Addison-Wesley, 1969.

Beer, S. "Death Is Equifinal: Eighth Annual Ludwig von Bertalanffy Memorial Lecture." *Behavioral Science*, 1981, *26*, 185-196.

Bell, D. *The Cultural Contradictions of Capitalism*. New York: Basic Books, 1976.

Bellow, G., and Moulton, G. *The Lawyering Process: Cases and Materials*. Mineola, N.Y.: Foundation Press, 1978.

Bennis, W. G. *Changing Organizations*. New York: McGraw-Hill, 1966.

Benson, J. K. "Organizations: A Dialectical View." *Administrative Science Quarterly*, 1977, *22*, 1-21.

Bettelheim, B. *The Uses of Enchantment*. New York: Vintage, 1977.

Beyer, J. M., and Trice, H. M. "A Re-Examination of the Relations Between Size and Various Components of Organizational Complexity." *Administrative Science Quarterly*, 1979, *24*, 48-64.

Bion, W. R. *Experiences in Groups.* London: Tavistock, 1961.

Blake, R., and Mouton, J. *Building a Dynamic Corporation Through Grid Organizational Development.* Reading, Mass.: Addison-Wesley, 1969.

Blanchard, K., and Johnson, S. *The One-Minute Manager.* New York: Morrow, 1982.

Blankenship, V., and Miles, R. E. "Organizational Structure and Managerial Decision Behavior." *Administrative Science Quarterly,* 1968, *13,* 106-120.

Blau, P. M., and Schoenherr, R. A. *The Structure of Organizations.* New York: Basic Books, 1971.

Blau, P. M., and Scott, W. R. *Formal Organizations: A Comparative Approach.* San Francisco: Chandler, 1962.

Blum, A. "Collective Bargaining: Ritual or Reality." *Harvard Business Review,* Nov.-Dec. 1961, pp. 63-69.

Blumberg, P. *Industrial Democracy: The Sociology of Participation.* New York: Schocken Books, 1969.

Blumer, H. *Symbolic Interaction: Perspective and Method.* Englewood Cliffs, N.J.: Prentice-Hall, 1969.

Bolman, L. "The Client as Theorist." In J. Adams (Ed.), *New Technologies in Organization Development.* La Jolla, Calif.: University Associates, 1975.

Bolman, L. "Leader Effectiveness in Group Dynamics Education." In C. L. Cooper (Ed.), *Developing Social Skills in Managers.* London: Macmillan, 1977.

Boulding, K. E. *Conflict and Defense: A General Theory.* New York: Harper & Row, 1962.

Boulding, K. E. "The Universe as a General System." *Behavioral Science,* 1977, *22,* 299-306.

Bowles, S., and Gintis, H. *Schooling in Capitalist America.* London: Routledge & Kegan Paul, 1976.

Bradford, L. P., Gibb, J. R., and Benne, K. D. *T-Group Theory and Laboratory Method.* New York: Wiley, 1964.

Brown, J. L., and Schneck, R. "A Structural Comparison Between Canadian and American Industrial Organizations." *Administrative Science Quarterly,* 1979, *24,* 24-47.

Brown, R. H. "Social Theory as Metaphor." *Theory and Society,* 1976, *3,* 169-197.

304

Brown, R. H. "Bureaucracy as Praxis: Toward a Political Phenomenology of Formal Organizations." *Administrative Science Quarterly*, 1978, *23*, 365-382.

Burns, T., and Stalker, G. M. *The Management of Innovation.* London: Tavistock, 1961.

Campbell, J. P., and Dunnette, M. D. "Effectiveness of T-Group Experiences in Managerial Training and Development." *Psychological Bulletin*, 1968, *70*, 73-104.

Caplow, T. *How to Run Any Organization.* New York: Holt, Rinehart and Winston, 1976.

Child, J. "Organization Structure and Strategies of Control: A Replication of the Aston Study." *Administrative Science Quarterly*, 1972, *17*, 163-177.

Clark, B. "The Organizational Saga in Higher Education." *Administrative Science Quarterly*, 1972, *17*, 178-184.

Clark, T. D., and Schrode, W. A. "Public Sector Decision Structures: An Empirically-Based Description." *Public Administration Review*, 1979, *39*, 343-354.

Coch, L., and French, J. R. P. "Overcoming Resistance to Change." *Human Relations*, 1948, *1*, 512-533.

Cohen, E. G., and others. "Structure and Technology in the Classroom." *Sociology of Education*, January 1979, pp. 20-33.

Cohen, M. D., and March, J. G. *Leadership and Ambiguity: The American College President.* New York: McGraw-Hill, 1974.

Cohen, P. S. "Theories of Myth." *Man*, 1969, *4.*

Collins, B. E., and Guetzkow, H. *A Social Psychology of Group Processes for Decision-Making.* New York: Wiley, 1964.

Corwin, R. "Organizations as Loosely Coupled Systems: Evolution of a Perspective." Paper presented at Conference on Schools as Loosely Coupled Organizations, Stanford University, November 1976.

Cyert, R. M., and March, J. G. *A Behavioral Theory of the Firm.* Englewood Cliffs, N.J.: Prentice-Hall, 1963.

Dachler, H. P., and Wilpert, B. "Conceptual Dimensions and Boundaries of Participation in Organizations: A Critical Evaluation." *Administrative Science Quarterly*, 1978, *23*, 1-19.

Davis, M., and others. "The Structure of Educational Systems." Paper presented at Conference on Schools as Loosely Coupled Organizations, Stanford University, November 1976.

Deal, T. E., and Kennedy, A. *Corporate Cultures.* Reading, Mass.: Addison-Wesley, 1982.

Deal, T. E., and Nutt, S. C. *Promoting, Guiding—and Surviving—Change in School Districts.* Cambridge, Mass.: Abt Associates, 1980.

Deutsch, M. *The Resolution of Conflict.* New Haven, Conn.: Yale University Press, 1973.

Dittmer, L. "Political Symbolism: Toward a Theoretical Synthesis." *World Politics,* 1977, *29,* 552-583.

Dornbusch, S. M., and Scott, W. R. *Evaluation and the Exercise of Authority: A Theory of Control Applied to Diverse Organizations.* San Francisco: Jossey-Bass, 1975.

Edelfson, C., Johnson, R., and Stromquist, N. *Participatory Planning in a School District.* Washington, D.C.: National Institute of Education, 1977.

Edelman, M. *The Symbolic Uses of Politics.* Madison: University of Wisconsin Press, 1977.

Enerud, H. "The Perceptions of Power." In J. G. March and J. Olsen (Eds.), *Ambiguity and Choice in Organizations.* Oslo: Universitetsforlaget, 1976.

Engel, G. V. "Professional Autonomy and Bureaucratic Organization." *Administrative Science Quarterly,* 1970, *15,* 12-21.

Etzioni, A. *A Comparative Analysis of Complex Organizations.* New York: Free Press, 1961.

Fayol, H. *General and Industrial Management.* (C. Stours, Trans.) London: Pitman, 1949. (Originally published 1919.)

Fiedler, F. E. *A Theory of Leadership Effectiveness.* New York: McGraw-Hill, 1967.

Fisher, R., and Ury, W. *Getting to Yes.* Boston: Houghton Mifflin, 1981.

Fleishman, E. A., and Harris, E. F. "Patterns of Leadership Behavior Related to Employee Grievances and Turnover." *Personnel Psychology,* 1962, *15,* 43-56.

Floden, R. E., and Weiner, S. S. "Rationality to Ritual." *Policy Sciences,* 1978, *9,* 9-18.

French, J. R. P., and Raven, B. H. "The Bases of Social Power." In D. Cartwright (Ed.), *Studies in Social Power.* Ann Arbor: Institute for Social Research, University of Michigan, 1959.

French, W., and Bell, C. *Organization Development.* (2nd ed.) Englewood Cliffs, N.J.: Prentice-Hall, 1978.

Freud, S. *On Dreams.* New York: Norton, 1952.

Friedlander, F., and Brown, L. D. "Organization Development." *Annual Review of Psychology,* 1974, *25,* 313-341.

Fullan, M., Miles, M., and Taylor, G. *Organization Development in Schools: The State of the Art.* Washington, D.C.: National Institute of Education, 1981.

Galbraith, J. *Designing Complex Organizations.* Reading, Mass.: Addison-Wesley, 1973.

Galbraith, J. *Organization Design.* Reading, Mass.: Addison-Wesley, 1977.

Gamson, W. A. "A Theory of Coalition Formation." *American Sociological Review,* 1961, *26,* 373-382.

Gamson, W. A. *Power and Discontent.* Homewood, Ill.: Dorsey, 1968.

Gephart, R. P. "Status Degradation and Organizational Succession: An Ethnomethodological Approach." *Administrative Science Quarterly,* 1978, *23,* 553-581.

Gibb, J. R. "A Research Perspective on the Laboratory Method." In K. D. Benne and others (Eds.), *The Laboratory Method of Changing and Learning.* Palo Alto, Calif.: Science and Behavior Books, 1975.

Goffman, E. *The Presentation of Self in Everyday Life.* New York: Doubleday, 1959.

Goffman, E. *Frame Analysis.* Cambridge, Mass.: Harvard University Press, 1974.

Gouldner, A. W. "Metaphysical Pathos and the Theory of Bureaucracy." *American Political Science Review,* 1955, *49,* 496-507.

Gouldner, A. W. "Organizational Analysis." In R. K. Merton, L. Broom, and L. S. Cottrell, Jr. (Eds.), *Sociology Today.* New York: Basic Books, 1959.

Gulick, L., and Urwick, L. F. (Eds.). *Papers on the Science of*

Administration. New York: Institute of Public Administration, Columbia University, 1937.

Hackman, J. R., and Morris, C. "Group Tasks, Group Interaction Process, and Group Performance Effectiveness: A Review and Proposed Integration." Technical Report No. 7. New Haven, Conn.: School of Organization and Management, Yale University, 1974.

Hall, D. T. *Careers in Organizations.* Pacific Palisades, Calif.: Goodyear, 1976.

Hall, R. H. "The Concept of Bureaucracy: An Empirical Assessment." *American Journal of Sociology,* 1963, *49,* 32-40.

Hall, R. H., Haas, J. E., and Johnson, N. J. "An Examination of the Blau-Scott and Etzioni Typologies." *Administrative Science Quarterly,* 1967, *12,* 118-139.

Hansot, E. "Some Functions of Humor in Organizations." Unpublished paper, Kenyon College, 1979.

Herzberg, F. *Work and the Nature of Man.* Cleveland, Ohio: World, 1966.

Hirschman, A. O. *Exit, Voice, and Loyalty.* Cambridge, Mass.: Harvard, 1970.

Jenkins, D. *Job Power: Blue and White Collar Democracy.* New York: Doubleday, 1973.

Jung, C. G., and others. *Man and His Symbols.* New York: Doubleday, 1964.

Kahn, R. L., and others. *Organizational Stress.* New York: Wiley, 1964.

Kamens, D. H. "Legitimating Myths and Education Organizations—Relationship Between Organizational Ideology and Formal Structure." *American Sociological Review,* 1977, *42,* 208-219.

Kanter, R. *Men and Women of the Corporation.* New York: Basic Books, 1977.

Katz, D., and Kahn, R. L. *The Social Psychology of Organizations.* New York: Wiley, 1966.

Katz, D., and Kahn, R. L. *The Social Psychology of Organizations.* (2nd ed.) New York: Wiley, 1978.

Katzell, R. A., and Yankelovich, D. *Work, Productivity, and Job Satisfaction.* New York: Psychological Corporation, 1975.

Kotter, J. P. *The General Managers*. New York: Free Press, 1982.

Landau, M., and Stout, R., Jr. "To Manage Is Not to Control: Of the Folly of Type II Errors." *Public Administration Review*, 1979, *39*, 148-156.

Lawrence, P., and Lorsch, J. *Organization and Environment*. Boston: Division of Research, Harvard Business School, 1967.

Leavitt, H. J. *Managerial Psychology*. (4th ed.) Chicago: University of Chicago Press, 1978.

Leifer, R., and Huber, G. P. "Relations Among Perceived Environmental Uncertainty, Organization Structure, and Boundary-Spanning Behavior." *Administrative Science Quarterly*, 1977, *22*, 235-247.

Leitch, J. *Man-to-Man: The Story of Industrial Democracy*. New York: B. C. Forbes, 1919.

Lepawsky, A. *Administration: The Art and Science of Organization and Management*. New York: Knopf, 1955.

Lewin, K., Lippitt, R., and White, R. "Patterns of Aggressive Behavior in Experimentally Created Social Climates." *Journal of Social Psychology*, 1939, *10*, 271-299.

Lieberman, M. A., Yalom, I. D., and Miles, M. B. *Encounter Groups: First Facts*. New York: Basic Books, 1973.

Likert, R. *New Patterns of Management*. New York: McGraw-Hill, 1961.

Likert, R. *The Human Organization*. New York: McGraw-Hill, 1967.

Lipsky, M. *Street-Level Bureaucracy*. New York: Russell Sage Foundation, 1980.

McGregor, D. *The Human Side of Enterprise*. New York: McGraw-Hill, 1960.

Machiavelli, N. *The Prince*. Baltimore: Penguin Books, 1961. (Originally published 1514.)

McManus, M. L. "Two Worlds of Organization Development: Contrasting East-West Organizational Intervention." Paper presented at First International Conference on International Organization Development, Toronto, 1978.

McNeil, K. "Understanding Organizational Power: Building on the Weberian Legacy." *Administrative Science Quarterly*, 1978, *23*, 65-90.

Maier, N. "Assets and Liabilities in Group Problem Solving." *Psychological Review,* 1967, *74,* 239-249.

Mangham, I. L. *Interactions and Interventions in Organizations.* New York: Wiley, 1978.

Manning, P. *Police Work: The Social Organization of Policing.* Cambridge, Mass.: M.I.T. Press, 1979.

March, J. G. "The Technology of Foolishness." In J. G. March and J. Olsen, *Ambiguity and Choice in Organizations.* Oslo: Universitetsforlaget, 1976.

March, J. G., and Olsen, J. *Ambiguity and Choice in Organizations.* Oslo: Universitetsforlaget, 1976.

March, J. G., and Simon, H. *Organizations.* New York: Wiley, 1958.

Marghlin, S. A. "What Do Bosses Do? The Origins and Functions of Hierarchy in Capitalist Production." *Review of Radical Political Economics,* 1974, *6.*

Marrow, A. J., Bowers, D. G., and Seashore, S. E. *Management by Participation.* New York: Harper & Row, 1967.

Maslow, A. H. *Motivation and Personality.* (2nd ed.) New York: Harper & Row, 1970.

Mason, R., and Mitroff, I. *Challenging Strategic Planning Assumptions.* New York: Wiley, 1981.

Mercer, J. L., and Koester, E. H. *Public Management Systems.* New York: AMACOM, 1978.

Meyer, J., and Rowan, B. "Institutionalized Organizations: Formal Structure as Myth and Ceremony." *American Journal of Sociology,* 1977, *30,* 431-450.

Meyer, J., and Rowan, B. "The Structure of Educational Organizations." In M. W. Meyer and Associates, *Environments and Organizations: Theoretical and Empirical Perspectives.* San Francisco: Jossey-Bass, 1978.

Meyer, J., Scott, W. R., and Deal, T. E. "Institutional and Technical Sources of Organizational Structure: Explaining the Structure of Educational Organizations." In H. Steen (Ed.), *Organization and Human Services: Cross Disciplinary Perspectives.* Philadelphia: Temple University Press, 1981.

Meyer, M. "Two Authority Structures of Bureaucratic Organization." *Administrative Science Quarterly,* 1968, *13,* 211-228.

Miller, J. G. *Living Systems.* New York: McGraw-Hill, 1978.

Mintzberg, H. *The Nature of Managerial Work.* New York: Harper & Row, 1973.

Mintzberg, H. *The Structuring of Organizations.* Englewood Cliffs, N.J.: Prentice-Hall, 1979.

Mitroff, I. I. *Stakeholders of the Organizational Mind: Toward a New View of Organizational Policy Making.* San Francisco: Jossey-Bass, 1983.

Mitroff, I. I., and Kilmann, R. "Stories Managers Tell." *Management Review,* 1975, pp. 18-28.

Moore, S. F., and Meyerhoff, B. G. (Eds.). *Secular Rituals.* Assen, The Netherlands: Van Gorcum, 1977.

Morrow, A. A., and Thayer, F. C. "Collaborative Work Settings: New Titles, Old Contradictions." *Journal of Applied Behavioral Science,* 1977, *13,* 448-457.

Nord, W. R. "The Failure of Current Applied Behavioral Science—a Marxian Perspective." *Journal of Applied Behavioral Science,* 1974, *10,* 557-569.

Olsen, J. "The Process of Interpreting Organizational History." In J. G. March and J. Olsen, *Ambiguity and Choice in Organizations.* Oslo: Universitetsforlaget, 1976a.

Olsen, J. "Reorganization as a Garbage Can." In J. G. March and J. Olsen, *Ambiguity and Choice in Organizations.* Oslo: Universitetsforlaget, 1976b.

Ortner, S. "On Key Symbols." *American Anthropologist,* 1973, *75,* 1338-1346.

Ouchi, W. G. *Theory Z.* Reading, Mass.: Addison-Wesley, 1981.

Parenti, M. *Democracy for the Few.* New York: St. Martin's Press, 1977.

Parsons, T. *Structure and Process in Modern Societies.* New York: Free Press, 1960.

Perrow, C. *Organizational Analysis: A Structural View.* Monterey, Calif.: Brooks/Cole, 1970.

Perrow, C. *Complex Organizations: A Critical Essay.* Glenview, Ill.: Scott, Foresman, 1972.

Peters, T. J., and Waterman, R. H. *In Search of Excellence.* New York: Harper & Row, 1982.

Pettigrew, A. M. *The Politics of Organizational Decision-Making.* London: Tavistock, 1973.

Pfeffer, J. *Organizational Design.* Arlington Heights, Ill.: AHM Publishing, 1978.

Pfeffer, J., and Salancik, G. *The External Control of Organizations: A Resource Dependence Perspective.* New York: Harper & Row, 1978.

Pinder, C. C., and Moore, L. F. "The Resurrection of Taxonomy to Aid the Development of Middle Range Theories of Organizational Behavior." *Administrative Science Quarterly,* 1979, *24,* 99-118.

Pondy, L. R., and Mitroff, I. I. "Beyond Open Systems Models of Organization." In B. M. Staw (Ed.), *Research in Organizational Behavior.* Greenwich, Conn.: JAI Press, 1979.

Porter, L. W., and Lawler, E. E. *Managerial Attitudes and Performance.* Homewood, Ill.: Irwin/Dorsey, 1968.

Pressman, J. L., and Wildavsky, A. B. *Implementation.* Berkeley: University of California Press, 1973.

Pugh, D. S., Hickson, D. J., and Hinings, C. R. "An Empirical Taxonomy of the Structure of Work Organizations." *Administrative Science Quarterly,* 1969, *14,* 115-125.

Pugh, D. S., and others. "Dimensions of Organizational Structure." *Administrative Science Quarterly,* 1968, *13,* 65-105.

Rallis, S. "Different Views of Knowledge Use by Practitioners." Unpublished qualifying paper, Harvard Graduate School of Education, 1980.

Ranson, S., Hinings, B., and Greenwood, R. "The Structuring of Organizational Structures." *Administrative Science Quarterly,* 1980, *25,* 1-17.

Rice, A. K. *Productivity and Social Organization: The Ahmedabad Experiment.* London: Tavistock, 1958.

Rice, A. K. *The Enterprise and Its Environment.* London: Tavistock, 1963.

Ritti, R. R., and Funkhouser, G. R. *The Ropes to Skip and the Ropes to Know.* Columbus, Ohio: Grid, 1979.

Rosenthal, R., and Jacobson, L. *Pygmalion in the Classroom: Teacher Expectations and Pupils' Intellectual Development.* New York: Holt, Rinehart and Winston, 1968.

Ross, F., and Deal, T. E. "The Effects of an Externally Directed Change Intervention on the Structure of a Small Elementary

School District." Unpublished paper, American Educational Research Association, April 1977.

Rubin, J. Z., and Brown, B. R. *The Social Psychology of Bargaining and Negotiation.* New York: Academic Press, 1975.

Salancik, G. R., and Pfeffer, J. "An Examination of Need-Satisfaction Models of Job Attitudes." *Administrative Science Quarterly,* 1977, *22,* 427–456.

Salancik, G. R., and Pfeffer, J. "A Social Information Processing Approach to Job Attitudes and Task Design." *Administrative Science Quarterly,* 1978, *23,* 224–253.

Sapolsky, H. *The Polaris System Development.* Cambridge, Mass.: Harvard University Press, 1972.

Schein, E. H. *Process Consultation.* Reading, Mass.: Addison-Wesley, 1969.

Schein, E. H. *Career Dynamics: Matching Individual and Organizational Needs.* Reading, Mass.: Addison-Wesley, 1978.

Schelling, T. *The Strategy of Conflict.* Cambridge, Mass.: Harvard University Press, 1960.

Schneider, B., and Alderfer, C. "Three Studies of Measures of Need Satisfaction in Organizations." *Administrative Science Quarterly,* 1973, *18,* 498–505.

Scott, W. R. *Organizations: Rational, Natural, and Open Systems.* Englewood Cliffs, N.J.: Prentice-Hall, 1981.

Selznick, P. *TVA and the Grass Roots.* Berkeley: University of California Press, 1949.

Selznick, P. *Leadership and Administration.* New York: Harper & Row, 1957.

Simon, H. A. *Administrative Behavior.* New York: Macmillan, 1947.

Simon, H. A. *Administrative Behavior.* (2nd ed.) New York: Free Press, 1957.

Simon, H. A. *The New Science of Management Decisions.* New York: Harper & Row, 1960.

Simon, H. A. *The Sciences of the Artificial.* Cambridge, Mass.: M.I.T. Press, 1969.

Stogdill, R. *Handbook of Leadership.* New York: Free Press, 1974.

Taylor, F. W. *The Principles of Scientific Management.* New York: Harper & Row, 1911.

Thompson, J. D. *Organizations in Action.* New York: McGraw-Hill, 1967.

Tregoe, B. B., and Zimmerman, J. W. *Top Management Strategy.* New York: Simon & Schuster, 1980.

Trist, E. L., and Bamforth, K. L. "Some Social and Psychological Consequences of the Long-Wall Method of Coal-Getting." *Human Relations,* 1951, *4,* 3-38.

Tushman, M. L. "Special Boundary Roles in the Innovation Process." *Administrative Science Quarterly,* 1977, *22,* 587-605.

Udy, S. H. "Administrative Rationality, Social Setting, and Organizational Development." *American Journal of Sociology,* 1962, *68,* 299-308.

Van Maanen, J. *Organizational Careers: Some New Perspectives.* London: Wiley, 1977.

Van Maanen, J. "The Fact of Fiction in Organization Ethnography." *Administrative Science Quarterly,* 1979, *24,* 539-550.

Vogt, E. Z., and Abel, S. "On Political Rituals in Contemporary Mexico." In S. F. Moore and B. G. Meyerhoff (Eds.), *Secular Rituals.* Assen, The Netherlands: Van Gorcum, 1977.

von Bertalanffy, L. *General System Theory.* New York: Braziller, 1949.

Vroom, V. H. *Work and Motivation.* New York: Wiley, 1964.

Vroom, V. H., and Yetton, T. *Leadership and Decision Making.* Pittsburgh: University of Pittsburgh Press, 1973.

Walton, R. E., and McKersie, R. B. *A Behavioral Theory of Labor Negotiations.* New York: McGraw-Hill, 1965.

Warwick, D. P. *A Theory of Public Bureaucracy: Politics, Personality, and Organization in the State Department.* Cambridge, Mass.: Harvard University Press, 1975.

Weber, M. *The Theory of Social and Economic Organization.* (T. Parsons, trans.) New York: Free Press, 1947.

Weick, K. E. *The Social Psychology of Organizing.* Reading, Mass.: Addison-Wesley, 1969.

Weick, K. E. "Educational Organizations as Loosely Coupled Systems." *Administrative Science Quarterly,* 1976a, *21,* 1-19.

Weick, K. E. "Cognitive Processes In Organizations." In B. E.

Staw (Ed.), *Research in Organizational Behavior*. Greenwich, Conn.: JAI Press, 1976b.

Weick, K. E. "On Repunctuating the Problem of Organizational Effectiveness." Unpublished paper, Cornell University, 1981.

Weiner, S. "Participation, Deadlines, and Choice." In J. G. March and J. Olsen, *Ambiguity and Choice in Organizations*. Oslo: Universitetsforlaget, 1976.

Weiss, C. H. *Social Science Research and Decision-Making*. New York: Columbia University Press, 1980.

Westerlund, G., and Sjostrand, S. *Organizational Myths*. New York: Harper & Row, 1979.

Whyte, W. F. *Money and Motivation*. New York: Harper & Row, 1955.

Whyte, W. F. *Organizational Behavior*. Homewood, Ill.: Irwin/Dorsey, 1969.

Wiener, N. *The Human Use of Human Beings: Cybernetics and Society*. New York: Avon Books, 1967.

Wilkins, A. "Organizational Stories as an Expression of Management Philosophy." Unpublished thesis, Stanford University, 1976.

Woodward, J. (Ed.). *Industrial Organizations: Behavior and Control*. Oxford: Oxford University Press, 1970.

Index

315